AMERICA /AMÉRICAS

DATE DUE

OCT - 7 1997	
OCT 21 1997	
NOV 2 1 1997	
APR 1 1 1998	
OCT - 7 1999	

Eldon Kenworthy

AMERICA/AMÉRICAS

*Myth in the Making of U.S. Policy
Toward Latin America*

*The Pennsylvania State University Press
University Park, Pennsylvania*

Library of Congress Cataloging-in-Publication Data

Kenworthy, Eldon, 1935–
    America/Américas : myth in the making of U.S. policy toward Latin
America / Eldon Kenworthy.
        p.   cm.
    Includes bibliographical references and index.
    ISBN 0-271-01414-8 (cloth)
    ISBN 0-271-01415-6 (paper)
    1. Latin America—Foreign relations—United States. 2. United
States—Foreign relations—Latin America. 3. United States—Foreign
relations—1981–1989. 4. Central America—Foreign relations—1979– .
5. Persuasion (Rhetoric)—Political aspects. 6. Reasoning.
7. Reagan, Ronald—Oratory. 8. Arias Sánchez, Oscar—Oratory.
I. Title.
F1418.K46   1995
327.7308—dc20   94-20971
                                                                      CIP

It is the policy of The Pennsylvania State University Press to use acid-free paper for
the first printing of all clothbound books. Publications on uncoated stock satisfy the
minimum requirements of American National Standard for Information Sciences—
Permanence of Paper for Printed Library Materials, ANSI Z39.48–1984.

This book is for Cynthia and Lauren,
companions on the long road.

Myth has in fact a double function: it points out and it notifies, it makes us understand something and it imposes it on us.

—Roland Barthes, *Mythologies*

When things die to function, they can resurrect as images of history.

—Thomas Moore, *Care of the Soul*

The past can only be told as it truly *is*, not was. For recounting the past is a social act of the present . . . affecting the social system of the present.

—Immanuel Wallerstein, *The Modern World System*

[W]hat [Gregory] Bateson's philosophy can teach us about our battles between good and evil is that "the difference that makes a difference" is difference itself. Evil is the destruction of differences; good is the creation of ever new differences. Differences are vital, and the good emphasizes diversity, individuation, integrity, and participation in the universal through the unique.

—William Irwin Thompson, *Pacific Shift*

Contents

List of Abbreviations		ix
Introduction		xiii
1.	Monroe's "Positive" Legacy	1
2.	The America/Américas Myth	13
3.	From Myth to Advertising	38
4.	Romance and the Hardball Player	54
5.	Mounting the Campaign	81
6.	The Campaign as an Ad Drawing on the Myth	114
7.	A Different Discourse	140
8.	Beyond the America/Américas Myth	159
	Appendix: The Reagan Speech	167
	Select Bibliography	175
	Index	181

List of Abbreviations

ARA
The "American Republics" bureau of the U.S. Department of State. During the period of this study the U.S. government's acronym for the Bureau of Inter-American Affairs, the branch of the State Department responsible for Latin America, then directed by Elliott Abrams.

CIA
Central Intelligence Agency. Agency of the U.S. government that generates reports on foreign situations of interest to the executive branch and that both manages and mounts clandestine military operations. A major supporter of the FDN during the period of this study.

CONDECA
Central American Defense Council. An organization of Central American militaries organized by the United States in 1963 in the wake of Castro's successful revolution in Cuba but moribund by the 1980s. Considered a possible vehicle for multilateral actions against the Sandinista regime.

Contadora
Name given the diplomatic efforts by Latin American governments—initially Mexico, Colombia, Panama, and Venezuela but the number grew to twelve—to peacefully resolve U.S.-Nicaraguan differences. Launched in 1983 on the Panamanian island of that name, the Contadora process generally was resisted by the Reagan administration. Esquipulas built upon Contadora.

Contra
Short for counterrevolutionary in Spanish. The most widely used term for the armed opposition to the Sandinista regime in Nicaragua mounted by Nicaraguan exiles and dissidents. Contra leaders and their U.S. supporters, including the Reagan White House,

preferred the terms "the resistance" and "freedom
fighters." Of the several Contra groups of differing
composition and goals, the U.S. government supported
the FDN.

DEA Drug Enforcement Administration. Agency of the U.S.
government mandated to halt the traffic of illegal narcotics into the United States.

Esquipulas Name given the diplomatic efforts of Central American
governments to resolve the standoff between Nicaragua and the United States and to end all civil wars in
that region. The name comes from the Guatemalan site
of two meetings of Central American heads of state,
the more important occurring in August 1987. Hence
this diplomatic process is called "Esquipulas 2" or "the
Central American peace initiative" or "the Arias Plan"
(after the Costa Rican president).

FDN *Fuerza Democrática Nicaragüense* or Nicaraguan
Democratic Force. The largest and most aggressive
of the Contra organizations and the anti-Sandinista
organization most supported by the U.S. government
from 1981 to 1988. To enhance its international standing the FDN was briefly folded into UNO.

FSLN *Frente Sandinista de Liberación Nacional.* Revolution-
ary/political movement that took power in Nicaragua
in 1979 and dominated that regime until 1990, when
the FSLN was voted out of office.

HP Hardball Practitioner. Lloyd Etheredge's term for a
personality syndrome found among top United States
policymakers involved with Latin America and the
Caribbean. Explained in Chapter 4.

IBC International Business Communications. Public relations firm created as a partnership of two former U.S.
government employees, Richard R. Miller and Francis
(Frank) Gomez, with Miller as president. IBC received
noncompetitive contracts from S/LPD to perform an
array of lobbying and publicity tasks, some of them
illegal for a branch of the federal executive. IBC
worked closely with Carl (Spitz) Channell and helped

	to launder some of the private donations made to the Contras.
NCPAC	Pronounced NiCPAC. National Conservative Political Action Committee founded by John Terry Dolan, with which Carl (Spitz) Channell worked. A highly successful fund-raiser for Reagan's presidential campaigns and for other conservative causes. Dolan drafted the strategy for the 1986 campaign that Channell executed.
NEPL	National Endowment for the Preservation of Liberty. Supposedly nonpartisan organization (with tax-exempt status) directed by Carl (Spitz) Channell. The single most important private fund-raising organization to support the Contras.
NSA	National Security Archive. Nonprofit, nonpartisan research institute that maintains a library of declassified U.S. government documents, selections of which it occasionally publishes. Source of many primary documents used in this book.
NSC	National Security Council. The agency within the White House command structure that advises the president on foreign and defense policies. Headed by a national security advisor who reports directly to the president and staffed by members of various federal agencies including the Pentagon.
OSS	Office of Strategic Services. Forerunner of the CIA. William Casey, the Reagan administration's Director of Central Intelligence from 1981 to 1987, "cut his teeth" with the OSS in World War II.
PRODEMCA	Friends of the Democratic Center in Central America. Set up as a nonpartisan foundation dedicated to developing public support for Reagan policies toward Central America, emphasizing themes that would attract Democrats. Received funds from Carl (Spitz) Channell's organizations to assume a lobbying role.
RIG	Restricted interagency group. Mechanism by which middle-level officials from different U.S. governmental agencies develop and oversee policies that require multiagency coordination. The Central American RIG

	included key players from the ARA, NSC, CIA, and the Pentagon during Reagan's second term. The inner core consisted of Oliver North, Elliott Abrams, and Alan Fiers.
S/LPD	Office of Public Diplomacy for Latin America and the Caribbean. Nominally an agency of the State Department but created to aid the NSC's public diplomacy operations and staffed by officials from State, the NSC, and military "psychological operations" specialists. When, in early 1986, this office was formally placed under State Department jurisdiction, its official abbreviation became ARA/LPD. Established in 1983, the Office of Public Diplomacy was disbanded in the wake of the Iran-Contra investigations.
UNO	*Unidad Nicaragüense Opositora.* United Nicaraguan Opposition. The acronym means "one" in Spanish. A new political command structure created for the FDN in June 1985 to influence the U.S. Congress and public. Ineffective in actually governing the FDN, UNO self-destructed in 1987.
USIA	United States Information Agency. Agency of the U.S. government mandated to promote U.S. foreign policy goals abroad through public relations and other means. An active member of the "public diplomacy" team on Central America coordinated by the NSC.

Introduction

In surprisingly few years Latin America passed from being a contentious issue in United States foreign policy to one scarcely discussed. While "trouble spots" remained, the deep ideological and diplomatic rifts that characterized the 1970s and 1980s vanished in a 1990s consensus on democracy, privatization, and free trade. A Democratic president carried forward policies initiated by his Republican predecessors while scholars heralded "a new era of U.S.–Latin American relations," "a new paradigm" of "partnership." (Chapter 1 offers citations.)

There have been similar moments in the past, for example immediately following World War II, when the White House and its Latin American counterparts seemed to share a basic consensus. Those moments have not lasted. When rhetoric must deal with new realities political elites throughout the Western Hemisphere discover, after all, that they understand "democracy," "development," and "independence" differently. Beneath those elites lie class-cleaved societies with yet more divergent understandings.

Rather than read each new situation afresh, Washington traditionally has refurbished its historic rhetoric regarding a common project that all "Americans" share. Such language comes naturally to U.S. leaders inasmuch as it evolved over centuries of use within the United States. For decades now Washington has attempted to unify Latin America behind U.S. leadership by employing the same discourse of identity and common purpose earlier used to pull the colonies together, to send the pioneers west and the marines south. (Chapter 2 fleshes this out.)

This book seeks to raise that discourse to full consciousness and to ask whose purposes it serves today. I write for those who see in the present moment an opportunity to reevaluate the underlying perception of the Americas that infuses U.S. policy. As Edward Said, writing about the Middle East, sensitized Western readers to strategies of control-through-difference, this work highlights the hidden strategies of control-through-sameness present in official U.S. constructions of Latin America. My thesis, then, is that this U.S. discourse not only contains assumptions traceable to the earliest days of the republic but that it reproduces those assumptions today when they offer a poor guide to reality. Old images and ideas comprise a founding myth of U.S.-hemispheric relations that has acquired paradigmatic status. I call this the America/Américas myth for its central confusion over who or what is American and (closely related) who speaks for this hemisphere. (Chapter 2 describes the myth in detail.)

How do myths perpetuate themselves? The answer lies in a symbiosis of the old and new. As Chapter 3 explains, advertising is a two-tiered semiotic system in which the familiar and accepted are deployed to sell the novel and the questionable. While advertising in U.S. electoral campaigns no longer is news, few seem to notice how far it has penetrated the workings of the state between elections, including such core activities as selecting policies and forging agreement between branches of government. The case study that anchors this book wades into the complexity of foreign policy, showing how a policy was sold to Congress and the U.S. public using a panopoly of advertising techniques that selectively drew upon (and thus reproduced) the America/Américas myth. This look at how a discourse actually is reproduced bridges the tendency of discourse analysts to stick to texts and the tendency of policy analysts to treat discourse as epiphenomena.

Myths chosen by policymakers not surprisingly cast them in heroic roles. The single case study method permits us to explore how a discourse selects policymakers as well as how policymakers select a discourse (see Chapter 4).

The Central American conflicts of the 1980s turned out the way they did largely (not wholly) because of differences in how key players constructed those conflicts. As hard as it is to reach firm conclusions in this matter, this book explores the impact of discourse on real-world outcomes. Chapter 7 contrasts the constructions of Nicaragua by two hemispheric presidents who otherwise shared key values: the United States' Ronald Reagan and Costa Rica's Oscar Arias. The realization of how differently the same situation can be perceived and of how differently the same values can be operationalized supports the book's overall contention that sameness is as dangerous a presumption as difference. In family, gender, and ethnic group relations many of us recognize this.

In the realm of U.S.–Latin American relations, however, this lesson is less understood. Fortunately the U.S. repertoire contains myths that emphasize diversity as well as unity. To tap other mythic founts, however, U.S. leaders would first have to become conscious of their use of the sameness myth.

The case selected is the Reagan administration's successful reversal of congressional prohibitions on U.S. military aid to the Nicaraguan Contras in 1986. The advantage of this case lies in the wealth of information that came to light in the Iran-Contra investigations. What I call the 1986 advertising campaign was never a central concern of those investigations, however. Rather than another book *on* Iran-Contra, this study takes advantage of the documents unearthed by Iran-Contra researchers to explore a different and broader question.

Here, then, myth will be wedded to advertising, the early nineteenth century to the waning twentieth. As the aphorism about weddings goes: "Something old, something new, something borrowed, something blue." The old and borrowed is the America/Américas myth; the new, advertising technique and the power drives of beltway insiders. As for "something blue," it is the outcome: dysfunctional U.S. policies toward Latin (in this case Central) America.

Throughout this work "Latin America" will refer to all the countries from Mexico to Tierra del Fuego, including those in the Caribbean Sea. In its origins a politically inspired term—and what isn't?—"Latin America" slights the many nonromance cultures in the region, but since no other term is more inclusive "Latin America" it will be. Apologies to Canadians and others for appropriating "hemisphere" to refer to the United States and Latin America. To minimize confusion regarding nation and hemisphere, "Americas" (plural) will refer to the hemisphere and "United States" to the nation. I avoid "America/n" even though this leads to an overuse of "U.S." and of "Washington." The myth in question I call America/Américas because it plays with this ambiguity. I realize that many Latin Americans use the singular "América" to refer to the Western Hemisphere, while some refer to U.S. citizens as "Americanos."[1] The difference that makes a difference is that Latin

1. A typical Latin use of "America" is heard in these words of Argentine musician Bernardo Rubaja: "When I was growing up, I was taught that the entire Western Hemisphere was called America, all one continent." See *The Narada Newsletter,* Spring 1992, 9.

Americans rarely equate being part of this hemisphere with *their* nationality, while U.S. officials manipulate that conflation within the U.S. discourse, adopting it for some purposes, rejecting it for others.

Many of the primary documents used in the case study were accessed at the National Security Archive in Washington, D.C., a private research organization that has opened to public scrutiny official documents that otherwise would not be noticed. I am grateful to Peter Kornbluh for guiding me through this collection, and I wish to acknowledge his seminal articles on themes close to this book's. My understanding of Costa Rica, important for writing Chapter 7, was furthered intellectually by Manuel Araya Incera (San José), and in other ways by Andre and Margarita Helfenberger (Turrialba) and doña Isabel (San Ramón de Tres Ríos), among others. An article published many years ago by Kenneth Coleman first set me to thinking about U.S. policy toward Latin America as myth.

No book is written without the stimulus of authors who often go unacknowledged. So let me thank Murry Edelman for his writing on political discourse before it was trendy to do so, William Appleman Williams for first showing me the links between U.S. territorial expansion and U.S. foreign policy, and Judith Williamson for presenting advertising as a semiotic system. For understanding the political uses of myth I am indebted to Roland Barthes. Key works of these authors are cited at appropriate places. Sanford Thatcher at Penn State Press patiently guided me through a process of revisions that were needed although resisted at the time. And when she sees these words in print Cynthia Witman will know that there will be fewer unanswered invitations for walks. Cynthia was the river that kept this boat afloat without altering her course.

1

Monroe's "Positive" Legacy

The United States enjoys a historic opportunity to promote democracy in the hemisphere unshackled by the fears of external threats.

—Richard E. Feinberg
Member, National Security Council, March 1994[1]

How does the United States talk about Latin America and what does it say? This book argues that official U.S. discourse not only reveals assumptions traceable to the earliest days of the republic but reproduces those assumptions today when they have become a poor guide to reality. Old images and ideas comprise a myth of U.S.-hemispheric relations that has acquired paradigmatic status, a myth I call America/Américas after its central confusion over identity. Who or what is American? Who speaks for America as a hemisphere? Is there *an* America?

This is not a work of history, although it draws on history. Here the focus is on official language, with the goal of explaining how a myth, premodern in origin, is perpetuated today. As an entry we begin with that most vexing of questions: Does discourse matter? Now that the Cold War has passed and Washington no longer sees Latin America

1. "Clinton Planning a Meeting of Hemispheric Leaders," *New York Times,* March 11, 1994, A7.

through the prism of big power rivalry, is there any need to analyze past language?

The "New Era Breaking" Thesis

Current writing on U.S.–Latin American relations assumes that, with the passing of the Cold War, Washington shed its penchant for interven- ing coercively in the internal affairs of Latin American countries. In this view the December 1989 invasion of Panama was an aberration, a last hurrah. "We are entering a new era of U.S.–Latin American relations," writes a trio of scholars; the "strategic denial" central to the Monroe Doctrine "is almost totally irrelevant."[2] Peter Hakim, president of the influential Inter-American Dialogue, claims that "what has clearly changed is the discourse of relations," with Washington now "showing greater respect for the countries of the region,"[3] a view echoed by Augusto Varas, for whom "a new paradigm" of "partnership" emerged "almost automatically" in the late 1980s in response to "world changes, and the suboptimal character of policies based on coercive paradigms."[4]

What has happened, one wonders, to the other elements encoded in the Monroe Doctrine? In that 1823 address President James Monroe not only warned European monarchs to stay away but expressed confidence that "our southern brethren, if left to themselves," would choose a political system much like that of the United States. At the time, Latin American leader Simón Bolívar was urging his countrymen to adopt constitutional monarchies and some Latin American nations were in fact ruled by monarchs, including Brazil and, for a time, Mexico.[5] So Monroe's prediction was normative, not descriptive. From

2. Jonathan Hartlyn et al., "Introduction," in *The United States and Latin America in the 1990s: Beyond the Cold War,* ed. Jonathan Hartlyn et al. (Chapel Hill: University of North Carolina Press, 1992), 13.
   3. Peter Hakim, "The United States and Latin America: Good Neighbors Again?" *Current History* 91 (February 1992), 49.
   4. Varas does recognize that elements of "counterproductive traditional policies" survived in the Bush administration. See his "From Coercion to Partnership . . . ," in Hartlyn et al., *The United States and Latin America,* 52, 57.
   5. Four years before Monroe's statement Bolívar recommended to Venezuela an executive that resembled the British monarchy. In other Latin countries as well he criticized "constitu- tional liberalism" and advocated "a constitutional monarch in all but name." See David Bushnell, "The Independence of Spanish South America," in *The Cambridge History of Latin America* (Cambridge: Cambridge University Press, 1985), 3:147.

its inception the Monroe Doctrine contained "hidden positives," including the notion "that the United States shall be . . . the sole directing power in both North and South America."[6]

Perhaps it was from Jefferson's dream of "an American system" as different from Europe in its domestic dynamics as in its foreign policies that this "positive" strand in U.S. thinking about Latin America arose,[7] or perhaps it can be traced back to the Puritans two centuries earlier. By "positive" I refer to the belief that Latin America's development would mirror the United States' and that united this hemisphere would become the world's most advanced. The negative "strategic denial," in contrast, merely places the hemisphere off limits to any foreign power that Washington, D.C., views as a threat.

How often have U.S. presidents from Theodore Roosevelt and Woodrow Wilson to Ronald Reagan, George Bush, and Bill Clinton used coercion (invasion, destabilization, and economic boycotts) to ensure that Latin Americans select the right regimes, "right" being defined variously but not just as an ally in international alignments? The 1989 invasion of Panama was justified as promoting democracy, with only the vaguest references made to protecting the canal and no allusions to foreign powers. Official U.S. discourse on Panama echoed statements Woodrow Wilson had made well before World War I. With no extra-hemispheric power threatening Latin America Wilson considered it a "duty" to impart "order and self-control" to the Latin states.[8] The positive strand in the legacy is no less associated with intervention than the negative.

The case that this book examines in detail, that of Reagan's policy toward Nicaragua in the 1980s, is more typical than Panama of that history in that "positive" and "negative" elements are conjoined. Such

6. Historian Richard Van Alstyne (*The Rising American Empire*) as quoted by Piero Gleijeses, "The Limits of Sympathy: The United States and the Independence of Spanish America," *Journal of Latin American Studies* 24 (October 1992), 489.

7. In an 1820 letter Jefferson noted that throughout the new world "room is abundant, population scanity, and peace the necessary means of life and happiness." While on earlier occasions Jefferson expressed doubts regarding the cultural underpinnings of Latin America, in retirement he seemed drawn by the logic of his spaciousness fosters self-government thesis to think that Latin America would opt for republics. See T. L. Schellenberg, "Jeffersonian Origins of the Monroe Doctrine," in *The Monroe Doctrine*, ed. Armin Rappaport (New York: Holt, Rinehart and Winston, 1964), 53.

8. A 1902 Wilson statement quoted by George Black, *The Good Neighbor* (New York: Pantheon Books, 1988), 28.

interaction is apparent in the original myth, which Chapter 2 spells out. The case study reveals, however, not just that admixture but the way in which newer themes are grafted onto the root stock of older legacies, including the "positive" heritage of the Monroe Doctrine.

The New World in the New World Order

The U.S. invasion of Panama was officially justified using the same language for explaining the collapse of communism in Europe and the dawning of a "new world order." Not just Panama in particular but Latin America in general exemplified a U.S. commitment to political democracy and free markets, a pledge Washington made as it assumed its post–Cold War role as the world's preeminent superpower. As President Bush called on "the United Nations, freed from cold war stalemate," to "fulfill the historic vision of its founders,"[9] so his ambassador to the Organization of American States, Luigi Einaudi, called on that body to respond to a historic opportunity in Panama: "The judgment of history will lay upon this organization. By improperly invoking the legitimate principle of nonintervention in this case, the OAS will find itself cast on the side of the dictators and tyrants of this world who are en route to extinction. . . . It is time this organization put itself on the right side of history."[10] In speaking later to the same organization Deputy Secretary of State Lawrence Eagleburger looked past the "paralysis" the OAS exhibited over Panama to urge the inter-American community to seize "the opportunity to redeem ourselves" by creating a hemisphere completely "democratic and free."[11]

While Bush's first Secretary of State, James A. Baker III, spoke of "a

9. Bush speech delivered to a joint session of the U.S. Congress, March 6, 1991, as reproduced in *Vital Speeches of the Day* 57 (April 1, 1991), 354–55.

10. "Panama: A Just Cause," *Current Policy* 1240 (Washington, D.C.: U.S. Department of State, Bureau of Public Affairs, 1990), 2–3. The ambassador omitted all reference to *how* "dictators and tyrants" had fallen in Eastern Europe, South America, and the Philippines. Most often unarmed citizens had toppled authoritarian states. Where violence was used it was generated locally. Latin Americans have brought down tougher regimes than Manuel Noriega's without the benefit of U.S. bombing, invasion, and occupation.

11. Address to the Twenty-first General Assembly of the Organization of American States meeting in Santiago, Chile, on June 3, 1991, as reproduced in *U.S. Department of State Dispatch*, June 10, 1991, 414–17.

new world order based on human and democratic values, thriving market economies, and peaceful international relations,"[12] Eagleburger (soon to succeed Baker) said of the Americas:

> We are the hemisphere which gave mankind a second chance. We are still, five centuries after Columbus, the New World. . . . We are, in short, the hemisphere of freedom, where liberty and democracy were reborn in the modern era but on a universal scale unknown to the ancients. . . . We are . . . on the threshold of a new world order today, following the defeat of totalitarianism and the global ascendancy of democracy and the free-enterprise system.[13]

The President himself echoed this theme on June 12, 1991:

> Here in the Americas we are building something unprecedented in human history—the world's first completely democratic hemisphere.[14]

And in a major address later that month Bush expounded:

> There's no accident of history here. From the northern tip of Alaska to the southernmost point of Tierra del Fuego, we share common heritages. . . . And now, as democracy sweeps the world, we share the challenge of leadership through example. We can lead the way to a world free from suspicion and from mercantilist barriers, from socialist inefficiencies. We can show the rest of the world that deregulation, respect for private

12. Baker's address to the Conference on Security and Cooperation in Europe (CSCE), Moscow, September 11, 1991, as printed in *U.S. Department of State Dispatch*, September 16, 1991, 681. Baker frequently coupled "rule of law" with "democracy" without addressing the tension between promoting both simultaneously in the international arena. In Panama, for example, Washington abandoned the former in its zeal to promote the latter. "[T]he United States is more than the greatest democracy in the world: We are the spokesman for the democratic community everywhere," Baker told the Senate Foreign Relations Committee on February 5, 1992, as reported in *U.S. Department of State Dispatch*, February 10, 1992, 85.

13. "Address to the Twenty-first General Assembly." A chosen people who lapse then redeem themselves, moderns who best ancients, a new world that is a beacon to the old—these are premodern ideas that carry teleological baggage.

14. Bush's public remarks on taking leave of Salvadoran president Alfredo Cristiani, as reproduced in *U.S. Department of State Dispatch*, June 24, 1991, 452.

property, low tax rates, and low trade barriers can produce vast economic returns. . . . [W]e can make our hemisphere's freedom first and best for all.[15]

Notice how this rhetoric not only invokes history but borrows the language of an earlier era, language burdened with teleological assumptions of Purpose in History that political leaders discern and implement.

Bush's vision of liberalism sweeping the globe (liberal democracy, privatized economies, free trade) was inherited from Reagan and passed on to Clinton. It is a bipartisan vision challenged in the United States by few beyond those whose immediate material interests are threatened. With Reagan and Bush this vision was linked to an action-oriented foreign policy that did not hesitate to use U.S. military power abroad. While preferring multilateral backing—as long as it left Washington in control—the White House was prepared to act unilaterally and did so when the relevant international organization and regional powers failed to perform according to the script, as happened in Panama in 1989.[16] Official rationales offered for invading Panama include issues likely to recur in the post–Cold War era: promoting democracy, protecting U.S. citizens abroad, and curbing international traffic in illegal narcotics—three issues cited by the Clinton administration in its dealings with Haiti.

If during the Bush years Washington dreamt of a unipolar world in which U.S. values triumphed and U.S. power was unchecked, by the Clinton inauguration that dream had been scaled down. It is important to discriminate, however, between hesitating for lack of resources and reevaluating the validity of the project. With its premises left unchallenged, the dream may return to be enacted in Latin America even if Washington lacks the resources to do so globally. Enhancing that possibility are the low perceived costs of attacking small nations with unpopular or divided governments within what many still regard as a U.S. sphere of influence. A Nixon battered in Vietnam destabilized Chile, a Reagan damaged in Beirut attacked Grenada, and the vision

---

15. Bush speech marking the first anniversay of the Enterprise for the Americas Initiative, delivered in Washington, D.C., July 27, 1991, as reproduced in U.S. Department of State Dispatch, July 8, 1991, 489.

16. "A desire for international support must not become a prerequisite for acting, though. Sometimes, a great power has to act alone." President George Bush speaking at West Point on January 5, 1993. See "America's Role in the World," U.S. Department of State Dispatch, January 11, 1993, 14.

Woodrow Wilson was unable to realize at Versailles he tried to impose closer to home.

Clinton's foreign policy may be more cautious, but its rhetoric retains the old language: a "global movement from despotism to democracy," "a hemispheric community of democracies linked by growing economic ties and common political beliefs," "a new convergence of values." Clinton even echoed Bush's "no accident of history": "It's no accident that our nation has steadily expanded the frontiers of democracy. . . . For it is our nature to reach out, and reaching out has served not only ourselves, but the world as well."[17] Of Cuba Clinton said during the 1992 presidential campaign that the Bush administration "has missed a big opportunity to put the hammer down on Fidel Castro."[18] During that campaign Clinton, more than Bush, favored tightening the U.S. economic blockade of Cuba in order to produce a change in Cuba's government.

As in the wake of World War II the early 1990s saw several Latin American leaders reinforce this propensity of their U.S. counterparts not just to believe in a common hemispheric project but in Washington's ability to promote it. If history is any guide such moments are short-lived. Latin America was more democratic in 1992 than it had been in 1972, but it also had been more democratic in 1962.[19] Similarly, the "neo" of neoliberal economic policies reminds us that Latin America earlier had opened itself to international economic forces, only to be

---

17. Secretary of State Warren Christopher, "Democracy and Human Rights: Where America Stands," *U.S. Department of State Dispatch,* June 21, 1993; Christopher (quoting Clinton), "NAFTA: A Bridge to a Better Future for the United States and the Hemisphere," *U.S. Department of State Dispatch,* September 13, 1993; Clinton, "American Leadership and Global Change," *U.S. Department of State Dispatch,* March 1, 1993. This last is a major foreign policy address delivered at American University on February 26, 1993. See also Peter Hakim, "NAFTA . . . and After," *Current History* 93 (March 1994), 97.

18. Earle Black and Merle Black, *The Vital South: How Presidents Are Elected* (Cambridge: Harvard University Press, 1992), 33.

19. The quality of what Washington considers "democracy" renders these judgments problematic. While President Bush was proclaiming "When Cuba embraces democracy, ours will become the first truly democratic hemisphere in the world," the *New York Times* reported that Peru under an elected civilian president led the world in the number of "disappearances" committed by public authorities. Elected and civilian Guatemalan and Mexican regimes, also embraced as democracies by the White House, continue to be criticized by human rights organizations for major violations of the rights of political dissenters. During the Bush years Haiti lapsed back into military rule and the Peruvian president closed that country's congress. One scholarly attempt to measure democracy over time is Ted Robert Gurr et al., "The Transformation of the Western State," in *On Measuring Democracy,* ed. Alex Inkeles (New Brunswick, N.J.: Transaction Books, 1991), 87.

deserted during the Depression and World War II. It is hard to equate Latin America's cycles with U.S. intentions other than to note the counterproductive nature of U.S. military intervention, which in time Panama may confirm.[20] A scholary survey of eight decades of U.S. efforts to democratize Latin America concludes that "the more interventionist the United States has been . . . the less it has been able to foster lasting democratic politics."[21] The January 1994 uprising in Chiapas, Mexico, brings back into focus a historic pattern of Latin nonelites claiming to be ill-served by such consensuses of U.S. and Latin elites.

What the case study in this book will demonstrate is what this introduction asserts: that a continuity exists in U.S. policymakers' views of what it takes to bring progress to Latin America, that the assumptions underlying this continuity are archaic, and that there is no compelling reason to think that this will end solely because the international system has entered a new configuration. Insofar as U.S. intervention is driven by "positive" elements in the legacy of the Monroe Doctrine, the post–Cold War absence of a major power challenging Washington in "its" hemisphere could lead to more, not less, intervention.

But Does Discourse Matter?

There is more to international relations than rhetoric and myths. Yet power and language are so intertwined that separating them is more an artifact of how we think than an accurate representation of political life. Power is present "in the way discussions are structured, agendas set, concepts selected, arguments developed"; thus power shapes discourse. But "power is not silent"; it expresses itself *through* language (including symbols of all kinds) and is shaped by that ongoing process.[22]

20. Three years after "Operation Just Cause" longtime Panama watcher Steve Ropp saw in the "rapid decline in legitimacy" of the U.S.-installed government an opportunity for "the old military populist coalition" to make a comeback. See "Things Fall Apart: Panama after Noriega," *Current History* 92 (March 1993), 104–5. A year later *The Economist* noted: "After the invasion, the Americans hoped to make Panama a model of democracy and free market-reform. It is neither." See "Back to the Future," *The Economist*, March 12, 1994, 48.

21. Abraham Lowenthal, "The United States and Latin American Democracy: Learning from History," in *Exporting Democracy: The United States and Latin America: Case Studies*, ed. Abraham Lowenthal (Baltimore: The Johns Hopkins University Press, 1991), 278.

22. Bjorn Gustavsen, *Dialogue and Development* (Stockholm: Arbetslivscentrum, 1992), 110. Many others make the same argument, including U.S. political scientist Murray Edelman in *Constructing the Political Spectacle* (Chicago: University of Chicago Press, 1988).

Listening to the official language sampled above, for instance, a Native American would recognize how language *constructs* a history that serves a specific set of power relations in the present. A different set of power relations would require a different reading of history. And so with Latin America: the "new paradigm," which Varas and others rightly desire, requires a new reading of the history of U.S. relations with Latin America on the part of U.S. leaders—not a reworking of who did what when, but a reconception of that history's meaning. Since the existing discourse was formed out of language used to create a *national* identity, such a fresh reading requires a degree of separation, a capacity for seeing Latin countries as other, as different. That unfortunately runs counter to the impulse most U.S. leaders have to stress unity and consensus. No less than Bush, Clinton speaks of "an unprecedented convergence of ideas" between hemispheric leaders fostering a hemispherewide "community."[23]

To sense the limits built into the inherited discourse, try reading the official language quoted above as if for the first time. "Here in the Americas we are building something unprecedented in human history." "We can show the rest of the world." "It is time this organization put itself on the right side of history."

How useful is it to think in terms of a regional enclave, especially an exemplary one carrying the torch for History, in an era when money, narcotics, atmospheric carbon dioxide, CNN, AIDS, and MTV circle the globe 24 hours a day, 365 days a year; when "globalism" has become a cliché in business circles; and when the harm done by national elites claiming to be History's agent is too obvious to need documentation? A "new world" separate from and superior to the European Union? Does that make sense when several European nations have higher per capita incomes and less poverty, preventable disease, and violent crime than the United States, not to mention Latin America?[24] Just where does Japan, whose per capita GNP is higher than

23. Phrase from a Clinton speech of December 2, 1992, which the Inter-American Dialogue, perhaps the most influential, multi-issue "lobby" on U.S. policy toward Latin America, incorporated into the title of its 1993 report *Convergence and Community: The Americas in 1993* (Washington, D.C.: The Aspen Institute, 1992).

24. In the United States in 1989 there were 31 homicides per million people, more than any of the other developed nations listed in this report. Compare, for example, West Germany with 15 and Great Britain with 6. An "Index of Social Health" measuring 16 indicators ranging from unemployment to drug abuse reveals a decline in the United States stretching from 1972 to 1990, the last year tabulated. A similar index for children shows a comparable

that of the United States, fit into this old/new world dichotomy?[25] On a multidimensional scale measuring quality of life the United States now ranks sixth in the world, while the highest Latin American country is thirtieth, behind some twenty "old world" nations.[26] Adam Przeworski's study of advanced industrial nations over two decades explains the European edge: "The welfare of the average adult, the average worker, and the average manufacturing employee was higher in social democratic countries."[27] While in recent years many of these high-scoring nations have trimmed their social budgets, they have not abandoned a model that is distinct from that of the United States.

Divorced from its inter-American context and set against the contemporary world, Washington's rhetoric seems as useful a guide to reality as the rules of croquet. Yet embedded within that language are presumptions that are far from innocent: that one national elite, largely Anglo-Saxon in origin, can speak for the interests of half a billion Latin peoples living at varying levels of economic development and in a multitude of cultural contexts; that Latin America should be more closely linked to the United States than to Europe or Asia; that global no less than regional well-being is furthered when Latin countries adopt neoliberal economic policies. The success of several East Asian NICs—the "newly industrialized country" status to which many Latin American nations aspire—suggests a different economic strategy.[28] If we assume a commitment to democracy that is as strong as the commitment to economic

decline. See "Guns and Deadly Violence in Ten Countries," *New York Times*, April 3, 1992, A15, and "U.S. Social Well-Being Is Rated Lowest since Study Began in 1970," *New York Times*, October 5, 1992, A16.

25. "In just 20 years, Japan has gone from having a per capita GNP only half that of the United States to one that is now 22 percent greater, if the two GNPs are evaluated using international currency values." See Lester Thurow, "The 21st Century Belongs to Europe," *Washington Post National Weekly Edition*, April 27, 1992, 23.

26. The United Nations' "human development index" based on 1990 data. See United Nations Development Programme, *Human Development Report 1993* (New York: Oxford University Press, 1993), 135.

27. "The Neo-Liberal Fallacy," in *Capitalism, Socialism, and Democracy Revisited*, ed. Larry Diamond and Marc F. Plattner (Baltimore: The Johns Hopkins University Press, 1993), 48.

28. Agrarian reform, a high investment in basic human resources, and a state-coordinated industrial strategy played important roles in the Asian success yet Washington discourages these measures in Latin America by pushing privatization (the dismantling of state organisms). For a full treatment of this complex topic see Stephan Haggard, *Pathways from the Periphery* (Ithaca: Cornell University Press, 1990).

growth, East Asian experience—and also Washington's advice—may be less relevant. Przeworski recognizes that "all countries cannot simultaneously have a positive balance of payments. The race to modernize will inevitably have its winners and losers . . . [who] will not be nation-states but regions, sectors, industries, and particular social groups." The stripped-down national governments of the world's south, however, no longer can "compensate losers and manage social tensions generally." As a consequence "democracy suffers."[29] Washington's projection of its experience and preferences onto societies dissimilarly situated in the world conjuncture might be overlooked were it not for the vanguard role embedded in official language: the presumption not just to advise but to "make happen," translated into action as recently as 1989.

Comparing the United States invasion of Panama to the last times U.S. troops openly warred on Latin American nations, the trend actually is one of increasing unilateralism. In the past Washington found some regional organization to endorse its intervention, as when the OAS sanctioned the 1965 invasion of the Dominican Republic. In the 1983 invasion of Grenada the United States had to settle for the smaller Organization of Eastern Caribbean States. Invading Panama in 1989, the White House went it alone, castigating the OAS for its noninterventionionist scruples while using vanguard rhetoric reminiscent of Leninism, democracy having "acquired the force of historical necessity."

What is it that permits a U.S. administration (in this case Bush's) to commit itself to a world order based on international norms backed by multilateral actions sanctioned by international organizations—the basis for repelling Iraq's invasion of Kuwait—*and* at the same time to undercut that commitment when dealing with a region that *has* established multilateral organizations and a clear body of international law? What leads U.S. leaders to fudge the ends-means nexus when addressing "their" region while cautioning other governments to observe it in theirs? Regarding Eastern Europe, for example, the Bush administration argued that "democratic means are the only way to achieve democratic ends," that "intimidation, illegality, and violence are not the handmaidens of democracy."[30]

---

29. Przeworski, "The Neo-Liberal Fallacy," 49.
30. Baker speaking to the Conference on Security and Cooperation in Europe in 1991 (see note 12 above), 679.

At least one part of that "something" consists of assumptions that linger in official thinking about Latin America—linger because they early acquired a paradigmatic status through association with the U.S. national project. As later chapters show, the U.S. discourse on Latin America both contains and cloaks those U.S.-centric assumptions.

Will statements regarding world order or hemispheric community spoken by U.S. leaders be credible if accompanied by a succession of Panamas or by subtler forms of vanguardism? In 1992 major U.S. allies voted with the plurality in the United Nations General Assembly to condemn a recent U.S. effort to force its trading partners and subsidiaries of U.S. corporations abroad to stop trading with Cuba—this from a country then lecturing the world on the benefits of freeing up world trade![31] In a multipolar world will Latin American governments follow a U.S. leadership burdened by such contradictions?

In early 1994 a new U.S. ambassador arrived in Managua, Nicaragua, and announced that since "there is no real security threat to the United States in this part of the world . . . we can get back to the real roots of U.S. values in foreign policy," which he equated with democracy, human rights, and rule of law.[32] Washington's counterproductive intervention in Nicaragua's internal affairs began well before World War II, at a time when there also was "no real security threat to the United States," and was expressed through similar-sounding attempts to promote democracy and rule of law. Washington went to great lengths to see to it that the 1990 election in Nicaragua would be clean. It had done the same in 1928. During the sixty years that intervened the relationship had been—as we now say—dysfunctional. "I married a socially acceptable man and had four kids. I tried to live through them, which meant I controlled everything they did. . . . Of course, I started to drive my husband and kids crazy. Who wants to be lived through?"[33]

---

31. On November 24, 1992, the General Assembly voted 53 to 3, with 79 abstentions, to repudiate the Cuban Democracy Act recently passed by the U.S. Congress and signed into law by President Bush. Voting with Washington were Israel and Romania. European Community governments, along with those of Canada and Japan, decreed this aspect of the "Cuban Democracy Act" null and void outside of the United States for its obvious violation of international norms and GATT agreements.

32. "U.S. Envoy in Nicaragua Asserts Washington Will Stop Meddling," *New York Times,* February 10, 1994, A8.

33. Katharine's story as told by Gloria Steinem, *Revolution from Within* (Boston: Little, Brown and Co., 1993), 86.

2

The America/Américas Myth

I only know two things about the Monroe Doctrine: one is that no American I have met knows what it is; the other is that no American I have met will consent to its being tampered with. That being so, I conclude that the Monroe Doctrine is not a doctrine but a dogma.

—Salvador de Madariaga[1]

What, then, is this America/Américas myth? In particular, what are the "positive" elements that remain in play when "negative" concerns are no longer salient? Listing the major ideas and images found in this myth is neither difficult nor controversial. To understand the force of the myth, however, we must see those elements emerging from the United States' *national* experience. The myth springs from and perpetuates a confusion regarding the boundaries of an "American" project launched long ago by and for the United States. First, however, "myth" needs defining.

Discourse refers to language viewed through the *meanings* it constructs. *Myth* is a discourse of some complexity "constructed from a semiological chain which existed before it."[2] I shall return to Roland

1. Salvador de Madariaga, *Latin America between the Eagle and the Bear* (New York: Frederick Praeger, 1962), 74.

2. Roland Barthes, *Mythologies*, tr. Annette Lavers (New York: Noonday Press, 1990), section "Myth Today," 114.

Barthes, whose words those are, after conveying these concepts though examples. In his analysis of the U.S. founding fathers' struggle with diversity Sheldon Wolin refers to the *unum* of *e pluribus unum* as a "mytheme," borrowing the term from Claude Lévi-Strauss. This particular mytheme, "woven of such primary elements as national unity, patriotism, centralization, and the state, . . . is profoundly mimetic of an older mytheme, that of Old Testament monotheism."[3] Hence the "presence of the past" in the title of Wolin's book, a presence that mirrors Barthes's understanding of myth as "a second-order semiological system" or "metalanguage."[4]

At first cut myth can be understood as a story that constructs meaning by mobilizing associations *already extant* in the culture and *redeploying* them toward new objects (public policies for example) that then acquire the authority of those older meanings. By this process the old concepts are both renewed and gutted; their hold on us grows as their content fades. For example, most Americans "believe in" the Constitution but no longer know what it says. Or, to use an example central to this study, in 1823 President Monroe announced a policy to deal with his cabinet's fears about Russian and British designs on lands that U.S. leaders hoped to annex to the United States. Seventy years later Grover Cleveland claimed that that policy applied "to every stage of our national life and cannot become obsolete while our republic endures." Then a secretary of state coupled the Monroe Doctrine with the Golden Rule as "cardinal guides of American diplomacy."[5] Finally, Woodrow Wilson universalized "the doctrine of President Monroe" as something all nations of the world "should with one accord adopt."[6] By Wilson's era Monroe's policy had become a guiding principle, a foundational myth.

In 1928–33 the U.S. State Department all but repudiated the much

3. Sheldon Wolin, *The Presence of the Past* (Baltimore: The Johns Hopkins University Press, 1989), 123.

4. Barthes, *Mythologies*, 114–15.

5. Elihu Root, Address to the Eighth Annual Meeting of the American Society of International Law, Washington, D.C., April 22, 1914, as reprinted in *American Foreign Policy,* publication 17 in a series edited and published by the Carnegie Endowment for International Peace (Washington, D.C., 1920), 28–29. The Secretary of State was John Hay, who served in that capacity from 1898 to 1905.

6. Walter LaFeber, *Inevitable Revolutions* (New York: W. W. Norton, 1993), 60. For Wilson—in theory, not practice—the doctrine guaranteed each nation's right to pursue "its own way of development, unhindered, unthreatened, unafraid."

amended Monroe Doctrine as a working policy, although during the Cold War efforts were made to revive it in a multilateral form. The "Miller Doctrine" of 1950, for instance, and later the Committee of Santa Fe's recommendations to the Reagan presidency, sought a multilateralized Monroe Doctrine to legitimate U.S. interventions in the post–Good Neighbor, post–Rio Pact era.[7] While increasingly marginal to diplomatic discourse, however, the Monroe Doctrine continued to be cited as a set of principles capable of guiding "every stage of our national life." A president might allude to the Monroe Doctrine in a State of the Union address, as Reagan did in 1987, in an attempt to elicit bipartisan support for a specific policy.[8] Or "abandoning the Monroe Doctrine" might be used to dismiss a policy alternative, as a ranking CIA official attempted in 1984: "If we have decided to totally abandon the Monroe Doctrine," Robert Gates advised William Casey "then we ought to . . . acknowledge our helplessness and stop wasting everybody's time."[9] "As valid today as ever," "part of our national honor," "cornerstone," "bedrock," "bipartisan" is how the Monroe Doctrine continues to be described.

The implicit claim is that this doctrine is as foundational to U.S. foreign policy as is the U.S. Constitution. Raymond Moley, who served Franklin Roosevelt's brains trust, wrote in the 1960s: "the Monroe Doctrine is an 'entailed' inheritance. It cannot be sold for the promise of good will nor given away, nor dissipated by reinterpretation. Those who speak for the nation now are not its creators, they are its trustees."[10] From a different point on the political spectrum a quarter of a

---

7. In Miller's formulation if "the organized community," meaning the OAS, invited Washington to intervene in a Latin American country, then "such a collective undertaking, far from representing intervention, is the alternative to intervention." On the Miller Doctrine see LaFeber, *Inevitable Revolutions*, 95–96. References to the Monroe Doctrine in the Santa Fe report are found in Committee of Santa Fe, *A New Inter-American Policy for the Eighties* (Washington, D.C.: Council for Inter-American Security, 1981), 3, 4, 10, 45, 52.

8. "Our commitment to a Western Hemisphere safe from aggression did not occur by spontaneous generation on the day that we took office. It began with the Monroe Doctrine." See "Address Before a Joint Session of Congress on the State of the Union, January 27, 1987," *Public Papers of the Presidents of the United States: Ronald Reagan, 1987* (Washington, D.C.: U.S. Government Printing Office, 1989), 1:57.

9. Robert Gates, "Nicaragua," December 14, 1984, document 15 in *The Iran-Contra Scandal: The Declassified History*, ed. Peter Kornbluh and Malcolm Byrne (New York: The New Press, 1993), 48.

10. Raymond Moley, "Perspective," reprinted in *The Monroe Doctrine*, ed. Armin Rappaport (New York: Holt, Rinehart and Winston, 1964), 118.

century later came this echo: "[Monroe] bequeathed to us a property that is part of our national honor. The Monroe Doctrine is a doctrine for all seasons. May it live forever."[11] Barthes calls this giving "the immobility of the world the alibi of a 'wisdom.' "[12] For these U.S. citizens, however, the strongest image of permanent value is not wisdom but property.

Thus there are at least two Monroe Doctrines today: the historically embedded one that the State Department repudiates, and the myth that appears in the *domestic* political discourse from time to time, where it is used as a talisman. As with the U.S. Constitution this second doctrine is invoked to lend authority to a variety of policy positions. Just as most citizens believe in a Constitution they cannot accurately describe, so the Monroe Doctrine conveys a vague, proprietary feeling of this being "our" hemisphere without the speaker taking responsibility for the diplomatic consequences. It may be less confusing if we find a name that distinguishes this mythic usage from the historic policy.

The founding myth I call America/Américas has this second Monroe Doctrine at its center. Sowing ground plowed by Barthes and by Wolin, I consider a *founding myth* any portion of the public discourse that transforms a part of a nation's history into a model for subsequent generations to follow. Founding myths are narratives "for which successful claims are made not only to the status of [historical] truth"— quoting Bruce Lincoln—"but what is more, to the status of *paradigmatic* truth."[13] Lincoln's "what is more" alerts us to the additive nature of myth and history, often misunderstood as opposites.

The Holocaust provides a founding myth for the state of Israel. That "all men are created equal" and thus are entitled to "life, liberty, and the pursuit of happiness" is a founding myth of the United States that Martin Luther King Jr. mobilized in his attempt to rally whites as well as blacks to end racial segregation.[14] The official U.S. account of the 1941 Japanese attack on Pearl Harbor as treachery out of the blue also

11. "Reaffirming the Monroe Doctrine," *The Phyllis Schafly Report*, May 1987, as reproduced in *Opposing Viewpoints: Central America*, ed. Carol Wekesser (San Diego: Greenhaven Press, 1990), 60–61.

12. Barthes, *Mythologies*, 102.

13. Bruce Lincoln, *Discourse and the Construction of Society* (New York: Oxford University Press, 1989), 24.

14. James Cone, *Martin & Malcolm & America* (Maryknoll, N.Y.: Orbis Books, 1993), 65–66.

is history transformed into myth. Throughout the Cold War U.S. leaders invoked Pearl Harbor in making deterrence of surprise attacks a keystone of defense policy, even though many analysts thought it unlikely that a war with the Soviet Union would start that way. Fifty years after the event the *New York Times* claimed that "Pearl Harbor has left its imprint on all that has followed."[15] Half a century after its conclusion the Vietnam War may be similarly encoded. For now its paradigmatic lessons remain contested.

Founding myths often form as a nation deals with what turns out to be recurring or traumatic situations. Myths form around experiences that demand explanation or expiation. Once an explanation has been selected and encoded it sets the terms of debate for generations to come. Eventually history is all but forgotten *qua* history. In its place arises a timeless solution attributed to demigods (e.g., "Founding Fathers") or to the workings of teleological forces, such as the History of Hegel's *Weltgeschichte*. From the vantage point of the consumer of myths, myth "transforms history into nature," transforms contingent sociopolitical acts into what seems natural or inevitable.[16]

It should be apparent, then, that Monroe's addressing Congress in 1832 marks the beginning of this particular founding myth no more than the Clark Memorandum or Franklin Roosevelt's Good Neighbor Policy ended it. Mythic elements on which Monroe drew antedate his proclamation, while the doctrine took on mythic proportions well after his presidency. "Founding" refers to a date in history no more than "myth" refers to a specific policy. Different policies can draw legitimation from the same myth, while different myths may be cannibalized by a single policy. Nor are myths static: every time a community responds to a situation by invoking a founding myth some elements of it are reinforced while others are neglected or reinterpreted.[17]

To recapitulate, history is a narrative about the past that possesses credibility with the relevant audience. A founding myth is a history (thus a narrative) that has acquired the additional authority of a

15. "The Imprints of Pearl Harbor," *New York Times*, December 1, 1991, E10.
16. Barthes, *Mythologies*, 129.
17. Those seeking to broaden the terms of a debate have two strategic choices. One is to reinterpret the myth afresh while reinforcing it, which is what Martin Luther King Jr. did by invoking the Declaration of Independence to promote racial equality. The other is to attack the myth head-on, as when American Indians counter "Columbus discovered America" with "Indians discovered Columbus."

paradigm. Such authority is in the eyes of the beholders. Thus the reproduction of myth is a *political* process not understood simply by examining texts. Politically, a discourse is irrelevant if it is not persuasive and, as Bruce Lincoln reminds us, "the question of whether the discourse is persuasive or not . . . is only partly a function of its logical and ideological coherence."[18] "Sentiment evocation" is Lincoln's term for the mobilization of publics, a mobilization that depends on the political techniques that merit the separate analysis they receive in this book.

The Deep Sentences of the America/Américas Myth

One way of describing a founding myth is through its deep sentences: general statements of its recurring ideas. What follows is the cognitive map of the America/Américas myth I have developed through years of crisscrossing the terrain of U.S.–Latin American relations. Others may construct this map differently. Obviously such maps serve a heuristic function, not an evidentiary one. Once the ideas are clear, we will turn to some of the images used to convey them.

As I interpret it the Americas myth has four sentences that interact in supportive and contradictory ways. While in any given moment some sentences are dominant and others recessive, over time all endure. Only one of the four carries the negative message of "strategic denial."

1. The Western Hemisphere is the geographical *tabula rasa* on which God (Providence, History) demonstrates civilization's advance through agents understood to be the descendants of Europeans.
2. The content of this advance is freedom and progress: forms of association favoring the self-determination of peoples and the liberty of individuals, which are linked to advances in material well-being.
3. The United States of America is where this project first began and where it still excels. The United States is the vanguard of a hemisphere that, following its leadership, is the vanguard region of the world.
4. Such an advance in civilization provokes enmity from an old world that clings to ways that are the antithesis of the new ways described in (2). The new world may be endangered by the old.

The "freedom" and "progress" of sentence two expand and contract in meaning; recently freedom has included democracy. "Vanguard" is a

18. Lincoln, *Discourse and the Construction of Society,* 8.

contentious term never spoken by proponents of the myth. I have yet to find another word that captures, however, the mix of membership and leadership assigned to the United States by the myth. The United States is of the hemisphere and for the hemisphere but not just another hemispheric nation. The same holds true, albeit more tentatively, for the hemisphere in relation to the planet.

In this schematic presentation conflicts that require the skillful use of language already may be spotted. Unless the United States restricts itself to moral suasion and example, its vanguard activity conflicts with the freedom of other governments in the hemisphere. If all nations are sovereign—surely a precondition for freedom existing in the new world—then whenever one or more of them reject the tutelage of the vanguard and the vanguard imposes its will by force, a contradiction appears. There is a recurring tension in the myth, then, between statements two and three, which official discourse tries to hide or alleviate. Here is how.

If the future of humanity is on the line in a drama ordained by God or History, should the vanguard not use all means at its disposal to assure the outcome? (Readers who wonder how human agency could be so crucial to a divinely or historically driven project must detour through Calvinist theology to find their answer.) So sentence one is implicated in the conflict between two and three, while sentence four often comes to the rescue. If the hemispheric community is threatened by an outside predator, especially a retrograde "old world" power, then the vanguard appears as the protector of the community's freedom even as it compromises the freedom of an individual hemispheric country.

But why must there be a vanguard state within a vanguard region? If the "new world" is so special, and if "we are all Americans" from pole to pole, why must one nation monitor, tutor, and discipline the others? The most frequently provided answer is linked to sentence four. When old world influences infiltrate Latin America, some Latins forget who they are; they stop acting as Americans. But there are moments— Panama 1989 and Haiti 1994 are two—when outside influences are weak to nonexistent and the blame falls squarely on the Latins for backsliding.

It is here that we arrive at the central preoccupation of the myth: boundaries. Not just geographical markers separate a "new world" from an "old" but moral boundaries, those that define an "American" identity. While these boundaries expand and contract over time, the general movement has been expansion as U.S. leaders redeployed a U.S. identity and a U.S. project to unify the hemisphere behind their leadership. The ambiguity built into the word "America" (nation and hemisphere) serves this process.

Who is American?

The Americas myth originated as a founding myth of and about the *United States*. Each of the four sentences originally described a conception that early U.S. leaders held of their nation as they engaged the continent of North America and the peoples native to it. The westward expansion of the United States also was a southward expansion. The fledgling United States not only confronted Spain on its southern and western borders but soon newly independent Mexico. A sizeable chunk of what we now consider the U.S. West, extending from Texas to California, was pried loose from a fellow American republic—not an old world monarchy—under the duress of U.S. military occupation.

So the movement from a national project to a continental and then a hemispheric one was incremental. The *referent* of the myth expanded without the *content* of the myth changing—and without Washington ceasing to be the principal *author and agent*. In providing examples to illustrate this process this chapter will emphasize the "positive" legacy found in the first three sentences, for reasons that Chapter 1 introduced. Of course Latin American elites have myths that interact with those of the United States, sometimes in complementary, sometimes in conflicting ways. This analysis assumes the perspective of Washington, D.C., throughout.

In the previous chapter we heard U.S. officials identify "democracy" with an "America" that is hemispheric. In explaining Bush's Enterprise for the Americas Initiative to South American officials, Vice President Dan Quayle called that policy "a declaration of independence for the peoples of our hemisphere." A decade before, a major Reagan speech on Latin America began with "We the peoples of the Americas," echoing the Preamble of the U.S. Constitution ("We the People of the United States"). Such borrowings are obvious manifestations of a U.S. myth being redeployed for a hemispheric purpose.

Following Reagan's "We the peoples of the Americas" were six uses of the word "common." From "our common past" has emerged "our common quest" to fulfill "a common destiny." Vice President Quayle, who visited Latin America nine times representing President Bush, once told a group of Latin officials: "The Americas, North and South, are destined to shape the future together. . . . [W]e are indeed on an irreversible course. . . . [A] new era is here, bringing with it an irreversible attitude of 'we Americans,' North and South; 'we Americans,' building on our common values."[19] Reagan's address made explicit what Quayle's "destined" and "irreversible course" imply: "I have always believed that this hemisphere was a special place with a special destiny. I believe we are destined to be the beacon of hope for all mankind."[20] So as not to be accused of overinterpreting one speech I offer Reagan once more, this time speaking to the Organization of American States in October 1987. Reagan appropriated these words of a Brazilian statesman—"It seems evident that a decree of providence made the western shore of the Atlantic appear late in history as the chosen land for a great renewal of mankind"—before adding his own admonition to the assembled leaders: "to keep watch over this chosen land, to keep it secure from alien powers and colonial despotisms, so that man may renew himself here in freedom."[21] I quote Reagan at length so that official references to a God-given mission will not be seen as an artifact of the 1992 quincentennial of Columbus's "discovery" of the "new world." The same images do appear, however, in Bush speeches.

For President Bush it was "no accident of history" that "here in the Americas we are building something unprecedented."[22] In speaking to the United Nations he interpreted the collapse of Soviet bloc communism as a "renewal" of history, echoing the assumption popularized by Francis Fukuyama that liberal values are universal and predetermined.[23] In Bush's words, "Communism held history captive for years, but now

19. "New Opportunities in Hemispheric Trade," *U.S. Department of State Dispatch*, August 26, 1991, 635.

20. "Remarks on the Caribbean Basin Initiative, February 24, 1982," *Public Papers of the Presidents of the United States: Ronald Reagan, 1982* (Washington, D.C.: U.S. Government Printing Office, 1983), 1:215.

21. Address to the OAS, October 7, 1987, reproduced as "Central America at a Critical Juncture," *Current Policy* 1007 (U.S. Department of State).

22. I quote from longer passages provided in Chapter 1. See Chapter 1 footnotes for sources.

23. Fukuyama served on the State Department's Policy Planning Staff before publishing a

history is free to resume its course."[24] No less than Reagan, Bush spoke of the Americas as having long shared a project that he defined as "the courageous quest for the advancement of man." In Chapter 1 we heard him proclaim that "we" in the Western Hemisphere "can show the world."[25]

No subtlety is needed to hear in these words the language used to unify the colonies that formed the United States and to justify the expansion of that nation across the continent. Then as now unity is tied to a project that must not be denied inasmuch as it is driven by forces nobler and more powerful than mere mortals. So let us review the history of this "myth of a single people and a single narrative" that Wolin identifies with *unum*,[26] concentrating on how the referent shifts from nation to hemisphere, from America to Américas.

History of a Myth

In a shipboard sermon to his Puritan band in 1630 John Winthrop preached, "We shall be as a city upon a hill, the eyes of all people are upon us."[27] Compare that to Reagan's "this chosen land" and Bush's "We can show the world" because (Bush said in a later speech) "it is our responsibility—it is our opportunity—to lead. There is no one else."[28] While leaving a contentious and censoring "old world" behind, many who settled New England believed that their experiment eventually would save humanity. "God, they thought, had singled them out to lead humankind. And He had given them an almost incredible opportunity. The New World was a vacuum, a clean slate on which humanity

---

1989 article subsuming the collapse of communism in Eastern Europe under a worldwide, history-climaxing triumph of Western liberal values. The U.S. "winning" the Cold War is evidence, he argued, for "a coherent and directional History of mankind." See *The End of History and the Last Man* (New York: The Free Press, 1992), xii.

24. "Excerpts from Bush's Address to General Assembly," *New York Times*, September 24, 1991, A6.

25. "Latin America: Debt Reduction," Bush's speech launching the Enterprise for the Americas Initiative delivered June 27, 1990, reproduced in *Vital Speeches of the Day* 66:20 (August 1, 1990), 612.

26. Wolin, *The Presence of the Past*, 136.

27. Roderick Nash and Gregory Graves, *From These Beginnings* (New York: 1990), 1:24.

28. Bush's first statement has been cited (see note 25 above). His second is found in "America's Role in the World," *U.S. Department of State Dispatch*, January 11, 1993, 13.

could write. . . . The New World gave them and all humankind another chance."[29] In Chapter 1 we heard an under secretary of state say in 1991, "We are the hemisphere which gave mankind a second chance."[30] Winthrop's vision was transmitted through such prolific writers and sermon givers as Jonathan Edwards and Cotton Mather, still active when those who drafted the Constitution were in their formative years. Adopting the Protestant practice of scanning the Old Testament for signs of things to come in the "new dispensation" set forth in the New Testament, these early myth weavers found in Israel, God's people in the wilderness, their model. "Winthrop's faith in America as a City on the Hill and then as another Israel was echoed by Jonathan Edwards 'that God might in [America] begin *a new world* in a spiritual respect.' "[31] Whether viewed as the reincarnation of Jerusalem or as the incarnation of Augustine's City of God, the American experiment was a construction against nature and against the "heathens" who lived in it. This was a city rising from the desert, a light thrust into the darkness, a repudiation of that wilderness which contemporary theologians at Oxford and Cambridge identified with hell.

This metaphor would cast the British as Pharaoh's men persecuting the American Israelites in their quest for freedom. As the Revolution was being fought Benjamin Franklin wrote that "our Cause is the Cause of all Mankind. . . . Tis a glorious task assign'd us by Providence."[32] On the Great Seal of the newly independent United States Thomas Jefferson wanted the Children of Israel led by a pillar of light. As it turned out, that seal, visible on the dollar bill, carries the mottoes "Annuit Coeptis" (He—God—has favored our undertaking) and "Novus Ordo Seclorum" (new order of the ages) surrounding an Egyptian pyramid with thirteen courses of stone. An official selling the North American Free Trade Agreement to Congress in 1992 noted this early reference to a "new world order."[33]

29. Nash and Graves, *From These Beginnings,* 32.
30. Lawrence Eagleburger's address to the General Assembly of the Organization of American States, reprinted in *U.S. Department of State Dispatch,* June 10, 1991, 414.
31. William Appleman Williams, *Empire as a Way of Life* (New York: Oxford University Press, 1980), 39, emphasis added.
32. Nash and Graves, *From These Beginnings,* 86.
33. Robert Zoellick, "The North American FTA [Free Trade Agreement]," *U.S. Department of State Dispatch,* April 13, 1992. Zoellick, the Under Secretary of State for Economic Affairs, gave virtually the same speech to the Senate Foreign Relations Committee one year before; see *U.S. Department of State Dispatch,* April 15, 1991.

Amply represented among the founding fathers were Free Masons who would have understood those symbols—especially the eye that tops the pyramid—to represent the divine, all-seeing Architect. Among these early leaders were deists who embraced the Newtonian concept of a Providence imparting movement to history while leaving humans the tasks of explicating its design through science and of manifesting its purpose through leadership. A concept that captures this sentence-one view of history is the invisible hand, today a metaphor for goods and services clearing in a market left unfettered by regulation but then literally God's hand. Replying to George Washington's first inaugural address, the House of Representatives acknowledged "the strongest obligations to adore the Invisible Hand which has led the American people through so many difficulties."[34]

By the 1840s this "sublime and friendly Destiny" was guiding America westward to "the country of the Future" (Ralph Waldo Emerson). Emerson penned the very sentiment that Reagan's speech writers later found in the Brazilian leader. "Our whole history," Emerson wrote, "appears to be a last effort of Divine Providence on behalf of the human race."[35] In our time U.S. leaders have become more comfortable ascribing the project to Nature—in recent decades "winds" and "tides"—than to God or Providence. But the implicit message remains the same: an American community moving inexorably toward a predetermined, transcendent goal. Indeed the nature imagery has antecedents in Hamilton's reference to the future growth of the United States as "the irresistible and unchangeable course of nature" and in John Quincy Adams's statement that "From the time when we became an independent people it was as much a law of nature that this should become our pretension [absorbing Mexico and Central America] as that the Mississippi should flow to the sea."[36]

Woven into this premodern vision, it is true, is the modern theme of

34. Washington used the phrase in his first inaugural address, to which each house of Congress responded. See *A Compilation of the Messages and Papers of the Presidents*, ed. James Richardson (n.p.: Bureau of National Literature, 1911).

35. Williams, *Empire as a Way of Life*, 53, 87; Patricia Hill, "Picturing Progress in the Era of Westward Expansion," in *The West as America*, ed. William Truettner (Washington, D.C.: The Smithsonian Institution Press, 1991), 97.

36. Alexander Hamilton, John Jay, and James Madison, *The Federalist Papers*, ed. Isaac Kramnick (Harmondsworth, Eng.: Penguin Books, 1987), 131. Adams's recollection of what he told a November 1819 cabinet meeting as quoted by Dexter Perkins, *The Monroe Doctrine, 1823–1826* (Cambridge: Harvard University Press, 1932), 9.

liberation: freedom from the monarch and from the contrictions of established religion. Talking *about* freedom, however, does not alter the implicit assumption of the myth that freedom is self-evident to the chosen few who will impose it on others. While Europe was moving toward positive law, early leaders of the United States clung to "the old idea of a fundamental law beyond human control," notes Samuel Huntington. Fundamental law was "given new authority by identifying it with a written constitution." Modern conceptions of democracy, in contrast, assume that no vision is privileged over others and that none is permanent. Consensus is forged through procedures rooted in assumptions of equality and change. "The certainty that one outcome is best for all," Adam Przeworski explains, is deeply antithetical to democracy.[37]

Originally the chosen *were* few. Not all of European stock qualified as Americans, much less the Africans brought as slaves or the indigenous peoples considered savages when not treated as invisible. For John Adams the Catholicism of Latin America's whites disqualified them from the American project because "a free government and the Roman Catholic religion can never exist together in any nation or country."[38] The Latin Americans with whom most U.S. citizens dealt were further disqualified by their Indian or African genes, *mestizaje* or race mixing being more common south of the border than north. When, in *Federalist* 11, Alexander Hamilton foresaw "one great American system superior to the control of all trans-Atlantic force or influence and able to dictate the terms of the connection between the Old and the New World," his "America" was hemispheric while his "Americans" were the whites of the soon to be reorganized United States.[39]

Two decades later Jefferson foresaw, "What a Colossus shall we be when the Southern continent comes up to our mark!"[40] John Quincy Adams found Jefferson's dream not at all fanciful: "Florida, he argued,

37. Samuel P. Huntington, *Political Order in Changing Societies* (New Haven: Yale University Press, 1968), 104; Adam Przeworski, *Democracy and the Market* (Cambridge: Cambridge University Press, 1991), 93.

38. Merrill Peterson, *Adams and Jefferson: A Revolutionary Dialogue* (Athens: University of Georgia Press, 1976), 118.

39. Hamilton, Jay, and Madison, *The Federalist Papers*, 134. While the context makes clear that Hamilton's "America" is hemispheric—one of the world's "four parts"—Hamilton's essay makes no mention of Latin America or Latin Americans. References to Americans as people—as in "the genius of American merchants and navigators"—clearly had U.S. citizens in mind.

40. Peterson, *Adams and Jefferson*, 118.

had been acquired from Spain in 1821, and there was reason to believe that Cuba, Texas, and perhaps all of South America would some day join the union."[41] The "America" now under discussion embraced Mexico, the Caribbean, and Central America all the way to the Panamanian isthmus, but *as territory*. Early U.S. leaders faced the same dilemma with contiguous Latin peoples as with indigenous peoples: how to incorporate the land but not the cultures.

In a world shaped by Luther and Locke to recognize the humanity of others is tantamount to admitting their rights. Convoluted legal arrangements treated tribes as sovereign foreign states for some purposes—obviating the need to make Indians citizens—while reserving to the federal government the right to move tribes from place to place as suited U.S. interests.[42] This "having it both ways" carried over into the federal government's treatment of sovereign Latin states, beginning with Mexico. If Latins were unable to bring progress to a landscape destined to advance progress, then someone's got to do it. Historian William Prescott justified the taking of one-third of Mexico on the grounds that "beggarly Mexico" lacked the energy to put that land to productive use.[43] To this day U.S. leaders refer to portions of Latin America as "yard" (front or back) or "grounds" ("fertile grounds," "breeding grounds").[44]

It was with regard to "our proper dominion" reaching as far south as present-day Panama that John Quincy Adams told Monroe's cabinet that "[f]rom the time when we became an independent people it was as

41. Nash and Graves, *From These Beginnings*, 154.

42. While on the one hand the United States treated the tribes as sovereign nations with which treaties could be signed, on the other hand the new federal government claimed ownership of the land on which those tribes had lived for generations as long as that land was not claimed by another "civilized" (i.e., European) government. Early on the U.S. Supreme Court made its peace with these "peculiar . . . distinctions which exist nowhere else." See *Cherokee Nation v Georgia* (1831) and the discussion of this and other cases by Stephen Pevar, *The Rights of Indians and Tribes* (New York: Bantam Books, 1983), 23 and passim.

43. Richard Slotin, *The Fatal Environment: The Myth of the Frontier in the Age of Industrialization, 1800–1890* (New York: Atheneum, 1985), 229.

44. In one use of this metaphor President Bush went from describing Latin America as "fertile ground" for democracy to describing a "battle for democracy" being fought on a "battlefield" that he defined as "the broad middle ground of democracy and popular government." Perhaps the tendency to describe Latin America as terrain over which others fight led the speech writers to forget that democracy is about people and uses methods the opposite of those found in warfare. See Bush addressing the Council of the Americas in Washington, D.C., May 2, 1989, as reproduced in *Current Policy* 1168.

much a law of nature that this should become our pretension as that the Mississippi should flow to the sea."[45] Yet Adams wanted nothing to do with Latin peoples who, he wrote in his diary, "are not likely to promote the spirit either of freedom or order by their example. They have not the first elements of good or free government. Arbitrary power, military and ecclesiastical, was stamped on their institutions. Civil dissension was infused into all their seminal principles."[46] Since Latin peoples could not be rounded up and put on reservations, what were those in charge of the project to do?

A partial, "nominalist" solution came from an idea that Hamilton and Jefferson expounded of an international regime in the "new world" so antithetical to that found in the "old" that whatever Washington did could not be labeled power politics or imperialism. This line was further developed by President Polk who presided over the annexation of much of Mexico.[47] While voices, including Thoreau's and Lincoln's, pointed out the contradiction in a project about freedom taking freedom away from those who already had it, the limiting factor was that too few U.S. leaders wished to make states of Latin lands until and unless there were enough white settlers to populate them. (The controversy over slave states versus free states entered here.) Most emigrants from east of the Mississippi preferred the Oregon Territory to hotter climes, so after the Southwest was annexed plans to do the same in Cuba, Hispaniola, and Nicaragua floundered, with unstable compromises found in protectorates and private governments.

When U.S. strategic and economic interests no longer could be satisfied in contiguous countries, annexation no longer offered a solution regardless of what was done with the people. Access to and the support of countries south of Panama began to matter, especially in time of world war. (Recall that the two world wars of the twentieth

45. Perkins, *The Monroe Doctrine*, 9.
46. As quoted in Lars Schoultz, *National Security and United States Policy toward Latin America* (Princeton: Princeton University Press, 1987), 122.
47. James Polk's first annual message to Congress, in 1845, contained this sentence-four logic: "The American system of government is entirely different from that of Europe. Jealousy among the different sovereigns of Europe, lest any of them might become too powerful for the rest, has caused them anxiously to desire the establishment of what they term 'the balance of power.' It can not be permitted to have any application on the North American continent, and especially to the United States." See *American Foreign Policy,* publication 17 in a series edited and published by the Carnegie Endowment for International Peace (Washington, D.C., 1920), 7.

century were low tech, requiring vast quantities of raw materials.) So
strategies of collaboration and control arose, with Washington's goal
being control *through* collaboration. In South America the British
already had demonstrated the efficacy of "the imperialism of free
trade": the ability to trade and invest on favorable terms in less
developed countries while avoiding the onus and expense of colonial
rule. Before the turn of the century Secretary of State James Blaine
announced that "our great demand is expansion" through trade, not
"annexation of territory." Blaine acknowledged that this would require
better relations with Latin elites.[48] Collaboration is hard to elicit while
assuming that would-be partners are defective.

Within the United States in the nineteenth century the prevailing
images of Latins were similar to whites' images of blacks: genetically
inferior ("a wild, wandering race, half Indian, half Spanish"), exces-
sively sensual ("indulgent, easy, and voluptuous life"), violent ("a
permanent *Riotocracy*"), and lazy ("lack industry, energy, and persever-
ance").[49] As World War II approached, however, the federal government
promoted positive images, casting Latins as fellow "Americans." New
York City's Sixth Avenue was renamed "Avenue of the Americas."
"Pan-Americana" was invented, fusing the Virgin Mary with the Statue
of Liberty. Pressure was brought to bear on Hollywood to revise its
stereotypes; Walt Disney obliged with a likeable parrot in a sombrero.[50]
The name of this movement, Pan-Americanism, says it all.

Fruit-hatted, air-headed Carmen Miranda still proved the better draw,
however, while Latin males continued to be identified with sleaze
and violence.[51] The boundary of American identity was and remains
contested, with different classes and regions of the United States continuing to view Latin Americans differently. What is said publicly may be
contradicted in private. Suggestive of ongoing ambivalence is the official
language already quoted, which "protests too much" that we are
Americans from pole to pole, that we are united, that we have common

48. LaFeber, *Inevitable Revolutions*, 33.
49. Fredrick Pike, *The United States and Latin America: Myths and Stereotypes of Civilization and Nature* (Austin: University of Texas Press, 1992), 68–71.
50. George Black, *The Good Neighbor* (New York: Pantheon Books, 1988), 69–70.
51. For Hollywood's construction of Mexicans see Carlos Cortés, "To View a Neighbor,"
in *Images of Mexico in the United States,* ed. John Coatsworth and Carlos Rico (San Diego:
University of California Center for U.S.–Mexican Studies, 1989).

values. In these speeches we hear echoes of George Washington exhort-
ing the regions of the young United States to "nourish" one another
when their unity was in fact far from assured.[52] For all these reasons it
is impossible to be precise in describing shifts in the identity boundary.
  Just how far official U.S. discourse had come by the 1990s, however,
can be seen in a speech made by an under secretary of state seeking
congressional support for the North American Free Trade Agreement.
Robert Zoellick began by describing an "original vision" born of the
American (i.e., U.S.) Revolution that inspired Latin Americans, who
nevertheless were unable to "realize" this vision in their lands. "Pre-
served by leaders with imagination on both sides of the border," today
that American (i.e., hemispheric) vision can be realized, starting with
the economic integration of the United States and Mexico. "After
200 years, history is coming full circle." Still, Zoellick anticipates
critics—"nay-sayers in the United States who grumble that Latin
America is in some way 'different,' or even a threat."[53] Lars Schoultz
found such "nay-sayers," albeit off the record, while conducting interviews in Washington in the 1980s: witness the State Department official
who told him that "What screws up Latin America is the Latin Americans. And they'll *always* screw it up, because *they're* screwed up."[54]

In Search of the *Latin* American

We have seen contradictions in the four sentences when rendered in
expository prose; we also have seen the boundary defining "American"
contested. It is through images that a discourse copes with these

52. A long paragraph in Washington's Farewell Address is devoted to demonstrating just
how much North and South, East and West "nourish and increase" one another, and how the
unity of these regions provides all "greater security from external danger."
  53. Zoellick, "The North American FTA." Zoellick's audience may have included Senator
Jesse Helms, who only a few years before had said "All Latins are volatile people." See
"Insulting the Latins," *Washington Post National Weekly Edition*, June 30, 1986, 22.
  54. Schoultz, *National Security and United States Policy*. Whereas Adams, father and son,
viewed Latin Americans' Catholicism as a defect, recent criticism by U.S. officials has found
the entire culture wanting. A good example of this is the book written by one long-involved
in U.S. AID programs in Latin America and the Caribbean. See Lawrence E. Harrison,
Underdevelopment Is a State of Mind: The Latin American Case (Lanham, Md.: Madison
Books, 1985).

problems. The ascendancy of images over ideas will lead us, in the next chapter, to consider the role that advertising plays in the reproduction of the myth today. Here it is enough to show that images too have genealogies.

Historically, the expansion of the American identity, checked by the vanguard's lingering fear that Latins may not live up to their (read: our) destiny has been handled by contrasting the "good" Latin with the "bad" and explaining the bad in terms of outside influences (sentence four). There is a long tradition of describing Marxism in Latin America as a virus or a cancer—that is, an alien element in an otherwise sound body. There is an equally long tradition representing the good Latin as a white female in need of protection. A recurring metaphor for the international relations of the region is a family in which the United States appears as brother while using the voice of father.

Researching U.S. editorial cartoons from the end of the nineteenth century to the middle of the twentieth, John Johnson found the larger Latin American nations frequently portrayed as female while the smaller countries were represented as children and, in the pre–Civil Rights era, as racially African.[55] The white señorita straddles the line of American identity: not quite "one of us" yet worthy of our protection, the stock situation of countless Hollywood films set in Mexico, where the white U.S. male saves the light-skin Mexican female from the dark Mexican male.[56] In political cartoons "old world" powers are Uncle Sam's rival for the señorita's affections.

With the Latin children Uncle Sam acts the tutor, disciplinarian, babysitter, or referee, showing the unappreciated forbearance captured in these words of a 1920s official: "[A]s these young nations grow and develop a greater capacity for self-government, and finally take their places upon an equal footing with the mature, older nations of the world, . . . they will come to see the United States with different eyes, and to have for her something of the respect and affection with which a man regards the instructor of his youth and a child looks upon the

---

55. John J. Johnson, *Latin America in Caricature* (Austin: University of Texas Press, 1993), chaps. 3–5. U.S. media portrayals of Cuba at the turn of the century presented these options: ". . . Spain as a stage villain, all black cloak and twirling mustachio. Cuba was a slender young woman—the kind who gets tied to railroad tracks. And the native population was portrayed as squalling, watermelon-eating imbeciles and infants . . . or 'pickaninnies,' a word derived from the Spanish *pequeño*, for little child" (Black, *The Good Neighbor*, 13–14).
56. Cortés, "To View a Neighbor."

parent who has molded his character."[57] As the 1981 cartoon suggests (Fig. 1), this pattern persists.

Family provides a bridge linking freedom and vanguard, equality and difference, while emphasizing unity. Children carry the family name and (the older generation hopes) learn parental values, even though children make mistakes along the way. Disciplining offspring is an act of love, not power.[58] This metaphor strengthens the sense of a common project found in the first two sentences while accounting for the existence of the vanguard nation within the vanguard region, inasmuch as families are not run democratically. Family also is a unifying symbol to fall back upon whenever control is shaky. Thus, when Los Angeles erupted in arson and looting in 1992, President Bush asked God to "give us the strength and the wisdom to bring the family together, the American family."[59]

Following World War II, when Latin governments asked for their reward for having kept the Allies supplied with cheap raw materials, they got not their own Marshall Plan but President Harry Truman promising "increased economic collaboration within the family of American nations." When Lyndon Johnson met with Latin American representatives in Washington following the assassination of John F. Kennedy, he termed it "a family gathering." "Family of free nations" and "family of nations in the Western Hemisphere" pepper Reagan-era discourse.[60]

57. Stokely Morgan, Assistant Chief of the Division of American Affairs, U.S. Department of State, as quoted by Walter LaFeber, *Inevitable Revolutions* (New York: W. W. Norton, 1984), 301.

58. There is obvious silencing in dismissing another as inferior, as Nixon's chief foreign policy adviser Henry Kissinger did when he told the Chilean foreign minister that Chile was "off the axis of history." But there also is silencing in speaking for others because you know them so well. Family is one of the sites where most of us experience this. Familiar examples occur in the traditional marriage where the Mr. and Mrs. speak with one voice, his, and where the parent tells the child "you need to" but really means "I want you to." At the core of silencing through identification is projection: attributing to another one's own needs and goals. In such a relationship I allow myself to know you only insofar as you mirror me. Speaking for the other because we know them so well slides into acting for the other when we have the power to do so, and finally into overriding their expressed desires in the name of defending their best interests, which is what Kissinger did in destabilizing Chile under Allende. See Seymour M. Hersh, *The Price of Power: Kissinger in the Nixon White House* (New York: Summit Books, 1983), 259, 265, passim.

59. "Bush Finds 'Horror' on Los Angeles Tour," *New York Times*, May 8, 1992, A1.

60. Truman's "Address Before the Rio de Janeiro Inter-American Conference . . . , September 2, 1947," *Public Papers of the Presidents: Harry Truman, 1947* (Washington, D.C.: U.S. Government Printing Office, 1963), 431. Johnson's "Remarks on the Alliance for Progress . . . , November 26, 1963," *Public Papers of the Presidents: Lyndon B. Johnson, 1963–64* (Washington, D.C.: U.S. Government Printing Office, 1965), 1:6. Reagan's "Mes-

Latin American nations are "sister republics" but rarely is the United States their sister. Official discourse prefers to cast Washington as "neighbor" or "brother" and, when these images become shopworn, to pile on adjectives. After using neighbor a dozen times in a major policy address on Latin America, President Reagan said, "I believe that my country is now ready to go beyond being a good neighbor to being a true friend and brother."[61] "President Clinton is committed to forging a true partnership of the Americas," a deputy secretary of state told the Council of the Americas.[62] Post-Orwell, it is inconceivable that a U.S. president would refer to the United States, as Franklin Roosevelt did, as Latin America's "guardian and big brother,"[63] but those images probably come closer to the role U.S. leaders actually see themselves playing than the less offending alternatives. So officials tolerate the compromise that is "Uncle Sam" (neither father nor brother but an elder relative) while addressing the region in a disembodied voice that often sounds parental without identifying the relationship.

In 1982, referring to the three then-Marxist governments of Latin America, President Reagan told a mixed audience of U.S. and Latin American officials: "We seek to exclude no one. Some, however, have turned from their American neighbors and their heritage. Let them return to the traditions and common values of this hemisphere, and we will welcome them. The choice is theirs."[64] Normalizing U.S. relations with Cuba must await Fidel Castro's "sincerely and honestly want[ing] to rejoin the family of American nations," Reagan repeated to the press.[65] The metaphor is the parable of the prodigal son and the voice that of the father, but the "we" remains ambiguous while responsibility for what ensues is placed on the children.

---

sage to the Congress on America's Agenda for the Future, February 6, 1986," *Public Papers of the Presidents: Ronald Reagan, 1986* (Washington, D.C.: U.S. Government Printing Office, 1988), 1:159. Additional Reagan sources appear in footnote 20 plus "U.S. and Cuba Gain an Accord," *New York Times,* December 15, 1984, A1.

61. Reagan, "Remarks on the Caribbean Basin Initiative," 215.

62. "Forging a True Partnership of the Americas," U.S. *Department of State Dispatch,* May 3, 1993, 305.

63. Black, *The Good Neighbor,* 60.

64. Reagan, "Remarks on the Caribbean Basin Initiative."

65. Reagan speaking to editors and broadcasters from Midwestern states, as reproduced in *Reagan on Cuba,* no. 18 in a series of pamphlets published by the Cuban-American National Foundation (Washington, D.C., 1986), 21.

Fig. 1. **1907:** "More Trouble in the Nursery" by Osborn, *Milwaukee Sentinel,* 1907. **1928:** "Welcome, Lindbergh!" by Cal Alley, *Memphis Commercial Appeal,* 1928, reprinted by permission of *The Commercial Appeal,* Memphis. **1981 and 1984:** "Sam's Sitting Service" by John Lara, *The Orange County Register,* 1981, and *The Washington Post National Weekly Edition,* 1984; reprinted by permission of *The Orange County Register.* The two earlier cartoons were first reproduced in John J. Johnson, *Latin America in Caricature* (Austin: University of Texas Press, 1980, 1993).

The Committee of Santa Fe's position paper for the Reagan administration referred to the hemisphere as a supportive wife in danger of
"sterilization" by outside influences, especially Marxism; it then singled
out the Caribbean as facing "the natural growing pains of young
nationhood."[66] While superficially the opposite of the virus metaphor,
sterilization continues the image of something from outside invading an
otherwise healthy body politic. Blaming "Bolsheviks" for "injecting" a
"virus" into Latin America was a stock metaphor of the 1920s. When
malaria existed in southern U.S. states as well as in the Caribbean
Basin, communism was an "infection" that "spread" from "breeding
grounds." In his address justifying the U.S. intervention in Guatemala
in 1954 Secretary of State John Foster Dulles claimed that "international
communism has been probing here and there for nesting places in the
Americas. It finally chose Guatemala as a spot . . . [from which] to
breed subversion which would extend to other American republics."[67]
   When malaria lost its power to frighten U.S. audiences, cancer
became the intruder who passes unnoticed until it is too late. While U.S.
officials originally saw Fidel Castro's triumphant revolutionaries as
"children" who "had to be led rather than rebuffed," for "like children,
they were capable of doing almost anything," in time Castro came to
represent "a cancer we cannot live with for another ten years."[68] In the
case study we shall encounter "the malignancy in Managua" in Reagan
speeches. Sometimes the invader remains formless, which is no less
frightening. One thing it cannot be is human. In his major address of
1982 President Reagan said, "A new kind of colonialism stalks the
world today and threatens our independence. It is brutal and totalitarian. It is not of our hemisphere but it threatens our hemisphere."[69]

66. Committee of Santa Fe, ii, 4, 10, 11, 53.
67. "International Communism in Guatemala," radio and television address of June 30,
1954, reprinted as publication 48 in the U.S. Department of State's Inter-American series,
August 1954. Consistent with this metaphor, Dulles spoke of "an alien despotism" using
Guatemala "for its own evil ends."
68. CIA Director Allen Dulles is recorded using the children analogy in "Memorandum of
Discussion at the 396th Meeting of the National Security Council, Washington, D.C., February
12, 1959," Foreign Relations of the United States, 1958–1960, vol. 5, American Republics
(Washington, D.C.: U.S. Government Printing Office, 1991), 80. The cancer remark made by
President John Kennedy is found in Lloyd Etheredge, Can Governments Learn? (New York:
Pergamon Press, 1985), 162.
69. Reagan, "Remarks on the Caribbean Basin Initiative."

"Family" may ironically feed the negative perception of the Latin American that it is intended to overcome. By persuading themselves that Latins are Americans just like them, U.S. leaders raise their own and their public's expectations. Should Latins fail, they sully the family name. Whether father, uncle, or older brother, Washington cannot shake its foreboding that, sooner or later, the Latin adolescent will (as the State Department official said) "screw up." Being ever vigilant, parents find—even generate—what they fear. Guatemala's government is caught purchasing Czech weapons, Nicaragua's government is caught with Marx on its postage stamps.[70]

In the early Clinton years columnists speculated on why a new administration from a different political party, in a post–Cold War setting, would continue the previous and by most accounts ineffective policy of attempting to liberalize Cuba by economically isolating it. This policy was creating problems for Washington's relations with its allies both in Europe and in the Americas. Part of the answer lay in domestic policies (the Cuban vote in key states). No less important, however, was the sense of betrayal burned into the psyche of U.S. leaders by Castro's being the prodigal who would not return.[71] Family metaphors moralize foreign policy in ways that often prove dysfunctional.

The Prejudice of Equality

While the America/Américas myth broadened the American identity to include Latins, agent and author remained in Washington, D.C. The

70. A classic case in recent years has been U.S.-Mexican "cooperation" on reducing the flow of illegal narcotics into the United States. For Washington it was a "war on drugs," for Mexico's government a problem to be handled while dealing with higher priority issues. Not finding Mexico's pursuit of narcotraffickers energetic enough, the United States insinuated its own agents into Mexico over the initial objections of the Mexican government. In the economic straits it was in Mexico could hardly afford to refuse an insistent Washington, and did not. Within Mexico the two different styles of operation clashed, convincing many U.S. officials that the Mexicans are corrupt and incompetent, while confirming many Mexicans' belief that Washington does not respect their country's sovereignty or view their officials as equals.

71. Salvador Allende also was viewed as an "errant child" within the policy-making circles of the Nixon administration according to a naval officer assigned to Kissinger's National Security Council. Kissinger viewed the entire Chilean electorate as children, as evidenced by

sentences have changed in some respects but not in others. What for devout colonists was a means (freedom to carry forth the mission commended to their conscience) has become transformed into an end: the freedom to be free. The residue of teleology means, however, that whatever the chosen people desire requires no further justification. Manifest Destiny took the project west while "freedom" and "development" carried it south. Facilitating this movement has been its lack of clear territorial boundaries. The myth survives to this day, however, not simply out of habit but because it continues to resolve problems Washington has with its hemispheric neighbors. Founding myths are reproduced because they provide not optimal solutions but familiar ones.

There are objective differences between societies and cultures in the Western Hemisphere, not the least being the unrivaled power and wealth of the United States. Aware of those differences, most Latin leaders are desirous of good relations with the region's largest market, banker, and military power. Not surprisingly the solution they offer to the common quest for order assumes a legal-institutional form. Examine the history of inter-American conferences and you will see a recurring dance in which Latin leaders try to commit Washington to binding rules interpreted by collective entities (even granting the United States more of a vote than others), while U.S. leaders intone the Americas myth and say, "Trust us, we're family."

As a world power the United States has wanted to be backed by its region but not to be bound by decisions collectively made by that region. Thus for Washington unity through language has been preferable to unity through procedures: it is easier to reinterpret promises than to fudge rules. Monroe's proscription of monarchy in the Western Hemisphere evolved into a ban on homegrown Marxism within Latin America, even when voted into power. That is how flexible discourse can be. But not any discourse will do.

At the close of the twentieth century and toward a region that shares a Western European genealogy, the United States cannot employ the control through otherness that Edward Said perceived in Orientalism, the West's construction of Asia and the Middle East.[72] While U.S.

his much-quoted remark "I don't see why we need stand by and watch a country go communist due to the irresponsibility of its own people." See Hersh, *The Price of Power*, 259, 265; and Schoultz, *National Security and United States Policy*, 284.

72. *Orientalism* (New York: Pantheon Books, 1978).

leaders initially used "otherness" in constructing Latin America, they soon found the contradictions too glaring and the resistance too strong. So Washington took the Americas myth in a different direction, emphasizing sameness rather than difference, inclusion rather than distance. While Tzvetan Todorov reminds us that this solution also has a long history, it is better suited than "otherness" for U.S.–Latin American relations of the mid to late twentieth century.

Control through conflation—through presumed identity—has serious shortcomings, which subsequent chapters explore. "Otherness reduced to sameness" is how Roland Barthes described "bourgeois myth" in Europe. Its flip side he accurately portrayed as difference constructed as criminality—the betrayal theme noted above. Others become our "analogues *who have gone astray*,"[73] as in Reagan's characterization of the Sandinistas as "betrayers" of their own revolution. Otherness reduced to sameness, when the otherness is real, is what Todorov calls "the prejudice of equality," which he defines as "identifying the other purely and simply with one's own 'ego ideal.' "[74] That same conflation William Connolly describes as "universalism subjugat[ing] the particularity of the other to its own particular code with universalist pretensions."[75]

While Connolly's formulation is less euphonious than Todorov's, it reminds us why America/Américas is associated with History or Nature, not just the United States. Adams's "as much a law of nature . . . as that the Mississippi should flow to the sea" becomes Bush's "rising tide of democracy sweeping the world" as History resumes its course. Following Kennedy's Secretary of State Dean Rusk, Reagan preferred "winds of freedom." Clinton keeps the practice alive with "winds of change."[76] Such language masks authorship and options.

While it is true that a common enemy or external threat helps solidify the hemispheric community and deflect attention from the vanguard, sentence four remains but one element in a versatile strategy of control that emphasizes identity. The America/Américas myth has four deep sentences, not one.

73. Barthes, *Mythologies,* 151–52; emphasis in the original.
74. *The Conquest of America,* trans. Richard Howard (New York: Harper & Row Colophon, 1985), 165.
75. *Identity/Difference* (Ithaca: Cornell University Press, 1991), 41.
76. President Clinton, "NAFTA: Embracing Change," *U.S. Department of State Dispatch,* September 13, 1993, 622.

3

From Myth to Advertising

From an anthropological perspective, ads are among the supreme creations of this era, standing in relation to our technological, consumer culture as the pyramids did to the ancients and the Gothic cathedrals to the medievals.

—Alan Thein Durning[1]

In U.S. politics today, media drive messages. Techniques used to sell a policy to targeted publics select both the language used to describe the policy and, through that selection, important elements of the policy itself. Thus an irony dogs this work. What I regard as an anachronistic conception of inter-American relations is reproduced using the latest techniques of political persuasion borrowed from the advertising, public relations, and entertainment industries. Myths premodern in their assumptions survive through a manipulation of communications so attentive to surfaces, so media-driven, so unconcerned with logical consistency that they could be termed postmodern. Advertising trades in simulacra, slogans, and logos; it is nothing if not eclectic.[2]

A central thesis of this book is the symbiosis of the old (myth) and

---

1. "Can't Live Without It," *Worldwatch* 6 (May–June 1993), 12.
2. A typical view of "postmodern capitalism" emphasizes "epistemological control" achieved "with the channeling of instincts into electronic sign-systems." See Carl L. Bankston III, "Intentionally Excessive," *American Book Review* 15 (December 1993–January 1994), 1.

the new (advertising). Each needs the other. Advertising cannot start from scratch but must cannibalize assumptions widespread in the culture, assumptions that sometimes crystalize into founding myths. Conversely, today the America/Américas myth needs advertising—an image-driven discourse that will deflect critical scrutiny. For reasons described at the end of Chapter 2 Washington prefers to pursue hemispheric unity through discourse rather than through rules and institutions. From their experience in electoral campaigns U.S. leaders now are able to bring more sophisticated techniques to this option. By tracing the osmosis that flows between myth, ideology, and policy—exchanges across permeable layers of discourse—the oft-noted anachronisms in U.S. policy toward Latin America are rendered less mysterious.[3] This focus on discourse is not novel, not even in studies of U.S. foreign policy.[4] Unlike other works, however, this one pays close attention to the political mechanisms used in reproduction.

Advertising permeates the public discourse of the United States yet still is underestimated as a semiotic system. The average U.S. citizen will see a million ads by age forty in a society that spends $140 billion a year on advertising in all formats, per capita much more than any other society. Even in nonpresidential elections a quarter billion dollars is spent on political ads, with the cost of entrance (i.e., what a nonincumbent running for the House of Representatives needs to be a contender) estimated at $200,000.[5] How likely is it that anyone who succeeds in reaching national office in the United States will be innocent of advertising or inept at using it? While advertising in electoral campaigns no longer is news, few notice how far it has penetrated the workings of the government in between elections, including such core activities as selecting policies and forging consent.

3. "Condemned to repetition" and "woefully outdated clichés" are two recent characterizations of U.S. relations with portions of Latin America. Fredrick Pike, *The United States and Latin America: Myths and Stereotypes of Civilization and Nature* (Austin: University of Texas Press, 1992), xvii, is the source of the second. "Condemned to repetition" is the title of Robert Pastor's book on U.S.–Nicaraguan relations in the Carter and Reagan years (Princeton: Princeton University Press, 1987).

4. See, for example, James Der Derian and Michael Shapiro, eds., *International/Intertextual Relations* (Lexington, Mass.: Lexington Books, 1989).

5. Durning, "Can't Live Without It," 13–14; Deborah Baldwin, "The Hard Sell," *Utne Reader* 49 (January–February 1991), 55; "A Forecast for '91 Spending," *New York Times,* December 10, 1991, C1; "Campaign Spending in Congress Races Soars to New High," *New York Times,* October 29, 1992, A1. The $140 billion total is my rounding of the 1993 figure of $139.3 billion found in an Associated Press graph published by the *Walla Walla Union-Bulletin,* June 15, 1993, 1.

From Myth to Ad

In his effort to get Congress to vote more money for his policies in Central America President Ronald Reagan liked to say that this region is not in our backyard but in our front. Reagan also cited mileages and flying times to make the point that Central America is close. The threat of "feet people" swarming into the United States to escape communism completed an ad that used proximity to arouse the fears of an otherwise apathetic public. What is the relationship of such advertising (detailed in Chapter 6) to the founding myth described in Chapter 2? "Yard" provides an example.

What meanings are likely to be invoked in a U.S. audience by "yard," front or back? While Reagan made no mention of a house, could a U.S. audience hear "yard" without assuming private property on which a house stood? Who lives in this house? Who owns the property? If the front yard is more picked up than the back and if special displays are mounted there on holidays, for whose benefit is that done? Is there a neighborhood, then? Why was Central America not in the neighborhood instead of in the yard, given that "good neighbor" is a stock phrase of U.S.–Latin American relations, a phrase that Reagan himself employed when addressing Latin Americans? Why was Central America not the house next door, if proximity is all that the President wished to convey?

What actually transpired between the President, his advisors, and speech writers need not detain us. Our focus is not on the modus operandi of the Reagan White House but on how certain ways of characterizing Latin America remain in the U.S. discourse, selected over and over again by politicians, speech writers, publicists, and, yes, by publics.

When one stops to think about it, "yard" is the international equivalent of calling an adult African American male "boy." Yet we rarely stop to think about it. There is something deeply familiar about this metaphor that permits most U.S. citizens to hear it, even repeat it, semiconsciously, perhaps even congratulating the President for upgrading Central America from back to front yard. "Yard" is a good example of what Michael Shapiro calls a "surviving textual practice" that serves to sustain "systems of meaning and value from which actions are directed and legitimated," actions that Shapiro understands to include foreign policy.[6] But what is "yard" a survivor of? As with "boy," genealogy draws us back to the nineteenth century.

The last chapter argued that a major concern of the young United States was westward expansion into what often was referred to as empty territory. We saw that westward expansion took a southern turn almost from the beginning through U.S. interest in acquiring Spanish possessions in Florida, Cuba, and Mexico. The largest addition of "western" territory after the Louisiana Purchase was land bought at bargain rates from a Mexico under U.S. occupation. Attempts were made to acquire land in Central America for canal building and commodity production. We also saw in Chapter 2 that U.S. leaders wanted the land but not the people. "Yard" evokes a time when Latin American no less than U.S. leaders used geographic proximity to argue that Washington was the "natural protector" of the nations that rim the Caribbean.[7] "Yard" maintains the assumption of inertness that also forms part of the myth: Central Americans are less actors than the stage on which the important players act (Fig. 2). "Fertile soil," "staging ground," "platform," and "beachhead" were 1980s ways of describing a region long considered a "yard."

It is fairly easy to pluck "yard" from the many speeches and television "spots" on Central America generated by the Reagan administration and demonstrate its relationship to the America/Américas myth. Those same speeches and media "spots," however, also contained references to Munich, the Truman Doctrine, Vietnam, and "freedom fighters" in Afghanistan. More than one myth was tapped by the campaign to sell Reagan's Central American policies. What is fascinating about advertising is its ability to mix and match, which may explain the difficulty we have recognizing the past in its products. The relationship between myth and advertising, then, is far from straightforward.

It may help to think of myths as reservoirs from which officials selectively draw images and lessons to address issues of the moment. A policymaker invokes a myth in order to capture its paradigmatic authority but selects only those elements that serve immediate needs. Into those mythic elements will be woven portions of other myths as well as contemporary material. The balance will shift with the audience. What mobilizes a U.S. public may not persuade Latin American officials and

---

6. "Textualizing Global Politics," in *International/Intertextual Relations,* 13.
7. Walter LaFeber, *Inevitable Revolutions* (New York: W. W. Norton, 1993), 33–34.

'He's mentioned a cousin in Orange County ... but I never knew about any brothers in Nicaragua'

UNCLE SAM: "Maybe I'll have to bring the boy into the house to keep him quiet."

The New Good Neighbor Policy

Fig. 2. Over the course of the twentieth century U.S. political cartoonists have portrayed Latin American countries or leaders as either in the yard or on the doorstep of the United States. The 1985 cartoon shows President Reagan's wife and butler surprised that the Nicaraguan Contras would take seriously his rhetorical embrace of them as brothers. The preferred place for Latin allies no less than enemies is outside, as seen in the 1904 and 1947 cartoons, one featuring a yard, the other a doorstep, while both reduce the Latins to children. In a 1986 speech reproduced in the Appendix, President Reagan asked, "Will we permit the Soviet Union to put a second Cuba, a second Libya, right on the doorstep of the United States?"

Sources. 1904: "Maybe I'll have to bring the boy into the house to keep him quiet," by G. W. Rehse, St. Paul Pioneer Press, 1904. 1947: "The New Good Neighbor Policy," © 1947 by Herblock in the Washington Post. 1985: "He mentioned a cousin in Orange County . . . but I never knew about any brothers in Nicaragua," by Paul Szep, The Boston Globe, February 21, 1985, reprinted courtesy of The Boston Globe. The earlier two cartoons were first reproduced by John J. Johnson, Latin America in Caricature (Austin: University of Texas Press, 1980, 1993), 183, 293.

vice versa. Or the mix may change in response to repetition's tendency to dull the message. While the analyst's attention is on the myth, the decision makers' remains on the policy. "Whatever sells" is the official's motto and "whatever" proves to be eclectic.

How Ads Work

Advertising may be defined as the conscious attempt to manipulate the choices a targeted audience makes without that audience resisting the manipulation. It is an activity elites consciously undertake to elicit behavior from large audiences voluntarily—behavior envisaged by those elites as a sale or a win. While the line is not a firm one, advertising belongs to that category of discourse in which intentional persuasion through manipulation of emotions and perceptions is the norm, in contrast to discourses more spontaneous, less outcome-specific, or more reasoned.

Advertisements framed to announce their presence might seem exempt from this definition. What lies within those frames remains manipulative, however. Apologists for advertising usually describe its function as information dissemination, and there are ads that do provide a great deal of objective data (e.g., performance specifications of an automobile). Such data, however, usually are in the ad to sell the image of the buyer that the ad constructs. "You're confident about your identity but you're different," says a Toyota commercial. What makes you different is that you are smart and discriminating. A full-page magazine ad for a bank shows a middle-aged couple in a luxurious drawing room with the text "Most of our clients are referred by a source far more compelling than any advertising."

Traditionally *advertising* had visible boundaries such as the caption "paid political advertisement" or the words "And now these messages." In contrast, *public relations* infiltrated spontaneous activities without giving notice. Whatever was being promoted just happened to appear at a talk show, an athletic event, or a community celebration—appear favorably of course. The private sector recognizes a third category known as *promotion,* with activities ranging from special seminars for physicians hosted by pharmaceutical companies to the person in the supermarket who hands out free samples.

Today when a television commercial (Taster's Choice Coffees) presents forty-five-second segments of an ongoing drama while a feature film ("Die Hard Two") contains nineteen paid placements of products, those traditional lines are blurred. A similar blurring occurs when advertising moves from commerce to entertainment to politics. Each activity adds its twist. Were advertising music we would talk of "fusion" and "crossovers." Recently a commercial advertiser recommended that practitioners of that craft study the way politicians present themselves to diverse publics in order to better sell brand name products in large markets.[8] "Infomercials" originated as television ads for products but evolved through the 1992 presidential campaign. In Washington today "the lobbying business is expanding to include advertising, news media contacts, and image making," for as one in the business put it, "The line between them is becoming grayer."[9]

National election campaigns in an era of unrestricted spending are the bridge across which techniques developed in commercial advertising found their way into policy discourse. Once politicians discovered that they could sell themselves using techniques devised to sell products they began selling policies in office using those same methods. "Permanent campaigns" fostered "permanent teams" of pollsters, speech writers, advance men, and media consultants who cycle in and out of government, political parties, and the burgeoning industry of *political* advertisers, now a specialty of its own employing over 50,000.[10] In the process skills are refined and exchanged. Advertising has spread like the Ice-9 of the Vonnegut novel, its pattern crystalizing in varied realms. "The heartbeat of America" appears here, "morning in America" there, one selling a product, the other a president.

Given fusions and crossovers, elaborating typologies is less useful than understanding how advertising works regardless of format. Most readers have experienced enough of it to judge the accuracy of the following description, which moves from a narrative to seven traits that serve as markers for my investigation of advertising in Reagan's foreign policy. Where those markers are present, I contend, a discourse may fairly be labeled advertising.

8. Stuart Elliott, "Turning the Issue Around: Politics as a Model for Products," *New York Times*, November 16, 1992, sec. C.

9. Gary Lee, "Supermarket Influence Peddling," *Washington Post National Weekly Edition*, January 14, 1991. "Supermarket" refers to one-stop shopping.

10. "The Boom in Political Consulting," *New York Times*, May 24, 1987, F1.

Ads work by engaging our attention with a "hook," to borrow a Jungian term. A successful designer of direct mail campaigns says he sprinkles words such as "sex," "death," and "free" throughout a text "to force the eye to stop."[11] With viewers hooked, most ads then juxtapose whatever is being sold with images that suggest to potential buyers the connection the seller wants them to make. If the ad is successful, buyers will make that connection using their own memories, fantasies, and fears. Those images may concern the thing sold, the buyer's identity, or feelings the buyer will experience when using the product. Rarely is the connection logically compelling, rarely is it based on life experiences.

When spending $40,000 on an automobile we are not just purchasing transportation but qualities our rational minds tell us are hard to buy, such as confidence, affection, or identity. Typically ads promise the unattainable on purchase of the attainable, explains Judith Williamson.[12] "What the advertiser needs to know is not what is right about the product but what is wrong about the buyer," that is, where the buyer is vulnerable.[13] "Business, through advertising, plays on human insecurity and fear."[14]

"I want to dream the impossible dream," opens a multipage ad for a New York department store over a photograph of a beautiful woman running. Attention captured, on the following page the transfer is completed with "Our exclusive dresses make dreams come true." Our product lets you "be all you can be," states another ad; "if you dream it, you can do it," says a third. Wear Nikes and you can even fly. Advertising did not invent this process of substituting the purchasable for the longed-for, the product for the panacea. Chocolates "stood for" love before advertising became pervasive; indeed, there may be a chemical basis for that association. Advertising builds on associations already present in the culture, extending them in the process. Taking chocolates-equal-love as a given, an ad may place a box of chocolates on a nightstand next to a bed made up with the sheets the advertisement is selling. A candidate for public office does the same with family or flag.

Thus advertising is a second-order semiotic system, which is to say

11. Randall Rothenberg, "Junk Mail's Top Dogs," *New York Times Magazine*, August 5, 1990, 40.

12. *Decoding Advertisements* (New York: Marion Boyars, 1983), 31.

13. Neil Postman, *Amusing Ourselves to Death* (New York: Viking Penguin, 1986), 128.

14. Carol S. Pearson, *The Hero Within* (San Francisco: Harper, 1989), 160.

that *advertising takes existing associations and redeploys them toward new objects, in the process building new meanings.* "Where's the beef?" was an ad for a fast-food hamburger that drew upon the cultural understanding that "real" hamburgers have a lot of meat in them. One could trace that understanding back to nineteenth-century associations of eating beef with well-being. In redeploying "where's the beef?" to criticize his opponent's economic proposals, 1984 Democratic candidate Walter Mondale treated the slogan as a folk saying that all Americans understood. Last year's ad, a commmercial appropriation of a cultural meaning, becomes next year's folk wisdom in so media-mediated a culture as the United States.

Ads are derivative in a second sense. We experience strong feelings as individuals. In fact, to see oneself as unique is an important component of most U.S. citizens' self-image, especially those who buy and vote more than the norm. *To work in this culture, ads must create the illusion that they are speaking to us individually, that they know our unique needs and aspirations.* One New York agency describes the "under-35 audience" as needing to "believe that an advertiser knows who they are. How they live. What excites them. And what they care about."

Implicit in what has been said so far is that *advertising works by engaging emotions and memories more than experience and reason.* This is often misunderstood as a claim that ads work subliminally. Consumers may be fully aware of encountering an ad—annoyed by it even—yet still be influenced by the ad in the ad-intended way. When casting ballots in presidential elections voters are affected by the negative campaigning they criticize. Surely those wealthy enough to buy expensive scotch or perfume know that wearing or serving a particular brand of same is not likely to transform their love life or advance their career. Yet ads based on those premises sell perfume and scotch to those people.

What sells may be the allure of a dream come true or a quick fix to a problem. But ads also sell identity. In the United States we wear corporate symbols, decorate our vehicles with logos larger than those the manufacturer installs, tattoo our skin with miniature logos, and pay to do this. Depending on the product/service being sold, the identity offered may be elitist or inclusionary. We may buy a product that addresses us as "busy professionals who demand . . ." Or we may buy a product that includes us in a generation or a nation: the Pepsi Generation, those "who still believe in this great country of ours," Cosmopolitan woman, "Americans who play by the rules," Concerned Parent, Family Farmer. On launching a new soft drink a Coca Cola official said the firm was marketing not a product but "an attitude about what people want from their beverages."[15]

Like moths to a flame we are drawn by the invitation ads offer to participate in their meaning. We incarnate our unique fantasies and fears as we fill in the blanks left to our imagination. *The cunning of modern advertising is to make us coauthors of the pitch.* That is why ads often invoke a mood rather than specify an outcome. On a cognitive level an ad may be puzzling. What happened to leave the model's clothes disheveled? What does the candidate mean by "values"? Notice how often ads tease with an ambiguous "it." One generation's "You can do it in an MG" becomes the next generation's "just do it." "Only in a Jeep." "Why ask why?"

Having made an ad ours by drawing on our deepest associations to complete it, we feel ourselves among the cognoscente who "get it." Ads speak to the needs of a mobile society of immigrant roots, in which people grow up being told that identities are what you construct, down to gender. What Coca Cola used to sell was a world of Little League fields and Connecticut kitchens. Those who want that now buy Heinz products. Heinz recently spent ten million dollars to position "the image of ketchup and gravy as being as American as baseball and apple pie."[16] Upscale items sell variations of "you're rich but you deserve it." "It's lonely at the top," states an airline selling first class seats. The political equivalent is the machine-generated letter inviting you to serve on your representative's special council of advisers.[17]

The irony of advertising is that it proclaims no value more than freedom, autonomy being a desired identity. "Express yourself," commands a Lord & Taylor ad that proceeds to tell you what to buy to stand out from the crowd. "Wrangler's purpose is not just to serve man.

---

15. "The Prose That Refreshes," *New York Times Magazine,* March 20, 1994, 17.

16. "Heinz's Focus on the Family," *New York Times,* November 27, 1990, sec. D.

17. These fund-raising devices flatter the recipient by asking, in effect, "Would you please fill out this questionnaire so that I may have the benefit of your views?" With the data this questionnaire provides, the "representative" will customize the pitch sent the constituent in future mailings.

But to set him free." The function of advertising, however, is to narrow the consumer's or citizen's choice to the one product, service, candidate, or policy that fulfills multiple needs. The options that ads offer exist in the number of functions one product can perform, as in "the wagon you'll want to drive even when there's nothing to carry." It is unthinkable that an ad would point out competing products that perform the same function equally well. Advertising sells the *illusion* of choice while structuring choice out of decisions, whether by omitting alternatives or by cannibalizing them.

To summarize, successful ads employ most of the following tactics. Advertising will:

1. capture attention by any means consistent with 2, usually with one or more attention-grabbing "hooks";
2. arouse fears, fantasies, and loyalties already present in the audience, leaving enough ambiguity so that most can read their individual desires into the ad;
3. transfer those aroused emotions and memories to whatever is being sold, taking care to do so through juxtapositions and substitutions (metaphors and similes) rather than through means that spark critical reflection;
4. position whatever is being sold as, if not the sole panacea, the most satisfying one, framing the choice so that competing alternatives are either excluded or co-opted;
5. motivate the sale by promising a catharsis through a sense of triumph or acceptance or some other positive feeling;
6. encourage the customer to feel that the decision to buy originates with him/her, that s/he automatically wishes to do what the ad asks be done;
7. and do all this by offering consumers multiple opportunities to participate in the ad, to own it by completing it with their own associations.

These elements form the ideal type of advertising, a way to recognize its presence in unfamiliar places such as a government's campaign to sell a foreign policy.

Advertising Capabilities of the Executive Branch

As president, Richard Nixon initiated a process that Ronald Reagan's handlers perfected and that journalist Sidney Blumenthal dubbed the "permanent campaign."[18] The use of advertising techniques *while in office* is what makes the campaign permanent. Few are the accounts of the Reagan presidency that could not easily be descriptions of corporate advertising or public relations. Of Reagan's second term Chief of Staff we read: "Don Regan was more of a professional salesman than anyone who had occupied his exalted post. 'He could sell it flat, or he could sell it round,' said one admiring colleague from the Treasury Department."[19] Foreign policy was not immune: " 'What was wrong with El Salvador,' says [Reagan consultant Richard] Beal, 'was the packaging of the activity in terms of policy and presentation to the public. It wasn't well staged or sequenced.' "[20] In all: " 'It was like sitting around a Madison Avenue advertising agency,' one [White House] speechwriter marveled."[21] These skills, used in the 1986 campaign on Contra aid, can be traced back (at least) to Nixon's appointment of Jeb Stuart Magruder to run his Office of Communications. While not all successive White Houses have followed Nixon's precedent, Reagan's second-term White House took the "permanent campaign" to new heights of sophistication.

There is no mystery to how one sells a foreign policy in an era of advertising: evoke the fears and fantasies present in the audience one hopes to persuade (e.g., fear of communism) and then transfer those emotions to new signifiers about which the audience knows little and perhaps cares less (e.g., Sandinistas). If the audience cared, there would be less need to sell; if it knew, there would be less scope for advertising. Those linked processes of emotion-evocation and transfer lie at the heart of how advertising constructs political discourse. We shall see them at work in Chapter 5 and Chapter 6.

The national election campaign in an era of unrestricted spending is the bridge across which techniques developed in commercial advertising and entertainment found their way into the public policy discourse. What is being sold may be a politician, a party, or a program. In truth,

18. Early in the Reagan years Blumenthal described the President "governing America by a new strategic doctrine—the permanent campaign. [Reagan] is applying in the White House the techniques he employed in getting there." See "Marketing the President," *New York Times Magazine*, September 12, 1981, 43. This article forms part of a book subsequently published as *The Permanent Campaign* (New York: Simon and Schuster, 1982).

19. Jane Mayer and Doyle McManus, *Landslide: The Unmaking of the President, 1984–1988* (Boston: Houghton Mifflin, 1988), 279.

20. Blumenthal, "Marketing the President," 111.

21. Mayer and McManus, *Landslide*, 204.

however, it always is some *image* of one or more of those. If the public trusts its image of the president, for example, a range of policies can be promoted the way a famous athlete sells gym shoes. Like most celebrities, however, leaders often become prisoners of their image. When, over the protest of Bush's economic advisers, public opinion consultant Roger Ailes persuaded candidate Bush to promise "Read my lips, no new taxes," parameters were put in place that Bush as president found as hard to break as to honor. What got him elected in 1988 contributed to his defeat four years later.[22]

Similarly, the confident, caring, yet principled father that most U.S. citizens believed Ronald Reagan to be was the artful construction of skilled aides working with a consummate actor.[23] As long-time Reagan adviser Edward Rollins put it, Reagan is "the perfect candidate. He does whatever you want him to do."[24] To work, an advertisement must hide such artifice, of course, which Reagan's did until the Iran-Contra scandal let "the house lights come on too early."[25] Our case study occurs in the months before that debacle, when "the Great Communicator" was counted among the "assets" available to those planning this campaign.[26]

A truly remarkable team had made Ronald Reagan a popular two-term governor of the nation's most media-infused state before moving

22. Bob Woodward, "The Anatomy of a Decision," *Washington Post National Weekly Edition*, October 12, 1992, 6.

23. Books on the Reagan White House portray a president who in real life was often indecisive and self-effacing, notorious for agreeing with whomever had seen him last. Reagan gave his approval so indiscriminately that his signature on memos carried little weight. When National Security Adviser Robert McFarlane tried to get the newly reelected Reagan to select one or two foreign policy priorities for his second term from a list of a dozen possibilities, Reagan replied, "Let's do them all," which McFarlane interpreted as "you choose." At Treasury Donald Regan had to turn to Reagan's public speeches to find out what the policy was. Reagan's press aide even invented, after the fact, comments the President "made" to Mikhail Gorbachev when the two leaders talked one-on-one. What Ronald Reagan actually said mattered less than what "President Reagan" should have said. Aides provided color-coded cue cards that carried Reagan through each day's encounters, telling him what to say to whom (including banter).

24. Mayer and McManus, *Landslide*, 7.

25. Ibid., 386.

26. Confidential memo to North and Reich from Jacobowitz of the Office of Public Diplomacy for Latin America and the Caribbean (S/LPD): "Public Diplomacy Action Plan: Support for the White House Education Campaign," March 12, 1985, National Security Archive 934. This document is from a collection on the Iran-Contra affair at the National Security Archive in Washington, D.C. In citing such documents I use the title, date, and fiche number given them by this source.

with him to Washington. Emblematic of the "permanent campaign" was Lee Atwater, who joined Reagan late but served both Reagan and Bush before becoming the first professional political consultant to be named chair of a national political party.[27] While our case draws attention to the advertising skills of Atwater, Rollins, and other Republicans, the trend is bipartisan and multilevel. In 1990 the Democratic Leadership Council—the spawning ground for that party's successful 1992 presidential ticket—hired an advertising firm because "we want people to feel good about the Democratic Party."[28]

At state and local levels as well the trend appears in the marketing of public celebrations and local heritages.[29] Cities in a financial pinch consider raising money "by renaming streets and parks for corporate sponsors, implanting high-tech advertising in city sidewalks, and sticking corporate logos on city garbage trucks."[30] Our case study includes similar instances of the "privatization" of public goods and roles, ranging from a corporate logo on an airplane donated to Nicaraguan rebels to funds raised by selling opportunities to have one's picture taken with the President. Other techniques that appear in the case study are: sophisticated opinion polls used to shape policy packaging; pretesting products (in this case speeches) on audiences chosen for the right demographics; creating at home and abroad events disguised as news; image manipulation through "sound bites," "spins," and "line of the day"; free satellite transmissions of propaganda masked as news to local TV stations.

Scattered throughout the planning documents of the foreign policy advertising campaign of 1986 are the words "advertising" and "markets." "What we need to do is to create the impression of . . . ," strategists would say as they discussed how to "frame the choice"

27. President Bush tapped Atwater to head the Republican National Committee. The only post to which Atwater ever had been elected was chair of South Carolina College Republicans while an undergraduate. Atwater is credited with inventing "negative campaigning" in 1978 and with perfecting such techniques thereafter (e.g., inventing damaging quotations attributed to an opponent, injecting racism into a campaign). See *Current Biography Yearbook 1989* (n.p.: H. W. Wilson Co., 1989), 25–29.

28. "New Product for Agency: Democrats," *New York Times*, March 26, 1990, D13.

29. For an example see "New York City's Campaign for Gulf Veterans' Parade," *New York Times*, April 8, 1991, C7. The decision to play down military images in this parade for military personnel returning from the Gulf War—so as not "to offend anyone who was against the conflict"—was made by the chairman of Wunderman Worldwide, an advertising firm.

30. "Adman in Atlanta Tries to Sell City," *New York Times*, February 9, 1993, A8.

before Congress and the public by using opinion surveys that identified the associations most likely to turn U.S. citizens against the Sandinistas and toward their opponents. Here, for example, are press releases from organizations central to the 1986 campaign that bracket the period when the campaign was most intense.

> WASHINGTON, D.C., FEBRUARY 27. The National Endowment for the Preservation of Liberty today launched a $1.2 million television advertising campaign, part of a $2 million public information program supporting President Reagan's position on Nicaragua which will reach an audience of 62.5 million Americans. The program is believed to be the largest privately funded public information campaign addressing a foreign policy issue ever mounted.[31]

And:

> WASHINGTON, D.C., JUNE 25. Eleven Congressmen created the margin of victory for President Reagan in yesterday's vote on aid to the Nicaraguan Freedom Fighters. Six of these Representatives came under intensive lobbying efforts sponsored by Sentinel, a Washington-based lobbying organization. Dan Conrad, Sentinel's Executive Director, said, "We undertook a broad-based program of personal contact, television messages and grass roots constituent education." . . . This new approach to address vital foreign policy issues is likely to become the way of the future for national security debates in Washington. "When we address issues vital to the President we intend to bring to bear a whole array of communications and political techniques," said Conrad.[32]

Given that this approach to lobbying Congress raises legal and constitutional issues, it is amazing that the practitioners were so open about their strategy. Consciousness of advertising on the part of prac-

31. "National Endowment for the Preservation of Liberty Supports Reagan on Nicaragua," February 27, 1986, National Security Archive 2401. Along with Sentinel, the NEPL was one of Carl (Spitz) Channel's organizations that collaborated with federal officials and other private parties in the campaign.

32. "News Release," June 25, 1986, National Security Archive 3053.

titioners is less important, however, than whether their discourse functions as an ad. To test that we will return to the ideal type of advertising offered here after the case study—the 1986 campaign—has been fully described.

4

Romance and the Hardball Player

Romantic . . . 2. having no basis in fact: being the product of invention or exaggeration . . . 3. impractical in conception or plan: unrealistic . . . 4. marked by the imaginative or emotional appeal of the heroic, adventurous, remote, mysterious, or idealized characteristics of things, places, people.
—Webster's Third New International Dictionary[1]

During Ronald Reagan's first term as president "rolling back" the Sandinista regime in Nicaragua was the illegitimate child of administration policies: nurtured by many in his administration while disowned by those in control of the White House agenda. The clumsy way in which this covert policy had been advanced by Director of Central Intelligence William Casey had turned Congress against the Contras, as the Nicaraguan rebels were known. For many, CIA mining of Nicaraguan harbors in March 1984 was the last straw. Thus, in October of that year Congress passed the most explicit of the Boland amendments, generally known as Boland II, suspending all official U.S. aid to the Contras.

"During fiscal year 1985," according to the Boland language that the President signed into law, "no funds available to the Central Intelligence Agency, the Department of Defense, or any other agency or entity

1. *Webster's Third New International Dictionary of the English Language, Unabridged* (Springfield, Mass.: Merriam-Webster, Inc., 1986), 1970.

involved in intelligence activities may be obligated or expended for the purpose or which would have the effect of supporting, directly or indirectly, military or paramilitary operations in Nicaragua by any nation, group, organization, movement or individual."[2] Over the following year and a half congressional prohibitions against U.S. assistance to the Contras were relaxed to permit "humanitarian" aid, communications support, and eventually intelligence sharing. But the involvement of U.S. officials in providing the equipment, logistics, and strategy of war remained off limits until October 1986, when new legislation setting aside the Boland prohibitions went into effect. This reversal resulted from the advertising campaign that provides our case study.

Rather than accept the Boland restrictions during the years when they were law, backers of the Contras among top U.S. officials sought a way around them, confident that they were fulfilling the President's desire (as expressed to National Security Adviser Robert McFarlane) to keep the Contras together "body and soul" until Congress could be brought around.[3] McFarlane and his successor John Poindexter later testified that they were carrying out the President's wishes through activities that flouted Boland II and deceived Congress, although neither claimed to have Reagan's explicit authorization. In his testimony over the years Reagan has been inconsistent; it is not clear whether he thought he was authorizing the Contras' physical survival or the maintenance of their war-fighting capability.[4] What he got was an expansion in the Contras' numbers, military fronts, and offensive capabilities.

As the administration would not accept Boland's strictures on the military track of the "two-track policy," so the administration refused to let the diplomatic track arrive at a solution that left the Sandinistas

2. Omnibus Appropriations bill signed into law by the President on October 12, 1984. Similar language is found in the Defense and Intelligence Authorization bills. Public Law 98-473, sec. 8066[A], October 12, 1984.

3. National Security Adviser Robert McFarlane transmitted the President's charge to his assistant, Lt. Col. Oliver North, according to McFarlane testimony to Congress and at North's trial in 1989. See Oliver North, with William Novak, *Under Fire: An American Story* (New York: Harper Paperbacks, 1992), 287, 463.

4. Ending his seven-year investigation into Iran-Contra illegalities, independent counsel Lawrence Walsh concluded that, while President, Reagan "created the conditions which made possible the crimes committed by others . . . by his open determination to keep the contras together 'body and soul' despite a statutory ban on contra aid." See George Lardner Jr. and Walter Pincus, "The Source of the Iran-Contra Mess Is Tracked to Reagan," *Washington Post National Weekly Edition*, January 24, 1994, 13.

in power. A 1985 *New York Times* article based on not-for-attribution interviews cited "high-level officials" as saying of the President "that despite his lack of a clear public stance, . . . he 'keeps coming back to internal democratization and national reconciliation.' They interpret that to mean that the Sandinistas must go."⁵ To these officials, the reporter concluded, the "democratization" of Nicaragua ruled out a "Yugoslavia solution," meaning tolerance of a Marxist regime that observed correct international relations. The administration's reasons for not accepting any of the diplomatic solutions offered at this time—solutions that many believe would have met the United States' legitimate security concerns—will become clear by the end of this chapter.

What the administration would not accept dictated what it had to do: proceed secretly at the margins of legality, hoping that Congress could be turned. If the advertising campaign worked, the secrecy could be set aside and the policy continued with no risk of impeachment. The 1986 advertising campaign sought the same goal as the secret activities of the Boland period but with more plausible evidence of public support—important for relations with other governments as well as with Congress. Both advertising and secrecy are substitutes for the open debate that the Constitution writers envisioned when they gave Congress and the executive joint control over foreign policy.

This propensity not to compromise, evident in the White House's relations with Congress and with other governments, had many roots. One was the policymakers' conviction that the situation was simple, that right was on their side, and that the power differential favored them. Why temporize? A propensity for the romantic (as the epigraph defines it) cemented the link between the dreamers and the doers. In setting the stage for the case study, then, this chapter both describes the objective situation that forced the policymakers to advertise and the subjective situation that made advertising so natural an option for them. The chapter moves from the objective to the subjective.⁶

5. "Reagan Aides See No Possibility of U.S. Accord with Sandinistas," *New York Times*, August 18, 1985, A1.

6. For the full history of U.S. policy toward Nicaragua in the 1980s see Roy Gutman, *Banana Diplomacy: The Making of American Diplomacy in Nicaragua, 1981–1987* (New York: Simon and Schuster, 1988), and Robert Pastor, *Condemned to Repetition: The United States and Nicaragua* (Princeton: Princeton University Press, 1987). While both relate events

The Policy Launched in Secrecy

The first substitute for congressional funding of the Contras' military campaign—weapons donated by the Pentagon through the CIA—did not pan out. The Defense Department's counsel found this ruse illegal.[7] Next, money and weapons were solicited from private citizens and sympathetic foreign governments, with the role of top U.S. officials kept secret even from each other. Without informing the Secretary of State, in May 1984 National Security Adviser McFarlane solicited funds from Saudi Arabia.[8] Beginning that July the Saudis contributed first a million dollars a month and then two. By May 1985 $17 million of the Saudi donation had been spent on weapons, munitions, and related gear and services, all to bolster the Contras' war-making ability. Other foreign governments contributed either money or the Soviet bloc weapons that matched those of the Sandinistas, while wealthy U.S. citizens bought high-ticket items, such as airplanes and helicopters.[9] Former Colombian

---

in Nicaragua to Washington debates, Pastor details the Sandinistas coming to power, Gutman the years that followed.

7. U.S. Congress, *Report of the Congressional Committees Investigating the Iran-Contra Affair*, 100th Cong., 1st sess. (Washington, D.C.: U.S. Government Printing Office, 1987), 34–35. The joint report bears the House number 100-433 and the Senate number 100-216. Hereafter referred to simply as the *Report*. Under Operation Elephant Herd, however, the Pentagon did sell the CIA, for transfer to the Contras, surplus weapons at a very low cost.

8. Later Shultz did participate in secretly raising funds from "third" governments, although he may have believed that the funds were solely for "humanitarian" aid. In a PROF note dated June 11, 1986, National Security Adviser Poindexter informs his assistant North that Shultz has agreed to the solicitation of a foreign government Shultz is about to visit, adding: "To my knowledge Shultz knows nothing about the prior financing. I think it should stay that way."

Electronic mail internal to the National Security Council were known as PROF notes. Officials using this system believed that their messages were erased when deleted on their computers. However, a backup file found during investigations into the Iran-Contra scandal produced many PROF notes. Subsequently these and other documents were assembled by the National Security Archive, a private research organization in Washington, D.C., where I accessed them. Document numbers cited in this book (in this case 2989) are those provided by the National Security Archive for its collection on the Iran-Contra affair. While many of these documents also may be found in the *Appendices* to the congressional *Report* on the Iran-Contra affair, if they are part of the National Security Archive I cite that source, which is available on microfiche from Chadwyck-Healey (Alexandria, Va., 1990) under the title *The Iran-Contra Affair: The Making of a Scandal, 1983–1988.* A selection of these documents has been published in book form as *The Iran-Contra Scandal: The Declassified History,* ed. Peter Kornbluh and Malcolm Byrne (New York: The New Press, 1993).

9. North, *Under Fire,* 322.

drug lord Carlos Lehder claimed that the Medellín Cartel contributed $10 million to the cause.[10]

In August 1985 the *New York Times* reported that the Contras had received $25 million in unrestricted monies "from private individuals in the United States and foreign sources" (all unnamed), complementing the $27 million in "humanitarian" aid voted by Congress in June of that year.[11] By April 1986 Oliver North calculated that $37 million in private individual and "third country" donations had been spent on Contra military needs.[12] Inasmuch as the leaders of the main Contra group, the FDN (*Fuerza Democrática Nicaragüense* or Nicaraguan Democratic Force), initially had asked for a million dollars a month to survive, it would seem that they were being held together, "body and soul," and then some.

When the Boland amendments forced the CIA to back off, responsibility for guiding and supplying the FDN devolved on to Lt. Col. Oliver North, a middle-level National Security Council staffer who interpreted the presidential charge as keeping the Contras "alive in the field," "field" meaning war zone.[13] North used the humanitarian aid approved by Congress as a cover for flights that brought the secretly purchased arms to the Contras. Illegal drugs entered the United States on some return flights, as North steered State Department contracts for delivering humanitarian aid to pilots known to U.S. drug enforcement officials as narcotraffickers.[14] A former aide to Senator Dan Quayle, Robert Owen, who served as Oliver North's "eyes and ears" in Central America from October 1984 to March 1986, also was paid from the State Department's humanitarian aid operation.

While shortages did occur in some Contra camps, they stemmed from the Contra leaders' "skimming" and from North's determination to

---

10. Peter Dale Scott and Jonathan Marshall, *Cocaine Politics: Drugs, Armies, and the CIA in Central America* (Berkeley and Los Angeles: University of California Press, 1991), x.

11. "Nicaragua Rebels Reported to Raise Up to $25 Million," *New York Times*, August 13, 1985, A1.

12. *Report*, 69.

13. North's testimony to the congressional committees jointly investigating the Iran-Contra scandal, as found in *Report*, 37.

14. This charge is documented by the April 1989 "Kerry report," officially entitled *Drugs, Law Enforcement, and Foreign Policy* and issued by the Subcommittee on Terrorism, Narcotics, and International Operations of the U.S. Senate Committee on Foreign Relations. Senator John Kerry chaired the subcommittee. Summarizing and amplifying that evidence is the 1991 book by Scott and Marshall, *Cocaine Politics*; see especially 10–11, 17, 118, 181.

open a southern front on the Nicaraguan–Costa Rican border. Bordering Nicaragua to the north, Honduras hosted the FDN's camps, warehouses, and headquarters, while Honduran officials kept a blind eye to their existence. The Costa Rican government, however, was less cooperative (see Chapter 7). Supplying the Contras' southern front, therefore, entailed long flights and difficult air drops. By the spring of 1986 the southern front finally was being supplied, however, as the larger northern front had been all along, with a few interruptions. By then North had discovered another source of funding: the diversion to the Contras of profits acquired by secretly selling U.S. missiles to Iran at high markups. The Contras, however, required more than money. They needed effective leadership and a presentable image.

Maintaining the Contras as an irritant that would bring the Sandinistas to the bargaining table was the rationale given Congress throughout these years in various presidential findings and letters of intent.[15] That was the "two-track" policy put into place during President Reagan's first term and never officially disavowed. For their part Congress was happy to see the Contras pressure the Sandinistas as long as U.S. officials and funds were not visible in the operation. After Reagan's reelection in 1984, and probably before, the administration's operative policy sought the Sandinistas' ouster whether through defeat or capitulation under military duress. It was this goal that motivated the expansion of the FDN's war-making capability and the refurbishing of its leaders' image.

As Oliver North coordinated a December 1985 trip to Central America for John Poindexter, newly elevated to National Security Adviser, North described the mission's goal as convincing key players in Central America that "we intend to pursue a victory." Poindexter was to reassure regional governments that they need not fear being

---

15. Required by a 1975 law, "findings" are the vehicle by which a president explains to the small number of senators and representatives charged with overseeing intelligence activities why a covert operation is needed. Originally Congress had been told that the Contras were a small force that would interdict arms the Sandinistas were sending Marxist guerrillas in El Salvador. As late as July 1983, even in closed sessions with small committees, Casey kept offering that rationale. The increasing size of Contra forces, along with their periodic operation along the southern front, undercut the credibility of that goal. On the advice of sympathetic senators, in September 1983 the White House generated a new finding. Now the rationale focused on inducing the Sandinistas to enter into negotiations with its neighbors and on the internal democratization of the Nicaraguan regime. Additional revisions followed, but the administration never formally acknowledged its goal of toppling the Sandinista regime.

pressured into diplomatic settlements.[16] Memos circulated within the National Security Council (NSC) suggest that Poindexter needed no convincing: for him diplomacy was a cover, not an option.[17] When a U.S. ambassador had asked CIA Director Casey point-blank "What's the real goal?" Casey did not hesitate to reply, "Get rid of the Sandinistas."[18] Casey always had held that goal, as most likely had Reagan.

This commitment to "victory" through expanding the Contra war put the Reagan administration on a collision course with reality, for the Contras had neither the intention nor the ability to play so central a role. While myths about "freedom fighters" fed "resolve" at the White House, they could not make the Contras other than what they were. And what they were, according to General Paul Gorman, Commander of the Pentagon's Southern Command from May 1983 through February 1985, was an ineffective military force. Recalling the 1985 testimony he had given Congress, Gorman remembers "saying in those days . . . that I did not see in the Nicaraguan resistance a combination of forces that could lead to the overthrow of the government or the unseating of the Sandinistas. . . . I didn't regard them as a very effective military organization, based on what I could see in reflections of battles, in communications on both sides. The Sandinistas could wipe them out."[19] Secretly the Contra leaders probably agreed with Gorman, for they banked on the U.S. military playing a decisive role in "liberating" Nicaragua.

Before North had him booted out of Central America for supporting the wrong Contra group, U.S. mercenary Jack Terrell (a.k.a. Colonel Flaco) came to the realization that the FDN's goal "was not victory on the battlefields of Nicaragua—it was direct United States military intervention as in Vietnam."[20] Reporting to North in March 1986,

16. *Report*, 64.
17. The strategy for the administration that Poindexter proposed in late 1984 advocated that we "continue active negotiations but agree to no treaty and agree to work out some way to support the Contras either directly or indirectly. Withhold true objectives from staffs." See "A Proposal for Resolving Inter-Agency Conflict," Poindexter's PROF note to McFarlane, November 23, 1984, National Security Archive 632.
18. Gutman, *Banana Diplomacy*, 157.
19. *Report*, 49.
20. Portion of a book prospectus written by *Houston Post* reporter Dan Grothaus, included with "Summary of Comments from Interviews—Jack Terrell," dated July 15, 1986, in U.S. Congress, *Report of the Congressional Committees Investigating the Iran-Contra Affair, Appendix:* vol. 1, *Source Documents*, 100th Cong., 1st sess., H. Rept. 100-433 (Washington, D.C.: U.S. Government Printing Office, 1987), 834–51. Terrell served as an officer in the

Robert Owen offered the following assessment of Adolfo Calero, Enrique Bermúdez, and other top Contra leaders: "This war has become a business to many of them; there is still a belief that the Marines are going to have to invade, so let's get set so we will automaticaly [sic] be the ones put into power."[21] The FDN leaders no doubt remembered what had happened in Guatemala in 1954, where a small exile army supported by the CIA crossed the frontier, set up camp, proclaimed itself the new government—then waited for Washington to do the rest. Or the model may have been Santo Domingo 1965, where Washington intervened militarily under cover of a token inter-American force, a pattern repeated in Grenada. (FDN military commander Bermúdez had led a contingent of Somoza's soldiers into Santo Domingo.)

The Honduran military chief, Gustavo Alvarez, formulated versions of this trip-wire strategy that he sold to Contra leaders, to CIA representatives in the field, and to North. One variant had the Contras provoking Sandinista attacks on Contra bases in Honduras, the Honduran army then retaliating and calling on U.S. forces to assist it under the Rio Treaty. Another had the Contras taking a sparsely settled corner of Nicaragua and calling on the U.S. military to help them defend "free Nicaragua" against Sandinista counterattacks. In either case U.S. troops would be joined by those of other Central American armies, making the operation appear as pan-American as possible. To set the stage Alvarez tried to revive the Central American Defense Council (CONDECA), which had lapsed into paper existence.[22]

Whichever plan, two things stand out. One is that the military leader of the largest Contra army "never had conceived of the FDN as able to conquer Nicaragua and doubted its ability to capture territory at any stage."[23] The other is that the Pentagon—both the Joint Chiefs of Staff

---

Civilian Military Assistance (CMA), a group of U.S. volunteers fighting alongside the Contras, but was also a member of an elite commando group that trained Contras to assassinate Sandinista personnel deep inside Nicaragua. With those skills Terrell claims that he was asked by John Hull to assassinate the FDN's rival, Edén Pastora. See Scott and Marshall, *Cocaine Politics*, 127–39.

21. Owen's "eyes only" memo to North of March 17, 1986, appears as "Overall Perspective," National Security Archive 2493.

22. Gutman, *Banana Diplomacy*, 55–57, 102, 176–79. Edgar Chamorro, *Packaging the Contras: A Case of CIA Disinformation*, monograph series 2 (New York: Institute for Media Analysis, 1987), 50.

23. Gutman, *Banana Diplomacy*, 305. Gutman recognizes in Bermúdez's posture the legacy of U.S.-Nicaraguan relations stretching back a half century: political leaders within Nicaragua had used U.S. intervention to dispose of local rivals.

and the Secretary of Defense—was not interested in participating in these plans. While FDN leaders saw U.S. airfields being built in Honduras by the Reagan administration and heard promises by U.S. officials, including Reagan, who called them brothers and heroes, they failed to understand that U.S. military construction served a psychological and logistical function: a way to intimidate the Sandinistas and to funnel U.S. weapons to the Contras through their Honduran military allies. While contingency plans included U.S. troops fighting in Nicaragua, the Sandinistas were careful not to do anything that would bring those contingencies into play.

The chosen instrument for overthrowing the Sandinistas not surprisingly consisted of Contra leaders that the CIA and later the NSC could control. An inverse relationship seemed to exist between controllability and competence. Other anti-Sandinistas—and there were several factions of different ethnic and political derivation—were denied U.S. support unless they submitted to FDN leadership, which consisted of Calero as political leader and Bermúdez as military commander. Faced with the shortcomings of these leaders, which Owen reported from the field, North responded by expanding his own role, not realizing the vicious cycle this induced: the more evident the hand of the U.S. government, the less credibility the FDN had in Central America, including inside Nicaragua.

In his 1991 book North recalls:

> It wasn't until the CIA started pulling out that both the contras and their supporters in Washington came to appreciate just how much the Agency had been doing. The CIA had provided everything from standard propaganda techniques like running a radio station and dropping leaflets to far more delicate tasks, such as providing liaison between the resistance and the governments of neighboring countries. . . . As the CIA began to withdraw, Calero and other resistance leaders began calling on me for everything from intelligence and communications support to weapons and liaison with neighboring governments.[24]

The first manifesto of FDN objectives was drafted by North and a couple of Contra leaders in North's Miami motel room in 1985.[25] When

24. North, *Under Fire*, 258, 296.
25. *Report*, 48; "Using the March 1 San José Declaration to Support the Vote on the Funding for the Nicaraguan Democratic Resistance," April 4, 1985, National Security Archive 1006.

the CIA and the Pentagon were prohibited from sharing U.S. intelligence with the Contras, North passed it along.[26] North functioned as the FDN's arbitrator, fund-raiser, treasurer, strategist, logistics manager, and public relations adviser.

In an "eyes only" report of February 1986 regarding a new political front being created to improve the FDN's image and broaden its political base, Owen wrote North:

> The Nicaraguan community at large see UNO [United Nicaraguan Opposition], as well as the FDN, as entities organized and bought and paid for by the USG [U.S. Government]. . . . Without the USG pushing and pulling Adolfo Calero and his people into an agreement to open up the leadership of the FDN and the UNO, there will be no trust, no unity, and no chance of defeating the Sandinistas without direct U.S. military involvement.[27]

Seeing no evidence of Calero's "open[ing] up the leadership" a month later, Owen informed North that those around Calero "are not first rate people; in fact they are liars and greed and power motivated. They are not the people to rebuild a new Nicaragua. In fact, the FDN has done a good job of keeping competent people out of the organization."[28] Consistent with this assessment, Owen concluded that "the heavy hand of the gringo is needed."

By the end of 1985 North no longer transferred private U.S. and "third country" donations to Calero's offshore bank accounts but routed them to another secret account that he controlled with his partner Richard Secord. A retired U.S. Air Force officer who ran an arms supply business, Secord joined North in what North dubbed "Project Democracy," the Central American subsidiary of "the Enterprise," Secord's lucrative and secretive arms trafficking operations. Ironically, Project Democracy was a secret operation to expand the Contras' fighting capability by circumventing the U.S. democratic process. What weapons the FDN received and when, which supplies went to which front—North reserved those decisions for Secord and himself.[29]

26. *Report*, 43.
27. "Update," National Security Archive 2335.
28. "Overall Perspective," National Security Archive 2493.
29. *Report*, 60, 65. A retired U.S. Air Force general who had been linked to CIA operations in the past, Richard Secord was the principal owner of an arms supply business that had many

Hundreds of thousands of dollars routinely passed through North's hands, with little of it accounted for owing to North's shredding of documents. North later claimed that he only reimbursed himself for legitimate expenses. When the dust settled from the Iran-Contra affair, however, Oliver North was a wealthy man.[30]

While the CIA saw to it that North received the latest encoding devices, word of North's expanded activities leaked not just in steamy Tegucigalpa, where the FDN was headquartered, nor in San Salvador, where the Contra supply flights shared the Ilopango airport with other planes, nor just in Miami where North regularly consulted Contra leaders and where the exile community was hungry for news, but also inside Washington's beltway. North's tightened control over the Contras generated disaffection, especially when Contra leaders learned that Secord-supplied weapons were more expensive than those available elsewhere. Occasionally the disaffected complained to *their* patrons (e.g., Félix Rodriquez to George Bush's aide Donald Gregg).[31]

By August 1985 rumors of North's activities were surfacing in the *New York Times,* setting off inquiries in the House where a liberal Democrat chaired the Subcommittee on Hemispheric Affairs. National Security Adviser McFarlane took the threat of exposure seriously enough to ask North to alter memos written during the preceding year that documented McFarlane's approval of his aide's Central American activities.[32] In March 1986 Owen warned North that "what you had hoped to remain quiet is now openly being discussed on the street," apparently referring to regional capitals, and then listed a dozen individuals and organizations being linked to North and Secord by such rumors.[33] On top of this North was suffering burnout and fearing that

---

fronts. Albert Hakim was Secord's partner specializing in the Middle East. At Casey's suggestion North turned to Secord as first the preferred, then the sole supplier of the Contras' military needs, relying on Secord to work out the logistics and hire the staff. Thus in Central America, recalls North, Secord was involved "with the entire resupply effort. Later on, congressional investigators and the press referred to this operation as 'the Enterprise'; we knew it as Project Democracy. It consisted of airplanes, a ship, warehouses, flight crews—the works." See North, *Under Fire,* 318.

30. Some of this wealth came from North's legal defense fund and some from book royalties. There is no way of knowing how much, if any, came from North's association with Secord and "the Enterprise." But it says something about North's ambition that his family moved into a $1.17 million estate in 1990, having lived modestly up until then.

31. *Report,* 71–74.

32. North, *Under Fire,* 376; *Report,* 124–26.

33. "Overall Perspective," National Security Archive 2493.

he was exposing his family to terrorist attack. In an internal memo to Poindexter North said "we have to lift some of this onto the CIA so I can get more than 2–3 hrs. of sleep at night."[34]

By 1986, then, even policymakers who approved of North's work wanted the CIA "to go back in," to replace this overexposed NSC staffer. Going back in, however, required congressional approval of a policy that bore little resemblance to the assurances the White House had given Congress over the years. Thus having Congress reverse itself both on aiding the Contras militarily and on the Boland prohibitions became a central goal of the White House, to be achieved by subjecting Congress to an intense advertising and lobbying campaign. A clear victory would legitimate CIA and Pentagon activities that had continued off the books. Unqualified congressional support also would reassure a wavering Honduran government that feared being stuck with tens of thousands of armed Contras and their families on its soil. Officially nonexistent Contra bases already had exposed that government to diplomatic embarrassment and military attacks. In the early months of the 1986 campaign the Assistant Secretary of State for Inter-American Affairs told the press that unnamed Central American governments were "afraid that we are going to walk away from this and leave them facing a communist government armed to the teeth."[35]

The Policy Drifts Toward Fantasy

While it embarked on a campaign that, if successful, would continue to expand a war that was killing ten thousand Nicaraguans a year (out of a population of three million),[36] the administration still had not reached consensus on where that expansion would lead. Did the administration really expect the Contras to overthrow the Sandinistas or merely bring them to the bargaining table? If the former, how? If the latter, when? At

34. *Report,* 68.
35. Press briefing by Elliott Abrams, 2 P.M., March 3, 1986, as reported in the microfiche version of *American Foreign Policy: Foreign Affairs Press Briefings, 1986, Supplement* (Washington, D.C.: Office of the Historian, U.S. Department of State, 1989), pt. 2.
36. In the three years of 1985–87 war-related deaths totalled 28,700 according to the *Statistical Abstract of Latin America,* Committee on Latin American Studies, vol. 27 (University of California, 1989), table 1077.

what point would Washington support negotiations? After 1984 it refused even to talk to Sandinista officials. If "democratizing" Nicaragua on Washington's terms was now a key demand—which it became in 1984 when hard-liners used it to sabotage State Department-led negotiations[37]—could future negotiations be anything but a euphemism for capitulation? What would induce the Sandinistas to bargain away their power when they were not losing ground in the war?

Now, as then, there is no scholarly consensus on how the policymakers answered such questions, if indeed they did. Most agree with journalist Roy Gutman that the administration lacked an endgame. When the dust had settled, one scholar concluded: "[T]he Reagan administration failed to establish a set of clear policy objectives or a consistent strategy for dealing with Nicaragua. Indeed, the U.S. decisionmaking process produced a confusing and decentralized policy by combining coercive diplomacy and containment objectives with a bullying strategy that was designed to roll back Sandinista rule."[38] It was not just a matter of pursuing maximum and minimum objectives within a single strategy, concludes Roberts, but "ambiguity" at the core of the strategy.

Both the FDN leaders and their Washington backers were pinning their hopes on low probability events outside their control. The White House hoped the Contras would acquire the capacity to hold significant amounts of Nicaraguan territory and to rally Nicaraguan dissidents to their organization. The Contras bet that this U.S. President, who cared deeply about his popularity, would order U.S. troops into battle against the advice of his Joint Chiefs of Staff and in the face of certain public repudiation. Both sets of leaders counted on the Sandinistas falling for some rather obvious traps.

The reality that few addressed was that Nicaragua was not Grenada. Sandinista rule was not self-destructing. Supporters of the Sandinistas, spread throughout the country, were armed and experienced in defeating a U.S.-equipped army (Somoza's National Guard). Two-thirds of the electorate had voted for the Sandinistas in 1984, and while some say that the absence of a high profile opposition candidate skewed those results, two-thirds seems a reasonable estimate of the number of

37. Constantine Menges, *Inside the National Security Council* (New York: Simon and Schuster, 1988), chap. 5.

38. Kenneth Roberts, "Bullying and Bargaining: The United States, Nicaragua, and Conflict Resolution in Central America," *International Security* 15 (Fall 1990), 73.

Nicaraguans who would align themselves with the Sandinistas to repel foreign invasion, especially one spearheaded by the Yankees. Thus U.S. forces could not be deployed to Nicaragua, achieve their objectives, and return home a few weeks after having suffered less than two dozen casualties (as happened in Grenada and would be repeated in Panama).

Other realities on the ground included the failure of CONDECA to revive, due to rivalries among Central American governments; Alvarez's being deposed as Honduran military chief as leaders there began pulling back from so exposed a role on the Contras' behalf; corruption and murder in the Contra camps, which began showing up in journalists' accounts by 1985; and the fact that, while the Contras claimed twenty thousand soldiers, no more than three thousand ever operated within Nicaragua at a given time due to reasons that Washington could not soon remedy.[39] The Sandinista army, on the other hand, numbered some sixty thousand and, led by ex-guerrillas, was adept at small-scale operations.[40] By 1985 the Sandinistas had revamped their tactics around newly acquired Soviet helicopter gunships and were sending retrained regular troops against the Contras instead of the militia previously used while regular troops defended the cities.

All this was known to the CIA, which produced four Special National Intelligence Estimates on Nicaragua in 1985, although North and Casey worked to keep these SNIEs as upbeat as possible. When Woodward tried to draw out the Deputy Director of the CIA by suggesting that the real reason for the Contra operation was "to overthrow the Sandinistas," the Deputy Director laughed and said, "No fucking chance of that. . . . Simple arithmetic."[41] By the time intelligence reached the top decision makers, however, those facts either were diluted or were countered by less representative but more vivid anecdotes. Woodward's account of the CIA under Casey's direction includes several instances in which intelligence was "cooked" to support the Director's preexisting

---

39. "Nicaragua Rebels, in Retreat, Viewed as Reduced Threat," *New York Times,* March 6, 1986, A1. Part of the problem, as this article points out, is that "the rebels are widely seen inside Nicaragua and abroad as a purely military force led by former members of the defeated Nicaraguan National Guard and by citizens who were loyal to Anastasio Somoza Debayle, the Nicaraguan dictator."

40. Bob Woodward, *Veil: The Secret Wars of the CIA, 1981–1987* (New York: Simon and Schuster Pocket Books, 1988), 459.

41. Ibid., 373. This interchange occurred in April 1984.

position, a practice documented later during Senate hearings into Robert Gates's qualifications for the director's job.[42] Casey also catered to President Reagan's propensity for reducing international relations to human interest stories.[43] Sitting astride the flow of intelligence, Casey fed Reagan a steady diet of Sandinista atrocities and Contra courage through vignettes that the President said "make my day."[44]

A World Simple Enough for Heroes

This inability of top policymakers to focus on Central American realities has several possible explanations. The difficulty of assigning each its due—the perennial problem of "overdetermination" in social science—recedes as we realize that they are three facets of a single reality. First, big nations dealing with little ones often substitute power for information and get away with it. The Reagan administration had just imposed its solution on Grenada without having accurate maps of the island. "America was involved in Vietnam for thirty years, but never

42. For an early attempt to blow the whistle on intelligence distortion, see the Staff Report of the House Subcommittee on Oversight and Evaluation (part of the Permanent Select Committee on Intelligence) entitled *U.S. Intelligence Performance on Central America: Achievements and Selected Instances of Concern*, September 22, 1982. Both Woodward, in his book on the CIA during the period, and McNeil, who spent 1984–87 as the second in command of the State Department's Bureau of Intelligence and Research, provide evidence of intelligence reports being shaped to serve Casey's political line with regard to Mexico and Central America. See Woodward, *Veil*, 393; Gutman, *Banana Diplomacy*, 188, 344; Frank McNeil, *War and Peace in Central America* (New York: Charles Scribner's Sons, 1988), 218.

43. Donald Regan remained sympathetic to Ronald Reagan, even after being fired, yet Regan's account of the inner working of the Reagan White House reveals a president whose "heart was easily touched," who was more animated at meetings if women were present, who liked to relate anecdotes recalled from film roles or found in countless letters ordinary citizens sent him (which he spent long hours reading), and who dozed off or remained silent when the talk turned analytical. In short, Regan's sympathetic account corresponds to more critical portraits, such as that of Mayer and McManus, which sums up Reagan's proclivities as "left to his own intentions, the president would confuse the human interest with the national interest, mistaking gestures for policies, romantic themes for strategies, and immediate emotional gratification for long-term strategic gains." See Jane Mayer and Doyle McManus, *Landslide: The Unmaking of the President, 1984–1988* (Boston: Houghton Mifflin, 1988), 226, 51, 98, and Donald Regan, *For the Record: From Wall Street to Washington* (New York: St. Martin's Press, 1988), 299–308.

44. The expression comes from Clint Eastwood movie westerns. Ronald Reagan not only had acted in Hollywood westerns, he remained an avid reader of Louis L'Amour western novels.

understood the Vietnamese."[45] Another explanation is that, while set *in* Central America, the conflict was really *about* another time and place. Rather than influencing Managua or Tegucigalpa, Washington sought to influence Moscow and Paris—and Miami and Dallas. A third explanation is that key decision makers were driven by the psychological dynamics Lloyd Etheredge isolated in his study of top-level U.S. policymakers of the 1960s: otherwise "intelligent men" who, in dealing with Cuba, "chose to avoid truths . . . in patterns suggesting, at a deeper level, they *did* know already what reality would be if they faced it. They stopped asking questions at exactly the point where the realistic answers would begin to be uncomfortable to know."[46]

The three complementary explanations shed light on the reproduction of myths such as America/Américas. For myths not only simplify a complex reality by reducing the novel to the known, they provide heroic roles for policymakers. If Etheredge is right, the process by which the United States selects its top foreign policymakers may reward an abnormal drive for "grandiosity" that includes a self-perception of "complete dominance of events of the world." What Etheredge's practitioner of hardball politics [HP] seeks is

> the experience of directorship atop the unfolding social and political drama of his times. . . . Although he may genuinely dedicate himself to certain kinds of grandiose accomplishment, these typically are stylistic and symbolic, and seldom involve thoughtful and well-elaborated programs. . . . [H]e imagines a better society to follow (he is vague about details) once his own will occupies the idealized "over-mind" location of high office.[47]

Myths that cast the United States in that role will be reproduced by policymakers who see themselves analogously situated. Thus we turn to the *subjective* conditions for launching the 1986 campaign.

Top Reagan aides formed their ideologies in the 1930s and 1940s around the traumas and controversies encoded in U.S. mythology such as "Munich," "Pearl Harbor," "Yalta," and "the Truman Doctrine." Reagan and Casey, along with Chief of Staff Donald Regan and Secretary of Defense Caspar Weinberger, were born in the second decade of

---

45. Loren Baritz, *Backfire: A History of How American Culture Led Us into Vietnam and Made Us Fight the Way We Did* (New York: William Morrow and Co., 1985), 19.
46. *Can Governments Learn?* (New York: Pergamon Press, 1985), 144.
47. Ibid., 149.

the twentieth century. Casey and Regan were marked by urban Irish-American boyhoods in an era when patriotism was that minority's best line of defense. Along with Weinberger, all had seen combat in World War II except the President, who made training films as a member of the Army Air Corps and played war heroes in Hollywood films. A portrait of Winston Churchill stared down on these 1980s policymakers as they met in the White House situation room.

Another Irish-American had been their contemporary—John F. Kennedy. Kennedy's foreign policy statements resemble Reagan's in positing a global confrontation between a free world and international communism and in seeing the Third World as a major theater of that conflict. As with Reagan and Casey, Kennedy saw this as "God's work" and preferred that other nationalities bear the cost in blood for executing it.[48] Like them, Kennedy was a proponent of special forces and proxy armies.

The Kennedy and Reagan presidencies are separated, however, not just by twenty years but by such major events as Nixon's opening to China, the Sino-Soviet rift, and the defeat of Marxist guerrillas throughout much of Latin America, of which Che Guevara's 1967 death in Bolivia is emblematic. Thus in Reagan's or Casey's mouth Kennedy's words were anachronistic. This may explain why Reagan policymakers avoided public use of "world communism" or even "Reagan Doctrine." Yet they acted as if those concepts informed their understanding of the Third World, including Nicaragua. Oliver North later would write disparagingly of "sophisticated Americans" who "snicker at any reference to an international Communist conspiracy."[49]

In the not-for-attribution interview quoted above "an Administration official" confided that "this goes beyond Nicaragua. If these people can stand up and throw off Communism, it goes beyond Managua. . . . The way to go after the Soviet Union is through the colonies."[50] In capsule, that is a statement of the Reagan Doctrine, of which Casey was the principal author.[51]

William Casey had been marked by his experience in World War II. As a member of the CIA's forerunner, the Office of Strategic Services (OSS), he conducted such heroic exploits as dropping spies behind

48. Baritz, Backfire, 42.
49. North, Under Fire, 319.
50. "Reagan Aides See No Possibility of U.S. Accord with Sandinistas."
51. The phrase itself apparently was coined by columnist Charles Krauthammer.

German lines. During and immediately after that war Ronald Reagan *acted* similar roles, as in the film "Desperate Journey." Serving under Casey in Europe had been John Singlaub, one of two retired U.S. military officers to whom Casey turned to supply the Contras when Congress clamped down on the CIA's involvement; Secord was the other. As head of the World Anti-Communist League, Singlaub actively promoted the Reagan Doctrine.

Through speeches he wrote himself and delivered to small, exclusive audiences Casey elaborated the view of the world that the right had inserted into the 1980 Republican party platform and that appeared in a position paper written that year to shape Reagan policy toward Latin America. According to the Committee of Santa Fe "World War III is almost over"; the Soviets are winning in this war's principal theater, the Third World. Washington is losing because it has denied itself full use of its capabilities, including covert warfare. It is past time for "a worldwide counter-projection of American power."[52] Similarly, the existence of a "third world war" was the premise of columns that James Burnham published in the *National Review*. In 1983 President Reagan bestowed the Medal of Freedom on Burnham, saying he owed him "a personal debt" for his writings.[53]

In a typical 1985 speech Casey divided the Third World into "occupied countries" (those with Marxist regimes) and "unoccupied countries" (the rest). Here is Woodward's recollection of hearing Casey speak: "In the occupied countries—Afghanistan, Cambodia, Ethiopia, Angola, Nicaragua—in which Marxist regimes have been either imposed or maintained by external force, has occurred a holocaust comparable to that which Nazi Germany inflicted in Europe some forty years ago."[54] At another opportunity Casey said: "In my opinion, Nicaragua can and should be a perfect example of how some of our experiences of World War II can be applied with great effect in support of a resistance movement."[55] Comparing the Contras to "the French Resistance that fought the Nazis" became a staple of Reagan rhetoric.[56]

52. Committee of Santa Fe, *A New Inter-American Policy for the Eighties* (Washington, D.C.: Council for Inter-American Security, 1981), 1, 2, 53.
53. "The Doctrine Is In," *Washington Post National Weekly Edition*, July 14, 1986, 24.
54. Woodward, *Veil*, 462.
55. Gutman, *Banana Diplomacy*, 268–70, including notes; Woodward, *Veil*, 426.
56. Reagan's "Address to the Nation on the Situation in Nicaragua, March 16, 1986," *Public Papers of the Presidents of the United States: Ronald Reagan, 1986* (Washington, D.C.: U.S. Government Printing Office, 1988), 1:355.

A core tenet of the "Reagan Doctrine" was that each side in this global struggle was interconnected. The hand of the Soviet Union lay behind all Marxist revolutionary movements and, it was claimed for awhile, all terrorist activities as well.[57] The less visible the hand, the more sinister its owner. In a 1983 speech to the nation following the bombing of marine barracks by Islamic terrorists and the U.S. invasion of Grenada, President Reagan said: "The events in Lebanon and Grenada, though oceans apart, are closely related. . . . Not only has Moscow assisted and encouraged the violence in both countries, but it provides direct support through a network of surrogates and terrorists."[58] Rather than note the downscaling of Soviet aspirations and capabilities, a trend recognized by professional analysts inside the CIA, Casey's speeches kept the Kremlin locked into vintage Khrushchev bravado of twenty years earlier. "This is not an undeclared war," Casey would say. "In 1961, Khrushchev . . . told us that communism would win . . . by wars of national liberation in Africa, Asia, and Latin America."[59]

As with the enemy, so with the "freedom fighters." Whether in Afghanistan, Angola, Cambodia, or Nicaragua, they were seen as parts of a single movement. In addition to Casey several in the administration were favorably impressed by Jack Wheeler, head of a Freedom Research Foundation linked to Singlaub's World Anti-Communist League.[60] After touring U.S.-backed resistance movements, including the Contras, Wheeler proclaimed that "anticommunist struggles worldwide were a single movement."[61] When, in his 1985 State of the Union speech, Reagan said that "support for freedom fighters is self-defense," he meant that by supporting freedom fighters anywhere—Casey hoped everywhere—the United States could counter the Soviet threat without risking nuclear war or exposing U.S. troops to combat.

Paradoxically, the global sweep of the Reagan Doctrine permitted the policymakers to proceed in a highly ad hoc manner in dealing with

---

57. North states that Casey was "enormously influenced" by Claire Sterling's book *The Terror Network*, which "described an international terrorist fraternity, a collection of groups who received extensive support from the Soviets and their Eastern European allies." See North, *Under Fire*, 215.
58. Woodward, *Veil*, 332–33.
59. Ibid., 462. See also Mayer and McManus, *Landslide*, 77.
60. Chamorro, *Packaging the Contras*, 53.
61. Gutman, *Banana Diplomacy*, 268–69.

Nicaragua. Means become detached from ends when the ends are so global. Without skipping a beat the administration could proclaim a worldwide communist movement and then facilitate surface-to-air missiles from Marxist China reaching the Contras to be used against Marxist Nicaragua. By casting the Contras as "freedom fighters," expanding the Contras' numbers (recruits, fronts, operations) became a self-evident good, as if the benefits of "more" were obvious.

Part of the attraction of the Reagan Doctrine was its familiarity to a generation born during one world war that came of age in another. The doctrine offered aging leaders a heroic role defending Western civilization, a role with few intellectual demands inasmuch as it extolled values over knowledge, resolve over skill. According to the doctrine any U.S. operation in any corner of the globe could be a world historic event. "Since 1945, Communism had prevailed just about everywhere it had tried its hand. But Ronald Reagan and Bill Casey insisted that if we could help an indigenous anti-Communist movement inflict a single major defeat, the entire Communist house of cards would come tumbling down."[62] That is North's version of the (by then discredited) domino theory. If the Contras held on to a corner of sparsely populated Nicaragua, North said it would send "a powerful psychological message to the entire world."[63]

A frequently criticized facet of Reagan's administrative style—his inattention to detail—now makes sense. Attention to the big picture was all that mattered. No need to register the difference between the Sandinistas coming to power through a popular revolution and Vietnam's military conquest of Cambodia. No need to discriminate between Soviet interests on its border (Afghanistan) and Soviet interests halfway around the globe in the shadow of U.S. power (Nicaragua). The Reagan Doctrine collapsed the variety extant in a world of receding superpowers and rising ethnic conflicts into a storybook struggle between good and evil that could be won militarily, with covert action and proxy armies playing the pivotal role. It was a blindingly simple view of the world that cast the U.S. leaders as directors.

When the decision whether or not to invade Grenada was being weighed, Casey could say "Hey, fuck it, let's dump these bastards," knowing little about the island.[64] Given a Third World divided between

62. North, *Under Fire*, 486.
63. Gutman, *Banana Diplomacy*, 337.
64. Woodward, *Veil*, 324.

"occupied" and "unoccupied" countries, all he needed to know was in which camp Grenada fell. Similarly, on hearing that the centrist Raúl Alfonsín had won the first election in Argentina following a period of military rule, Casey's only question was, "Is he a Marxist-Leninist?"[65] In reality Alfonsín was a committed democrat with a track record of supporting human rights. Because the Reagan Doctrine required it, "the Soviets" went on "challenging the United States to a test of wills over the future of this hemisphere" well after Mikhail Gorbachev had provided evidence that such an objective was inconsistent not only with his priorities but with Soviet capabilities. "[A]nyone searching for evidence that the Soviets remain expansionist—indeed, imperialist— need look no farther than Nicaragua," President Reagan said as late as October 1987,[66] having signed important agreements with Gorbachev in the meantime.[67]

The pivotal role of Oliver North, a decorated veteran of a later and different war, raises the question of how the Reagan Doctrine sat with those younger officials who fleshed out the President's ambiguous directives in the interagency battles that shaped the policy actually applied. Like North a marine veteran of Vietnam combat, McFarlane was only six years older than his aide. Adding Poindexter, McFarlane's replacement as National Security Adviser, Michael Ledeen comments

65. Ibid., 393. Argentina had no serious Marxist party or movement; the new president represented a centrist liberal democratic party with a long history.

66. Two Reagan speeches reprinted by the U.S. Department of State as *Current Policy 952* and 1021 (May and November 1987).

67. Basing his periodization of Soviet foreign policy on information that would have been available to U.S. government analysts at the time, Jan Adams writes: "The coalition of interventionists managed to dominate Soviet policymaking toward the Middle East and the Third World for almost a decade, from 1973 into Brezhnev's last year, 1982. In mid-1982, however, a new power configuration formed within the Politburo, and the policy pendulum began to swing back toward a less militant posture." Adams believes that Leonid Brezhnev "provided helpful groundwork for Gorbachev's subsequent policy preferences and initiatives." A major change in Soviet policy toward far-flung Third World countries, visible in 1982, was strengthened by Gorbachev's rise to power in early 1985, which brought with it a sharper focus on domestic reforms, a more imperative search for superpower cooperation, and a cutback on overseas expenditures. Gorbachev's "new political thinking" included explicit disavowals of "world revolution" and of armed revolution as a path toward socialism in the Third World. Conflicts should be resolved by "a just *political* settlement" that "take[s] the interests of all sides into consideration." The Twenty-seventh Congress of the Communist Party of the Soviet Union, held early the following year (February 1986), ratified this as the dominant Soviet position. See Jan S. Adams, *A Foreign Policy in Transition: Moscow's Retreat from Central America and the Caribbean, 1985–1992* (Durham: Duke University Press, 1992), 23, 27, 110.

that they "were all military officers [who] . . . came from small-town America, and . . . went to military academies."[68] What NSC consultant Ledeen implies, and Reagan's popularity with young voters supports, is a symbiotic relationship between segments of two generations: an older one confident of its values attracting a younger one seeking reassurance that the country remained strong and good after the self-critical "sixties" and the defeat in Indo-China. While liberal Democrats compared Central America to the "quagmire" of Vietnam, where local nationalism and poverty are more salient than international alliances, those who worked for the Reagan administration interpreted Vietnam as a politically induced defeat, a betrayal of the U.S. troops who bravely fought there and of their Vietnam allies. Both North and McFarlane spoke of not abandoning the Contras the way the South Vietnamese army had been abandoned. Hence Reagan's emphasis on "resolve" appealed to them, as did the President's loyalty to U.S. citizens held hostage in the Middle East.

Conversely, Reagan and Casey drew assurance from North that World War II-style heroism was still relevant. Said presidential aide Michael Deaver of North: "He'd fly to Beirut, be back twenty-four hours later, and brief the president. Reagan loved him, [loved] the style."[69] Casey's feelings for North were recalled by his top aide, Clair George: "[Casey] loved North very much. He liked action people." North reminded Casey of his own "swashbuckling days" in the OSS: "He saw in Ollie North a part of that."[70] (George's own professional estimate of North was harsher.)[71]

If Casey cloaked his romanticism under an appearance of indifference (mumbling advice, refusing to "stroke" Congress), North wore his on his sleeve as Reagan was wont to do. But "Casey's convictions," no less than Reagan's in Woodward's estimation, were fueled by "nostalgia" and "willfulness."[72] Nostalgia of a different sort pervades North's account of the Norman Rockwellesque childhood from which he and his wife emerged. By his account North married someone "like me,

---

68. *Perilous Statecraft: An Insider's Account of the Iran-Contra Affair* (New York: Charles Scribner's Sons, 1988), 81.
69. Mayer and McManus, *Landslide*, 69.
70. Ibid., 81–82.
71. *Report*, 37.
72. By the fall of 1985 the CIA director knew he had cancer of the prostate and that "the chances were not very good at his age, seventy-two." See Woodward, *Veil*, 483, 586.

[who] had grown up in a clean-cut, rural, common sense small-town environment."[73] The eldest son of a decorated World War II veteran, North served as an altar boy at his mother's church. After two years at a small state college he entered the Naval Academy, where he spent the sixties. Those years at Annapolis—to him "a combination monastery and prison-work camp"—were prolonged by North's slow recovery from an auto accident.

Commissioned a Marine officer, North soon married and left for Vietnam. North fought near the DMZ, an area by then devoid of Vietnamese who were not soldiers; he experienced few of the ambiguities that U.S. personnel confronted further south among peasants.[74] Thus North's Vietnam bore little resemblance to Central America. Posted to the NSC in a minor role, by 1983 North was that agency's liaison with the Kissinger Commission, a blue-ribbon panel that the Reagan administration hoped would generate bipartisan support for its Central American policy. From there North's involvement with Central America grew.

Of Oliver North his NSC colleague Ledeen wrote: "He was not familiar with the history and culture of Latin America and did not speak Spanish, which made it difficult for him to make independent evaluations of people and the exceedingly delicate political decisions he faced in the Central American project."[75] The same could be said of McFarlane, Poindexter, and Casey, and more pointedly of Dewey Clarridge and Alan Fiers of the CIA, Elliott Abrams at State, and North's man on the ground Robert Owen, all personnel specifically chosen to work *in* Central America. Former U.S. Ambassador to Costa Rica Frank McNeil noted that "[n]one of the principals in making the Contras into a substitute for foreign policy . . . knew a damned thing about Latin America."[76]

North acquired a reputation for forging ahead anyway, for being

---

73. North, *Under Fire*, 101.
74. Ibid., 76–141.
75. Ledeen, *Perilous Statecraft*, 79.
76. McNeil, *War and Peace in Central America*, 221. North once interpreted an aerial photograph showing baseball diamonds at Nicaraguan military facilities as evidence of a Cuban presence, since "Nicaraguans don't play baseball. Cubans play baseball." Baseball has been a popular sport in Nicaragua since the turn of the century when U.S. soldiers introduced it. Not knowing that Nicaraguans play baseball is like not knowing that Canadians play ice hockey. See George Black, *The Good Neighbor* (New York: Pantheon Books, 1988), 149–50, 160.

what State Department professionals call a cowboy. North reciprocated by calling them shoe clerks and mice. When he could not make things happen North made it *seem* as if they were. Through his frenetic movement he created the illusion of the policy's working: taking overnight flights to Miami to consult Contra leaders, calling meetings on Sundays, sleeping at his NSC "command center" with its multiple computers, secure telephones, and encryption devices. If victory was not here, such behavior made it seem just around the corner. One NSC colleague evaluated North as "about thirty to fifty percent bullshit." Journalists Mayer and McManus, who report this and other appraisals by North's coworkers, conclude that "he was a relentless selfpromoter and a spellbinding storyteller, almost as good as Ronald Reagan himself."[77] Among the code names North chose for himself were "Colonel Rambo," "Steel Hammer," and "Blood and Guts."[78]

Myth and the Hardball Player

When Oliver North ran for the U.S. Senate in 1994, several associates from the Reagan days took the unusual step of publicly questioning his fitness. Their complaint was not ideological; in their eyes North lacked the ethics and reliability for the job. North had lied not just to Congress but to them.[79] Both Casey and North operated "with cool, even cold, detachment" toward colleagues (all quoted phrases are from Etheredge's description of the "hardball practitioner" [HP] written before Iran-Contra), structuring relationships in terms of loyalty/betrayal. "Funda-

77. Mayer and McManus, *Landslide,* 67–70. Congruent with this portrait of North is one later provided by another NSC staff member working on Central America. See Menges, *Inside the National Security Council,* 350–63. After his exhaustive study Theodore Draper came to the same conclusion. See *A Very Thin Line: The Iran-Contra Affairs* (New York: Hill & Wang, 1991), 532.

78. Gutman, *Banana Diplomacy,* 207; "Owen Memos Detail Rancher's Activities in C.R.," *The Tico Times* (San José, Costa Rica), March 17, 1989, 8.

79. "What Reagan Could Say about North," *Washington Post National Weekly Edition,* February 28, 1994; Rachel Wildavsky, "Does Oliver North Tell the Truth?" *Reader's Digest,* June 1993. Previous memoirs by Constantine Menges and Michael Ledeen collaborate what journalists suddenly discovered in 1993–94: that North's associates at the Reagan NSC found him untrustworthy in ways that broke even Washington norms. One pattern recurring in these accounts is North's pretending to close and personal associations with Reagan and Casey, including private sessions that never occurred.

mental disagreement is perceived as disloyalty."[80] North's "close" relationships with his idols, Reagan and Casey, turned into scorn or
scapegoating once those superiors lost power.[81]

Casey's business practices had drawn more than one legal investigation, while in government his willingness to manipulate others, including the President, was legendary. Descriptions of the CIA under Casey
are classic "hardball," including the distortions that arise when policymakers outdo each other in being tough. Regarding Qaddafi's Libya,
Woodward writes, "There was lots of tough talk. No one wanted to
sound weak." Not to be outdone, North drafted a document for
President Reagan advocating that CIA-trained teams of foreign nation-
als "neutralize" terrorists thought to be planning attacks on Americans.
"In North's language, it was time to kill the 'cocksucker' terrorists."[82]
Rattling Qaddafi's cage, as seasoned CIA analysts realized, was just
inviting trouble. The United States' 1986 bombing of Tripoli, in which
dozens of civilians died, is thought to have motivated Libyan participation in the downing of Pan Am flight 103 two years later, in which
many more Americans died.

"But this is not to say the HP lacks a sense of morality. The fantasies
embedded in the grandiose self include an almost religious sense of
moral justification," according to Etheredge. Both Casey and North
concluded internal memos with "God bless America," both raised
patriotism to a law higher than the Constitution. While North, during
the campaign described in the next chapter, paraded his concern for
"protecting" or "saving" Nicaraguan lives, he meant only "his" Nicaraguans.[83] At the NSC North planned attacks on urbanized areas within
Nicaragua, the sole purpose of which was to impress Congress with the

---

80. Etheredge, *Can Governments Learn?* 150.

81. It is on the basis of North's testimony at the Iran-Contra hearings that many assume
that Casey was plotting an ongoing, unmonitored covert action capability, an assumption that
conveniently deflects responsibility from North and onto the one superior who no longer
could defend himself, Casey having died by then. Why North didn't mention Casey's scheme
to Attorney General Edwin Meese at their November 23, 1986, meeting is strange, since it
would have been to North's advantage to do so and hardly an act of disloyalty given Meese's
close ties to Reagan. In a book coauthored after his conviction on felony charges had been set
aside, North continued to assert that "Ronald Reagan knew everything," while supplying no
evidence for a charge that contradicts Reagan's statements. For a skeptical review of North's
testimony regarding Casey see Menges, *Inside the National Security Council*, 365–70, and
Wildavsky, "Does Oliver North Tell the Truth?"

82. Woodward, *Veil*, 412, 419.

83. North, *Under Fire*, 447, 483–85.

Contras' mobility and audacity.[84] As described earlier, North over-looked drug running into the United States when it served the cause. The key to understanding the HP policymaker lies in the "structural split into two selves (grandiose/depleted)" that leads him to project an "imperial, absolute self-confidence" while privately harboring deep insecurities about himself. To keep his confidence up the HP is hyperactive and hyperbolic: "He over-schedules himself. He works long hours" on projects "he considers heroically important." Especially important for this analysis, the HP "appears caught up powerfully in a world of his own imagining," so much so that "there is a slight drunkenness to his thought when he thinks or declaims about important issues."[85] Recall the Reagan Doctrine being used to magnify Nicaragua into a world historic event.

Etheredge's description so closely fits these and other Reagan-era officials dealing with Nicaragua that it is easy to forget that he wrote about an earlier attempt to tame a Latin American revolution: the policy making that produced the Bay of Pigs. It is not that Etheredge's portrait is so unusual. Many accounts, such as Seymour Hersh's of Henry Kissinger during the Nixon era, show the same tendencies.[86] Where Etheredge breaks fresh ground is in postulating the psychological underpinnings of what often is assumed to be situationally caused behavior. The HP person not only is preoccupied with power but has advantages in the competitive pursuit of power. He projects an image of confidence and tough-mindedness that wins assent from others, especially in dealing with foreign governments perceived as dangerous.

84. In March 1985 an upcoming vote in Congress on Contra aid appeared headed for defeat. Along with others in the administration North planned a two-week public relations, advertising, and lobbying blitz aimed at altering the impression held by many in Washington that the Contras remained ineffective. As a part of this campaign North hired British mercenary David Walker, who in turn hired agents of Panamanian dictator Manuel Noriega. These agents entered Nicaragua and blew up ammunitions stored at a military complex in Managua. The explosion not only ripped through barracks and officers' quarters but also a hospital, for which reason it was decided that it was unwise to have the Contras take the credit as they had for the earlier attack on oil storage in Corinto masterminded by the CIA. North, one of whose official tasks was to prevent terrorist attacks in the world, spent $50,000 in public monies on this event. See Malcolm Byrne and Peter Kornbluh, eds., *The Iran-Contra Affair: The Making of a Scandal, 1983–1988* (Alexandria, Va.: Chadwyck-Healey, 1990), 42, 108; Gutman, *Banana Diplomacy*, 281; "Noriega and North," *Newsweek*, January 15, 1990, 22.

85. Etheredge, *Can Governments Learn?* 151–55.

86. *The Price of Power: Kissinger in the Nixon White House* (New York: Summit Books, 1983).

The HP's "analytically rational intelligence operates in connection with a larger part of his mind that functions as if he were sleepwalking: manipulating vaguely defined, emotionally laden, symbols." Such policymakers "are psychologically predisposed to be caught in their own imaginations." "An almost religious confidence in his own eventual success" accompanies the policymaker who is driven by these "internal fantasies."[87]

Those statements could just as well describe the America/Américas myth. For "policymaker" substitute "the United States" and you have an adequate gloss of the four deep sentences. As we saw in Chapter 2, this myth has its roots in insecurities that the young nation experienced, insecurities prolonged by desires for expansion. The Americas myth delivered the United States from those insecurities by projecting a grandiose mission and by insisting on loyalties of the with-us or again'-us kind. "Imperious vanity and anger is the psychology of the grandiose self," according to Etheredge.[88] And so with the nation.

In dealing with major international actors these attributes of policymakers usually are checked by their aides. At the Reykjavik summit in 1986, for example, when President Reagan got carried away in conversations with Soviet leader Gorbachev and promised more than he was programmed to, his words quickly were "reinterpreted" by senior aides. In dealing with "lesser nations," however, especially those within Washington's sphere of influence, such "drunkenness" not only is less checked by bureaucratic processes but seems to serve as an outlet for HP policymakers' need to wax grandiose. The more careful and reciprocal U.S. relations are with major nations in the post–Cold War era, the more "imperious vanity and anger" may be vented on hemispheric targets, particularly those less able to fight back.

Thus the reproduction of the America/Américas myth responds to factors that are global on the one hand yet Washington-based on the other. Myths are reproduced by people, and the people with greatest access to the reproductive mechanisms described in the next chapter often have distinct psychological profiles.

87. Etheredge, *Can Governments Learn?* 154.
88. Ibid., 153.

5

Mounting the Campaign

No part of the money appropriated by any enactment of Congress shall, in the absence of express authorization by Congress, be used directly or indirectly to pay for any personal service, advertisement, telegram, telephone, letter, printed or written matter, or other device, intended to influence in any manner a Member of Congress, whether before or after the introduction of any bill or resolution . . .

—United States Code 18, 1913[1]

We are using the methodology of national political campaigns. . . . We are using advertising and public affairs programs. . . .

—"Central American Freedom Program"
Plan of action for Carl Channell's organization[2]

If private and "third country" funding bought the time in which to mount a campaign to turn Congress around on this issue, Reagan's landslide victory in November 1984 suggested the method: mobilize the public's anticommunist and pro-Reagan feelings to pressure wavering legislators, particularly House Democrats in southern and sunbelt states where Central America holds greater saliency due to immigration, trade, and proximity.

As the second term got under way, conservatives awaited the "un-

1. Reproduced in a letter to Representative Dante Fascell from the Comptroller General, dated September 30, 1987, with regard to the legality of activities of the Office for Public Diplomacy for Latin America and the Caribbean, forming part of the Comptroller General's report to Congressman Dante Fascell, Chair of the Foreign Affairs Committee, House of Representatives, September 30, 1987, numbered B-229069.

2. "Central American Freedom Program," February 16, 1986, National Security Archive 2354, 6. The same document may be found in Appendix A of *Source Documents*, volume 1 of U.S. Congress, *Report of the Congressional Committees Investigating the Iran-Contra Affair*, 100th Cong., 1st sess., H. Rept. 100-433, S. Rept. 100-216 (Washington, D.C.: U.S. Government Printing Office, 1987).

leashing" of the Reagan they imagined the President to be. The inability of conservatives to ride Reagan's coattails into Congress hindered their chances of promoting their social agenda, however, other than through appointments to the Supreme Court. By now major pieces of Reagan's economic program had been enacted. Thus foreign policy emerged as an attractive target of opportunity, for here the President would be less hampered by the Democratic majority in the House of Representatives.

An arms agreement with the Soviet Union would secure the President's place in history, his wife and other advisers thought, as well as maintain his popularity at home.[3] As early as 1983 Reagan confided to Secretary of State George Shultz his desire to improve relations with Moscow.[4] For both the President and his conservative supporters, however, any melting of the Cold War had to be perceived as a Kremlin defeat inflicted by the President's unyielding resolve. Nearby Central America and the Caribbean provided a safe place to demonstrate such "resolve," since the Soviets showed little inclination to defend their assets in the Western Hemisphere other than in Cuba, as demonstrated by the weak Soviet response to the 1983 U.S. invasion of Grenada.

White House toughness could not rest on Grenada alone, but the popularity of that invasion shaped the administration's belief that U.S. public opinion was malleable. "Standing tall" would be supported by a public still trapped in "Vietnam syndrome" as long as U.S. casualties were minimal. Polling numbers should not be considered the final word, since *this* president had proven his ability to shape public opinion through a combination of decisive action and avuncular homilies. With an upcoming election facing the House 1986 was the year to bring Congress on board by making Nicaragua a test of "communism vs. freedom."

Reagan's first-term Chief of Staff, James A. Baker III, might have discouraged such a campaign for the risk it carried of rekindling the public image of Reagan as trigger-happy, an image Baker's team worked to overcome in 1981–82. But in the second term Baker went to Treasury to escape battles with hard-liners at the White House, in a trade that brought Donald Regan from Treasury to be the President's Chief of

3. In 1986, 86 percent of the U.S. public favored negotiating an arms control treaty between the two superpowers. See Eugene R. Wittkopf, *Faces of Internationalism: Public Opinion and American Foreign Policy* (Durham: Duke University Press, 1990), 33 (table 2.7).

4. "If We Knew Then What We Know Now," *Washington Post National Weekly Edition,* October 7, 1991, 25.

Staff. Not the ideologue on foreign policy that his golf partner William Casey was, Regan consolidated his power by "letting Reagan be Reagan" on issues that did not centrally concern him, a category that included Central America. Casey liked the change, finding the President "more liberated": "Don Regan drew out the President. Reagan talked more; his exact notions were given priority. What do you want? the new chief of staff frequently asked."[5] What Reagan wanted, of course, was being shaped by the misinformation Casey fed him.

In preparation for the National Security Council meeting preceding the full campaign to turn Congress around, Casey asked his staff to provide him with "intelligence" that will "make the insurgency choice stark" and demonstrate why Washington should "get out of" supporting the Contadora negotiations. "Either we go all out to support them [the Contras], or they'll go down the drain."[6]

Rather than circumvent Congress as Casey had done, Don Regan rose to the challenge of turning it around, having been a marketing specialist in the private sector. Similarly, Robert McFarlane's replacement as National Security Advisor in late 1985, John Poindexter, was less inclined than McFarlane to compromise with congressional leaders, an attitude shared by the new White House Director of Communications, Patrick Buchanan. So, with the targeting of Congress firm Poindexter and Buchanan made sure the arrows were not blunted. There would be no settling for "humanitarian" aid this time around.

In December 1985 the Reagan administration served notice that it would request from Congress full military funding of the Contras before the current "humanitarian" aid ran out in 1986. In February the White House officially asked for $100 million, $70 million earmarked for military purposes. That represented more military aid to the Contras in a single year than had been provided (officially) in Reagan's five years in office. During the campaign that followed, reports Roy Gutman, "the political energies consumed were staggering."[7] Notes William LeoGrande, "the administration went all out to win its full request."[8]

---

5. Bob Woodward, *Veil: The Secret Wars of the CIA, 1981–1987* (New York: Simon and Schuster Pocket Books, 1988), 459.

6. "NSC Pre-Brief," January 9, 1986, National Security Archive 2124. For an explanation of this source see note 8 of Chapter 4; Roy Gutman, *Banana Diplomacy: The Making of American Diplomacy in Nicaragua, 1981–1987* (New York: Simon and Schuster, 1988), 321.

7. Gutman, *Banana Diplomacy*, 321.

8. William LeoGrande, "The Contras and Congress," in *Reagan Versus the Sandinistas*, ed. Thomas Walker (Boulder: Westview Press, 1987), 213.

According to Ben Bradlee Jr. the campaign included "a dramatic exten-
sion of earlier White House efforts to blend public relations with policy
on the Central American front."[9] Journalist or scholar, all who write
about this episode recognize that the Reagan administration's campaign
to convert Congress on the issue of Contra military aid exceeded
previous efforts to manipulate, in tandem, public opinion and congressional voting.

By this time most members of Congress had adopted public positions
on Contra aid. Only some thirty votes in the Democrat-controlled
House could be considered "swing," many of them southern or border
state Democrats. In the Senate the White House could count on votes
closely following party lines, which meant fifty-three votes for the
administration, a majority. The previous year the White House had
won over sufficient swing votes in the House by offering a series of
compromises, the most important being the deletion of the military
component from the Contra aid package. The President had also sent
Congress letters of intention designed to pick up votes by promising to
resume negotiations, disclaiming intent to seek a military victory, and
pledging to monitor the Contras' human rights record. (Such letters
have no legal force.) This time the task the Reagan team set for itself
was to win enough swing votes while holding firm on *military* aid.

What made this a "quantum leap in U.S. backing" of the Contras, as
Cynthia Arnson labels it, is that the CIA was designated the distributor
of the aid.[10] The figures of 70 million and 100 million had been pulled
from the air as large enough to signal the importance the White House
attached to this legislation yet small enough that the money could be
diverted from other Pentagon accounts, permitting the Reagan team to
argue that it was not "new" money that Congress was being asked to
provide. But in point of fact passage of the legislation legitimated a
host of other CIA and Pentagon projects benefiting the Contras. One
Republican source estimated that half a billion dollars in aid to the
Contras was released by this legislation—half a billion to help at most
15,000 Contras assault a country of 3 million.[11]

9. Ben Bradlee Jr., *Guts and Glory: The Rise and Fall of Oliver North* (New York: Donald
Fine, 1988), 221.
10. *Crossroads: Congress, the President, and Central America, 1976–1993*, 2d ed. (University Park: Pennsylvania State University Press, 1993), 205.
11. Quoting that source, the *Washington Post* reported that the one hundred million dollar
figure "reflected an assessment of what the political traffic would bear, not an assessment of
what the requirements are." "It was to some extent pulled out of thin air," Elliott Abrams

It took the White House two attempts to win on its terms. When the administration fell twelve votes short on March 20, 1986, the campaign was intensified. A concession made by Democratic leaders of the House to moderate Democrats, who wanted to vote for *some* support for the Contras in an election year, led to a second vote after much parliamentary maneuvering. On June 25 the House of Representatives finally did what on four previous occasions it had refused to do and approved military aid to the Contras. The margin was a comfortable 221 to 209.

Stalled by a Democratic filibuster, the Senate followed suit in August, approving the House-passed measure by the predicted 53 to 47 margin. Stalled once more by Speaker Thomas (Tip) O'Neill, the bill did not reach President Reagan's desk until October, with the most restrictive Boland amendment remaining in effect. Reagan signed the bill into law on October 25, 1986. Official military aid to the Contras, ready to roll since September, resumed. All aspects of official U.S. involvement in the Contra operation once more had Congress's imprimatur, allowing the CIA to legally resume its multiple roles on the Contras' behalf.

With the Democratic leadership of the Congress reduced to stalling maneuvers the White House claimed victory for its strategy of going over the legislators' heads to mobilize the public. After the June 25 vote Secretary of State George Shultz saw a "shift of view" throughout the nation, adding, "We're seeing a growing breadth of support for the basic policy in Central America."[12] At most 6 percent of public opinion shifted, however; the majority of Americans still opposed military aid to the Contras, as will be demonstrated later in this chapter. The White House succeeded *by redefining the terms of the debate* so that many people, especially opinion makers and legislators, came down on a different side of this question without changing their overall estimate of the situation in Nicaragua.

The secret measures that had kept the Contras armed during the Boland period now could be phased out or (as North testified that Casey intended) redeployed elsewhere.[13] The Contras had been held

---

admitted later. Oliver North had used the figure a year before, "arguing that the very act of requesting a large amount conveyed greater seriousness to the endeavor." See "The Winds of War Blow through Washington," *Washington Post National Weekly Edition*, July 28, 1986, 9–10; Gutman, *Banana Diplomacy*, 321–22.

12. "The Winds of War Blow through Washington," 9.

13. North may have been attributing to Casey—who was dead by the time the congressional hearings began—North's own fantasies. A close associate of Casey's at the CIA during most

together "body and soul," as the President had requested in 1984 when Congress had cut off all U.S. aid. Two years of supporting the Contras on the sly, and of lying to Congress about it, could come to an end.[14] National Security Adviser Poindexter talked of transferring North from the NSC, where he was attracting press attention, to the CIA. North and Secord's "Project Democracy" asked Casey to buy out its $4.5 million in Contra-related assets.[15] It was time to close the back-alley shop and move the operation to the mall now that Congress had opened the store there.

Ad Agencies in the Executive Branch

Coordinating the 1986 campaign were overlapping agencies and committees at the National Security Council. A veteran of CIA media operations overseas, Walter Raymond Jr. came to the NSC in 1982 to create a "public diplomacy" program there. A secret National Security Decision Document (NSDD 77), signed by President Reagan in January 1983, legitimated Raymond's role as Special Assistant to the President for National Security Affairs with responsibility for International Communications.[16] Operating out of Raymond's shop was an interagency committee, the Central American Public Diplomacy Task Force, which met weekly and, among other things, coordinated the work of the Office

---

of these years provided different testimony. See Theodore Draper, *A Very Thin Line: The Iran-Contra Affairs* (New York: Hill & Wang, 1991), 531.

14. One of the more egregious examples of lying occurred in August 1986 when, writing on behalf of the President, Poindexter explicitly assured Congress that "the actions of the National Security Council staff were in compliance with both the spirit and the letter of the law," referring to the second Boland amendment. Questioned by the House Intelligence Committee, North repeated this denial, earning Poindexter's "well done." See Jane Mayer and Doyle McManus, *Landslide: The Unmaking of the President, 1984–1988* (Boston: Houghton Mifflin, 1988), 253–54.

15. While estimating its assets at $4.5 million, Secord offered "Project Democracy" to the CIA for $2.2 million. The CIA refused, fearing being tainted by the equipment's source. Secord and Hakim had paid themselves well, however, for procuring the equipment and supplies for the Contras. See Woodward, *Veil*, 544; Mayer and McManus, *Landslide*, 262.

16. In a rebuttal to an article by Parry and Kornbluh, Raymond emphasized his break with the CIA on accepting the NSC position. But as Parry and Kornbluh point out and internal memos sustain, Raymond and the CIA director consulted each other on "public diplomacy" through August 1986. See Robert Parry and Peter Kornbluh, "Iran-Contra's Untold Story," *Foreign Policy* 72 (Fall 1988); for the exchange of letters see no. 73 (Winter 1988–89).

of Public Diplomacy for Latin America and the Caribbean, known by the acronym S/LPD.

While formally under the aegis of the State Department (the "S" of S/LPD), most of the staff came from other agencies, including the Department of Defense, while the S/LPD functioned under Raymond's direction at the NSC. The close working relationship that Raymond and North had with the first S/LPD coordinator, Otto Reich, was maintained when the S/LPD was formally transferred to the State Department in 1986. The Assistant Secretary of State for Inter-American Affairs, Elliott Abrams, to whom the relabeled ARA/LPD was responsible, was a major supporter of the Contras who later pleaded guilty to unlawfully withholding information from Congress to protect "Project Democracy." After the move and after Reich's replacement by Robert Kagan (April 1986), Raymond commented in an intra-NSC memo that the LPD continues to function under the "interagency mandate" created by the NSC.[17]

For decades the U.S. executive has concerned itself with public opinion abroad. Manipulating opinion and information outside the United States has entailed a panoply of methods, many deemed inappropriate for use within the United States. So while "disinformation," "perception management," and "psychological operations" are recognized aspects of what the Pentagon, the CIA, and even the United States Information Agency (USIA) do abroad, specific laws and regulations prohibit these organizations from influencing domestic audiences. As the epigraph to this chapter indicates, additional laws restrain executive agencies from manipulating the legislative branch through advertising while leaving the door open for information—an admittedly problematic distinction. Scattered through the federal bureaucracy are public relations personnel whose salaries total some $100 million.[18] Therefore, guarding the line between informing and propagandizing is important if "separation of powers" and "consent of the governed" are to have meaning.

The activities that Raymond coordinated at the NSC dealt with both realms, foreign and domestic. The public diplomacy group for Central America was concerned with opinion in Europe and Latin America as well as with public and congressional opinion at home. The term

17. From a PROF note of July 1986, "Otto Reich," National Security Archive 3087.
18. Benjamin Ginsberg, *The Captive Public* (New York: Basic Books, 1986), 227.

"public diplomacy" connotes overseas activities as well as some regard for diplomatic conventions. By 1986, however, "public diplomacy" had become administration code for a massive advertising-cum-lobbying campaign to influence Congress both directly and through the U.S. public. This evolution parallels the transfer to the NSC of the CIA's management of the Contras. In both instances the executive bypassed prohibitions by transferring functions from a more regulated agency to a less regulated one. With regard to the campaign the NSC became the coordinating agency for public relations and lobbying, functions normally centered in the White House with its Office of Communications, its Legislative Strategy Coordinator, and its Office of Public Liaison. While officially part of the White House, the NSC's national security mandate allows its staff to do two things that would raise eyebrows were the White House proper to do them: to function in great secrecy and to draw staff from the Pentagon and the CIA. The S/LPD followed NSC practice in both regards, while the Central American Public Diplomacy Group was interagency by design.

Heading up the innocuous-sounding "public diplomacy" program was Raymond, a veteran of CIA disinformation campaigns abroad, and assigned to an agency that presented itself as a part of the State Department (the S/LPD) were five members of the army's Fourth Psychological Operations Group based at Fort Bragg. These PSYOPs specialists were employed by an agency that defined its purpose as "coordinat[ing] government-wide efforts to ensure that the public and Congress understand U.S. policy in Central America."[19] In explaining why the S/LPD needed such skills coordinator Reich attributed to "strategic PSYOP" training a rare ability to combine "intelligence analysis and production of persuasive communications."[20] It is not surprising, then, that the S/LPD's Deputy Director secretly boasted of his shop's "white propaganda" or that the Comptroller General later

19. "Denial of Detail of Personnel by DOD," January 5, 1986, National Security Archive 2089. In this memo S/LPD head Otto Reich enlists Raymond's help in reversing a Pentagon decision not to replace the five military detailees who worked for the S/LPD in 1985. Another document reveals that the S/LPD had "two senior military officers" assigned to it "on a permanent basis," along with six more junior-level DOD personnel on temporary assignment. See "FY 1986 Financial Plan," November 26, 1985, National Security Archive 1905.

20. "Denial of Detail of Personnel by DOD." Here Reich identifies the S/LPD's mission as "cordinat[ing] government-wide efforts to ensure that the public and Congress understand U.S. policy in Central America."

would discover that the S/LPD had engaged in "prohibited, covert propaganda activities" within the U.S.[21]

The following recur as participants at meetings to frame plans to turn Congress around on Contra aid. Using the nicknames found in the record, they are Walt Raymond, Ollie North and Ray Burghardt of the NSC; Don Mathes of the USIA; two representatives of the CIA whose names remain censored; and from the S/LPD Otto Reich, John Blacken, and Jake Jacobowitz. Daniel "Jake" Jacobowitz was a senior military specialist in "psychological operations" on "permanent" loan to the S/LPD; Jacobowitz drafted several of the campaign plans. The weekly meetings that Raymond chaired "to sustain the public diplomacy effort" with regard to Central America included representatives of "DOD, CIA, USIA, and NSC," along with the S/LPD director and representatives from the White House (e.g., its Office of Communications). Either directly represented or kept informed was the Latin American bureau of the State Department (ARA), directed by Abrams.[22]

A second stream feeding the 1986 campaign came from a different source. It drew on executive branch personnel with no less manipulative attitudes toward public and congressional opinion but with a different set of skills derived from "the permanent campaign" described in Chapter 3. The 1986 campaign involved the symbiosis of these streams when joined by a third: private individuals and organizations that functioned as financiers and "cutouts," paralleling the administration's method of keeping the Contra war effort alive. It is to this third stream that we now turn.

Contractors and Cutouts

We have seen how, confronted with congressional opposition in the form of the Boland prohibitions, the Reagan administration "privatized" Contra military aid. Secord's weapons business took responsibility for the Contras' supplies and logistics, using resources raised privately along with secret "donations" from other governments. In the advertising campaign privatization played a similar role for the same reason: to

21. *Report of the Congressional Committees Investigating the Iran-Contra Affair*, 34.
22. "Otto Reich."

circumvent legal obstacles and avoid political embarrassment. It is a violation of federal statutes to spend public funds trying to influence congressional votes or to shape public opinion in partisan ways. This limitation posed a problem for an administration intent on selling a specific policy needing a specific vote from Congress. For this reason important elements of the campaign were conducted by private firms and individuals who were paid to do what officials are forbidden to do. Since these cut the link between the sponsoring agencies and the prohibited activity, they are known as "cutouts."

During 1985–86 the Office of Public Diplomacy gave secret and noncompetitive contracts ("sole source" in government jargon) to International Business Communications (IBC), a private firm created by two recently resigned federal employees, one who had worked as a public relations specialist for USIA down to the day IBC was created. International Business Communications used the nearly half million dollars in public funds it received from S/LPD contracts to generate several unobjectionable products that the S/LPD apparently filed away as often as it used. Mostly, however, IBC acted as the S/LPD's retainer, handling activities from which that federal agency had to keep distance, partly for legal reasons but also to maintain the credibility of the public relations being purchased. Contra leaders' press conferences and op-eds would be less effective, for example, if the administration's heavy hand in orchestrating them were known.[23]

Through IBC and other cutouts, the S/LPD arranged for op-eds to be ghostwritten for Contra leaders and U.S. notables, then placed in the *New York Times,* the *Washington Post,* and the *Wall Street Journal.* Consultants were hired to visit Central America, then feed their "news" to "NBC News with Tom Brokaw." Computerized lists of grass-roots organizations favorable to the administration's policy were generated and distributed. Even floor speeches were drafted for sympathetic members of Congress to give. International Business Communications squired Contra leaders and Sandinista defectors on trips to the home districts of congressional "swing votes," always with the official hand

23. In arguing the necessity of keeping some of its contracts with IBC secret, interim S/LPD coordinator John Blacken claimed that "release of the general nature of the contract could allow elements unfriendly to the United States to deduce sensitive interagency operations of S/LPD, the secrecy of which is fundamental to their success." See "Proposed Contract with International Business Communications, Inc.," February 24, 1986, National Security Archive 2382.

hidden.[24] International Business Communications's contract with the S/LPD for calendar year 1986, the peak period of the campaign, totaled over three hundred thousand dollars. These were tax-derived revenues used to propagandize the U.S. public and the Congress.[25]

In escorting Contra representatives and other select Central Americans to the home districts of targeted members of Congress the S/LPD was only continuing what the CIA began. The CIA had paid private firms to promote the Contras with an eye to congressional decisions. A Miami PR firm received $300,000 to generate film footage, press handouts, glossy information kits, newsletters, even bumperstickers and T-shirts.[26] Edgar Chamorro had resigned from the FDN leadership by the 1986 campaign, but his insider description of a previous attempt to influence congressional votes is instructive:

> The CIA encouraged us to take advantage of the vulnerability of a Member of Congress to the charge that he or she was "soft on communism." FDN Directors were advised by CIA operatives how to influence Members of Congress by focusing on the districts of those Members considered vulnerable. We were able to have articles published in the local press of those districts which defined the issue, from the *contras'* point of view, for the constituents of that Member. We met with leaders in the district who would bring pressure to bear on the Member.[27]

24. This information comes from investigations into the S/LPD conducted by the State Department's Office of Inspector General, by the staff of the House Committee on Foreign Affairs, and by the General Accounting Office (Comptroller General). Key reports are, from the first source, Audit Report 7PP-008, "Special Inquiry into the Department's Contracts with International Business Communications and its Principals," July 1987; from the second source, "Final Staff Report," in *State Department and Intelligence Community Involvement in Domestic Activities Related to the Iran/Contra Affair,*" September 7, 1988; from the third, "State's Administration of Certain Public Diplomacy Contracts," B-229069, a report to Jack Brooks, Chair of the Committee on Government Operations, and to Dante Fascell, Chair of the Committee on Foreign Relations, House of Representatives, October 1987.

25. "International Business Communications Contract Proposals for State Department," February 7, 1986, National Security Archive 2323. To place this amount in perspective, the S/LPD's operating funds ran around one million dollars a year.

26. Edgar Chamorro, *Packaging the Contras: A Case of CIA Disinformation,* monograph series 2 (New York: Institute for Media Analysis, 1987), 10–21.

27. Ibid., 42. Chamorro does not specify when these activities took place, but he resigned from the Contra directorate on November 21, 1984.

So much for executive order 12333 and other regulations that bar the CIA from influencing "United States political processes, public opinion, . . . or media."[28]

In a similar pattern Oliver North raised millions of dollars for the 1986 campaign by literally selling wealthy citizens meetings with President Reagan. (The price for a face-to-face meeting was $300,000.)[29] Then, through private "foundations," money North raised was funneled to advertising agencies and public relations firms that prepared commercials aimed at specific members of Congress. In this case the principal cutout was Carl (Spitz) Channell and the various organizations he ran, such as the National Endowment for the Preservation of Liberty (NEPL), American Conservative Trust (ACT), and Sentinel, the first a tax-exempt "foundation" prohibited from engaging in partisan activities.

A Reagan campaigner in 1980, Channell had cut his political teeth with John Terry Dolan's National Conservative Political Action Committee (NCPAC), an early and highly successful political action committee, and the two remained associates. In 1985, teaming up with Oliver North, whom Channell code-named "Green" for his ability to shake large donations from wealthy conservatives, Channell wined and dined wealthy widows whom privately he derided as his "blue-rinse brigade." After North softened up donors with sob stories of Contra privation and heroism Channell would make the pitch. North discreetly left the room while the checks were written, as if that took care of his conflict of interest as a federal employee.

While the funds raised paid Channell and his organizations well, millions remained to buy military supplies for the Contras and to fund the advertising campaign. Using NEPL's tax-exempt status to attract private donations, Channell also passed dollars along to organizations engaged in open lobbying, such as his Sentinel and Bruce Cameron's Center for Democracy in the Americas. Channell hired ad agencies (e.g.,

28. Parry and Kornbluh, "Iran-Contra's Untold Story," 5.

29. Mayer and McManus, *Landslide,* 201–3; Peter Kornbluh, "The Contra Lobby," *Village Voice* October 13, 1987, 27. Channell paid David Fischer, who recently had been the President's personal assistant, a half million dollars to deliver the President for these photo-ops. Reagan acknowledged participating in solicitations to raise money "to put spot ads on television in favor of the contras in an effort to try and influence Congress." The President's counsel apparently advised Reagan's staff that "objections may be raised that the President is violating the spirit of the anti-lobbying provisions" of the law.

the Goodman Agency) to make attack ads for television just as he hired other firms (e.g., Miner and Fraser Public Relations) to organize the "grass-roots" pressure brought to bear on members of Congress.

Reagan's complicity did not end with the sale of photo-ops at the White House. International Business Communications's Richard Miller drew up a "Central American Freedom Program" for Channell in February 1986, which served as the overall guide to one of the campaign's "two tracks" (on this more below). Reagan wrote an endorsement of this plan that Channell then used in soliciting funds. Here is a portion of a typical appeal, this one to a business executive from NEPL staffer Jane McLaughlin, dated March 4, 1986:

> Dear Ralph:
>   Thought you might want a copy of the President's response to our Central American Freedom Program. . . . Spitz met with the President and UNO leaders yesterday. They need our help. . . .[30]

Reagan, of course, played a central role in legal aspects of the campaign, giving an unprecedented number of speeches on Central America, for example.

Holding this web of cutouts together was their practice of contracting jobs to one another. Channell's NEPL, for example, retained IBC for various purposes. Equally important was the close working relationship between public officials and these private entities. Names such as Channell, Miller, and Cameron frequent North's log of daily activities. A typical North list of "things to do" starts with fund-raising in association with Channell's operation, then addresses the needs of two Channell-controlled organizations, before passing to a cryptic reference to putting money into Senate races—hardly typical activities for a middle-level National Security Council staffer.[31]

---

30. "Fundraising Letter Soliciting Money . . ." March 4, 1986, National Security Archive 2442.

31. "Fundraising," August 1, 1985, National Security Archive 1382; "Agreement to Help Gain Legislative Clearance," February 26, 1986, National Security Archive 2390; "Proposal to Carl Channell," June 12, 1986, National Security Archive 2998; "To Do," June 3, 1986, National Security Archive 2946.

Manipulative Polling

The ultimate cutouts are the political parties themselves. National committees of both parties buy a variety of advertising expertise in order to manipulate citizens and the media. As long as this expertise is purchased by a party, the White House may use it for any purpose without disclosing content. Secret White House polls guided the 1986 campaign. North, operating out of the NSC, was in frequent contact with Patrick Buchanan, the White House Director of Communications, who along with Chief of Staff Don Regan had regular access to Richard Wirthlin, long-term Reagan pollster.

A March 1985 plan, which served as the precursor to the 1986 campaign, called for a "public opinion survey to see what turns Americans against the Sandinistas," the results of which would be used to "review and restate" the campaign's "themes." Responsibility for this survey was delegated to Ed Rollins, who had run the President's reelection campaign.[32] In connection with this plan North informed McFarlane of the analysis Wirthlin has made of "recent polling data."[33] Among the 1986 television ads purchased through the Channell cutouts was one showing Soviet missiles rising from silos while the voice-over asked, "What can you do if the Communists use Central America as a base for nuclear missiles?"[34] Soviet missiles in Nicaragua was one contingency that opinion polls indicated would lead a majority of citizens to support policies that risked U.S. military involvement in Central America.[35]

Richard Wirthlin had served as the President's consultant on public

32. Given the interagency coordination of "public diplomacy," plans such as this went through various drafts. The description you find here is drawn from two that contain a good deal of overlap. One drafted by Jacobowitz and sent to North and Reich is entitled "Public Diplomacy Action Plan: Support for the White House Education Campaign," March 12, 1985, National Security Archive 934. A second involves North's cover memo to McFarlane "Timing and the Nicaraguan Resistance Vote," which is attached to "Chronological Event Checklist," both dated March 20, 1985, National Security Archives 967 and 968.

33. "Timing and the Nicaraguan Resistance Vote."

34. "Inside Washington," *Human Events*, March 1, 1986, 4.

35. Wittkopf, *Faces of Internationalism*, 28 (table 2.4). According to this source, in 1986 52 percent of the public would favor sending U.S. troops if the Nicaraguan government permitted the Soviets to install missile bases there. That ranked just below the Soviet Union invading Japan (60 percent) and well above the one question that came close to Nicaraguan reality: Sandinista troops invading neighboring Honduras to wipe out Contra base camps (29 percent).

opinion for two decades, including Reagan's two terms in the White House, without ever becoming a federal employee subject to federal regulations. Wirthlin was paid by the Republican party, which kept his polls and advice private.[36] Using computer software to link polling to census data, Wirthlin helped the White House manipulate, not just respond to, public opinion. With this system speeches could be tailored to individual markets, a big advantage in going after "swing" members of Congress.[37] When, for example, opinion surveys showed citizens in the sunbelt to be worried about an influx of illegal Latin American immigrants, Reagan speeches began warning of a "tidal wave" of "feet people" "swarming into our country" should the Sandinistas remain in power.[38]

By Reagan's second term Wirthlin developed a "speech pulse" method for pretesting the public's response to individual words the President might use. He would gather forty to eighty citizens in a room where they were handed sensitive, computerized devices that enabled Wirthlin to chart their responses to speeches moment by moment.[39] With this information presidential speech writers knew what "resonators" to put in Reagan's mouth while White House aides knew what themes to play up after the speech. As Mayer and McManus observe, Wirthlin's methods closely resemble "market research done in the entertainment business by movie and television producers."[40]

Such combinations are common in corporate advertising where market research links demographic data to opinion surveys and where product testing in selected markets fine-tunes the packaging and positioning of the product. Unlike a private agency, however, the White House is able to present many of its ads as news. "What most people call television news programs those in the campaign business call 'free media,'" stated a former president of NBC News.[41] An audience's susceptibility to an advertisement obviously increases when it is not perceived as such. News programs and interview shows are ideal opportunities to advertise while neither paying for it nor alerting the audience to the carefully scripted origins of what they are seeing.

36. Mayer and McManus, *Landslide*, 43.
37. Johan Carlisle, "Marketing Reagan," *Propaganda Review* 1 (Winter 1987–88), 10–11.
38. Parry and Kornbluh, "Iran-Contra's Untold Story," 7.
39. Mayer and McManus, *Landslide*, 44.
40. Ibid.
41. Reuven Frank, "On Sound Bites, Strategizing, and Free Media," *New York Times,* November 6, 1988, H31.

Putting It All Together

Through cutouts and secrecy, and through a willingness to employ at home propaganda techniques developed for use abroad, the 1986 campaign amassed an unprecedented range of talent and skills. The documentary record, which the principals tried to keep secret, reveals money, ideas, and data flowing freely across an official/private boundary honored in appearance far more than in practice. The precursor for the 1986 campaign, the plan drafted in March 1985, contains examples worth citing, since most of those who worked on the 1985 campaign went on to work on 1986's as well. For complex reasons, including doubts that National Security Advisor McFarlane harbored regarding the Contras' effectiveness, only portions of this March 1985 plan were put into action at that time. Poindexter's replacing McFarlane set the stage for the all-out effort that followed.

Overlapping versions of the 1985 plan drafted by Jacobowitz and by North contain diverse activities coordinated through a two-week timetable set to culminate with a vote in Congress on Contra aid. There would be a $2 million media ad purchase orchestrated by Channell, which the North version of the plan describes as a "national television commercial campaign in 45 media markets." "Specific editors, commentators, talk shows, and columnists" were targeted (i.e., the "free media" just discussed). North's cover memorandum to McFarlane mentions "four communications/media meetings we have now had with Pat Buchanan's *ad hoc* working group."

The plan also included a "targeted telephone campaign in 120 congressional districts" carried out by Citizens for America (CFA), a grassroots organization with a "close working relationship" with the S/LPD. Unabashedly partisan, CFA had three other assignments in this NSC-coordinated plan, pages from which showed up in IBC's files.[42] While

---

42. U.S. Department of State, Office of Inspector General, "Audit Report No. 7PP-008, Special Inquiry into the Department's Contracts with International Business Communications and Its Principals," July 1987, 24. Also see page 14 of Otto Reich's comments on an earlier version of this report, which is appended to it as Exhibit B, and page 3 of Robert Kagan's comments, included as Exhibit C. When investigation into the Office of Public Diplomacy's activities began, according to Kagan, IBC was asked to provide files of its work under S/LPD contracts. The March 1985 chronological checklist turned up in those files. Kagan claims that "no one presently in ARA/LPD [the Office of Public Diplomacy] had ever seen those checklists before." "Presently" removes several key players from consideration, including Otto Reich and Jonathan S. Miller.

IBC was to assist partisan organizations such as CFA, it also was given responsibility for a "media/speaking tour" by an anti-Sandinista Nicaraguan editor and asked to "encourage U.S. media reporters to meet individual FDN fighters with proven combat records and media appeal." In addition the S/LPD would "prepare dummies" for articles that Zbigniew Brzezinski and other notables would author. With unintended irony the 1985 plan also had the S/LPD releasing a "paper on Nicaraguan media manipulation."

The task of drawing up a "list of publicly and privately expressed Congressional objections to voting for the aid" was assigned to Arturo Cruz Jr., son of a major Contra (UNO) leader. The son received contracts from the S/LPD, while the father was paid by the CIA. Office of Public Diplomacy personnel were to "construct themes for approaches to Congressmen based on [those] overall listed perceptions," "themes" that would "attack the reasons" for their not supporting Contra aid. To further galvanize Congress and the public North projected "special operations attacks against highly visible military targets in Nicaragua" "timed to influence the vote" in Congress.[43] In other words, lethal photo-ops staged on other peoples' soil.

More traditional activities included the President phoning key representatives two days before the vote in addition to hosting White House breakfasts. Beyond the agencies and individuals mentioned, the March 1985 plan held roles for the Justice Department, the Vice President's office, the Latin American Bureau and the Bureau of Public Affairs at State, USIA, the U.S. Ambassador to the Organization of American States, and White House speech writers. The memo traffic included the National Security Adviser, the Director of the CIA, and the President's Chief of Staff.

The glue holding this diverse array of people together included hardball themes of loyalty and betrayal filtered through an ideology that redefined a domestic debate into a foreign conflict. As the Reagan Doctrine described the Third World, so the architects of "public diplomacy" viewed the U.S. citizenry: as a battlefield on which the forces of good and evil contend. Such a perception not only galvanized the principals but justified their using all methods available to them. In classic "mirroring" they attributed to their domestic opponents all that they did that violated the norms of democratic debate.

---

43. "Timing and the Nicaraguan Resistance Vote"; Gutman, *Banana Diplomacy*, 281.

One hears this in the 1986 "Central American Freedom Program" that President Reagan endorsed. After acknowledging that "the American public remains woefully ignorant about Nicaragua," this document links such ignorance to the enemy's design: "An ignorant and misinformed public is one of the principal objectives of the communists." (In point of fact, domestic opponents of the Reagan policy were attempting to *rouse* public interest, as evident in the work of an organization known as Neighbor to Neighbor.) The "Central American Freedom Program" went on to construct domestic public opinion as the battleground for international rivals: "The American public is the victim of an intense, sophisticated multimillion dollar disinformation campaign. It is being conducted by opponents of the President. . . . The Soviets and Cubans already spend tens of millions of dollars to shape public opinion in America. Their actions are supported by a vast network of communist and leftist activist sympathizers."[44] Other than as "sympathizers," domestic opponents of Contra aid drop out of this picture of a struggle between Reagan loyalists and the combined forces of Nicaraguan, Cuban, and Soviet communism. So framed, why not import into a U.S. debate the "perception management" techniques used abroad? Off the record one "public diplomacy" official recognized that the campaign was conceived as a "vast psychological warfare operation."[45]

While battlefield metaphors are common in U.S. political discourse, they were taken to new lows. To potential donors Oliver North claimed the President was up against the "most sophisticated disinformation and active-measures campaign that we have seen in this country since Adolf Hitler."[46] ("Active measures" are covert actions such as the CIA conducts abroad.) "Destroy Barnes—use him as object lesson," scribbled Channell on one 1986 memo, referring to the liberal Democrat who chaired the House Subcommittee on the Western Hemisphere and who was legitimately inquiring into North's activities on behalf of the Contras.[47] In his plan for the 1986 campaign strategist Terry Dolan

44. "Central American Freedom Program," February 16, 1986, National Security Archive 2354, 2–3, 5.

45. Parry and Kornbluh, "Iran-Contra's Untold Story," 5.

46. A statement from North's often-repeated slide show, as quoted by Bradlee, *Guts and Glory*, 243.

47. Testimony of George P. Shultz and Edwin Meese III, U.S. Congress, House and Senate, "Public Affairs Strategy for Spitz Channell & NEPL," *Joint Hearings on the Iran-Contra Investigation*, 100th Cong., 1st Sess. (Washington, D.C.: U.S. Government Printing Office, 1987), Appendix A: Exhibits GPS–81, p. 1075.

counseled targeting as few in Congress as possible, then using them "to intimidate other Congressmen into voting right, based on what they see happening to their colleagues."[48] The President himself characterized his domestic opposition as part of "a great disinformation network at work throughout the nation," identifying "disinformation" as a "custom established by the Soviet Union."[49]

Assumptions Underlying the 1986 Campaign

The "Ninety-Day Plan" circulated by the S/LPD in December 1985 noted that "awareness of Central America among the U.S. people remains low" but believed that "informed Americans" were becoming "disenchanted with the Sandinistas." Among the themes that the domestic opposition could be anticipated to use were "parallels with Vietnam," fear of a military buildup leading to "an American invasion and consequent loss of American lives," and the Somocista connection and poor human rights record of several Contra leaders.[50]

Terry Dolan, a "leading force in the New Right," had a more precise take on the same phenomena.[51] In a January 1986 plan that provided a model for Channell's strategy, Dolan wrote: "There is little doubt that

48. John Terry Dolan cofounded the National Conservative Political Action Committee, one of the earliest and most effective PACs that contributed $7 million to Reagan's 1984 reelection. Dolan remained what the *New York Times* called "a leading force in the New Right" and would have played a more prominent role in our case study had he not become ill in mid-1986. He died in December 1986 at age 36. See "Central American Proposal," January 6, 1986, National Security Archive 2095; "John T. Dolan, Founder of Group That Backed Conservatives, Dies," *New York Times,* December 31, 1986, D16.

49. "Remarks and a Question-and-Answer Session with Regional Editors and Broadcasters on United States Assistance for the Nicaraguan Democratic Resistance, March 11, 1986," *Public Papers of the Presidents of the United States: Ronald Reagan, 1986* (Washington, D.C.: U.S. Government Printing Office, 1988), 1:319.

50. "Ninety-Day Plan," December 17, 1985, National Security Archive 2006. This confidential document is marked "rev. 5," suggesting previous drafts.

51. Both Channell and Dolan were closet homosexuals whose early deaths were caused by AIDS, Dolan's in 1986, Channell's in 1990. The political causes they supported ranged from neutral to hostile on gay rights. Dolan's advice on turning Congress included a form of political "outing." The way to get some members of Congress to "vote right" was to "intimidate" them with the "threat of political exposure back home" ("Central American Proposal," 2, 3, 5). See also Chris Bull, "Red, White, and Lavender," *Utne Reader* 53 (September/October 1992), 44.

Congress and the public are plagued with the Vietnam Syndrome. They are very reluctant to get America involved in any Central American conflict, despite the potential dangers of failure to act. But, in fact, there are two competing majorities on Central America: one majority is isolationist, while the other is anticommunist." Given a public that "is grossly ignorant about Central America," which of these "competing majorities" is mobilized will depend on the campaign's ability to "frame the debate about Central America on our terms, not on the opposition's terms."[52]

Public ignorance *was* rife. Of the adults polled, as many identified the Sandinistas as a right-wing dictatorship as a Marxist regime.[53] Dolan was also correct in viewing anticommunism as the position of the majority. An early 1987 Gallup poll commissioned by the Times Mirror Center confirmed that. Respondents were asked how much they identified with each of sixteen labels, using a scale of one (none) to ten (completely). To "anticommunist" 70 percent of this national sample of adults responded with an eight or higher. At that level no other label was adopted by more than 50 percent of those surveyed.[54]

How could an anticommunist public be so complacent about a "communist government" in "our own backyard?" The U.S. public continued to view the Soviet Union as a major threat. Three-fourths said they would support sending U.S. troops into battle should the Russians invade Western Europe.[55] Where the Reagan administration had its work cut out was in convincing the public that Marxist regimes *in Central America* posed a comparable threat. The prospect of such a regime in *Mexico* was considered serious by many, as was the prospect of Soviet *bases* and *missiles* in Central America. Half the public would support sending U.S. troops into battle to prevent these contingencies,

---

52. Dolan, "Central American Proposal," 2, 7.

53. In a March 1985 Gallup poll only 37 percent of the sample knew which side Washington supported in Nicaragua. One year later, according to a CBS-*New York Times* survey, half the respondents did not know whether the Sandinistas ran a right-wing dictatorship or were a Marxist regime. After the campaign was over, still less than half the public could correctly identify which side the White House supported in the Nicaraguan conflict. See "Poll Shows Confusion on Aid to Contras," *New York Times*, April 15, 1986, A6; Norman Ornstein et al., *The People, the Press, and Politics* (Reading, Mass.: Addison-Wesley, 1983), 54 (note 23); Brad Lockerbie and Stephen Borrelli, "Question Wording and Public Support for Contra Aid," *Public Opinion Quarterly* 54 (Summer 1990), 196.

54. Ornstein et al., *The People, The Press, and Politics,* 113.

55. Wittkopf, *Faces of Internationalism,* 28 (table 2.4).

which never happened. But Marxist regimes *per se* in Central America did not upset the public. That the public disliked them was clear; that the public would not expose U.S. troops to danger to dislodge them also was apparent. Only 30 percent thought that a Marxist regime in El Salvador would pose a "great threat" to the United States, virtually the same number who saw a "major threat" in "the situation in Nicaragua" (where a Marxist regime *was* in power and receiving Soviet military aid).[56]

Two interpretations are possible. One is Dolan's: that the U.S. public contained overlapping majorities of anticommunists and isolationists, suggesting that a sizeable group of U.S. citizens struggled with competing impulses. The "focus-group" research of pollster Stanley Greenberg sheds some light on the isolationist side of the overlap. Greenberg detected "a strong aversion to the region [Central America] that goes from misinformation to racism." Both the Contras and the Sandinistas were perceived as "unsmiling, dirty, armed Spanish people" on which U.S. citizens "don't want to spend their money," much less their lives.[57] By 1986 Central American conflicts had become drawn-out affairs marked by repeated votes in Congress and endless charges and counter-charges in the media. There was no culminating crisis, no television footage of Central Americans welcoming U.S. troops, as Grenada and later Panama provided. With few visible results Washington was pouring a billion dollars annually into the region (1985), ten times the amount spent in the seventies—this at a time when the domestic budget was being slashed by "Reaganomics" and by the Gramm-Rudman plan to rein in the federal deficit.

Alternatively, it is possible that the public was taking its cues from the President himself who, by 1986, was praising the new Soviet leader, Mikhail Gorbachev, while simultaneously arguing that the Kremlin retained imperialistic designs on Central America—a classic case of the modern leader's inability to isolate discourses intended to construct different issues. One might argue that the public was being discriminat-

56. Ibid., 32 (table 2.6); "Central America and the Polls," a special report of the Washington Office on Latin America (Washington, D.C., March 1987), table 34; "Relax, Democrats: The Public Supports You on Nicaragua," *Washington Post National Weekly Review*, April 7, 1986, 37; "American Opinions on Aid to the Contras," *New York Times*, April 20, 1986, E3.

57. David Moberg, "The Grassroots Push," *In These Times*, September 2–8, 1987, 2. As the article's title suggests, some grass-roots groups opposing Reagan's policy appealed to the sentiment that Central America just was not worth it given domestic needs.

ing in attaching differing levels of threat to various expressions of "communism." Nicaragua *wasn't* Cuba, much less the Soviet Union. Its importance to the U.S. *wasn't* comparable to Mexico's. Soviet missiles *are* more threatening to U.S. cities than Soviet tanks or helicopters.

Whatever interpretation is correct—and the data will not resolve that—the Reagan administration faced a difficult task. Staying with the most relevant question—that of U.S. military aid for the Contras—polls show 24 percent supporting it in June 1985. At the height of the 1986 campaign one poll showed support increasing to 42 percent. When it was all over and Congress had been turned around, public support fell back to 29, a gain of only five percentage points over June 1985.[58] By mid-1986 the Reagan team apparently had convinced a majority of the public that the Sandinistas were bad guys who threatened their neighbors (56 percent) but had failed to persuade a majority that this constituted a significant threat to *them* (32 percent).[59]

Age separated respondents on this issue more than party affiliation or region, suggesting that "Vietnam Syndrome" may have been a factor, the young not remembering the war.[60] The largest constituency in favor

58. Polling data show the "yes" response rising from 24 percent in June 1985, through the 34 to 42 percent of March 1986, and falling back to 29 percent a year later, while the "no" response declined from 66 to 62 percent, with the dip in the "no" column evident by April 1986. The 1986 campaign may have converted some "no" responses to "undecideds" and from there on to "yes"—before most people reverted back to previous positions. From aggregate data such inferences are only guesses. As Lockerbie and Borrelli demonstrate, how questions were worded played a role ("Question Wording and Public Support for Contra Aid").

59. For the analyses of others see ibid., and Gordon Bowen, "Presidential Action and Public Opinion about U.S. Nicaraguan Policy," *PS: Political Science and Politics* 22 (December 1989). Bowen indiscriminately mixes responses to different questions, while Lockerbie and Borrelli demonstrate the difference wording makes. I checked individual polls taken during the months critical to this case study. In addition to those already cited these include "Most Americans in Survey Oppose Aid," *New York Times,* June 5, 1985, A8; "In Poll, Public Approves Denial of Contra Aid," *Washington Post,* March 26, 1986, A12; "Poll Shows Confusion on Aid to Contras," *New York Times,* April 15, 1986, A6; "Public Would Preserve SALT II Treaty," *Washington Post,* June 25, 1986, A16; and George Gallup Jr., *The Gallup Poll: Public Opinion 1986* (Wilmington, Del.: Scholarly Resources, 1987), 65–67. While Lockerbie and Borrelli find a "modest increase over time" in public support for aiding the Contras, in order to avoid being "contaminated by the Iran-Contra scandal" their analysis stops in mid-1986. Extending the purview to the end of the Reagan era reverses their secular trend, although the line might best be described as a bumpy ride through flat terrain.

60. For all the emphasis in the campaign on the Southeast and sunbelt only three points separated the support for Contra aid visible in various regions of the country, although the South held more undecideds. A March 1986 Gallup poll on military aid to the Contras found

of military aid to the Contras were those aged 18 to 29. What also characterizes this under-thirty population, however, is a thin and personalized approach to public issues. What some call the MTV generation receives its news from *People Magazine,* TV drama, and talk shows, if at all. By 1990 only a third of those aged 18 to 29 read a newspaper or looked at such television news programs as "20/20" or "Sixty Minutes," in contrast to over half of those aged 50 and up.[61] Conservative campaign media adviser Don Sipple, 35 years old in 1986, claims: "We are in an era when voters are intensely driven by personal qualities—trust, feeling comfortable with the individual, feeling they know them well."[62] Reagan always did well with the young, no doubt for the reasons Sipple lists. Judged by its low propensity to vote, however, this was not a group that would go to the barricades over Central America. For the young, foreign affairs is a spectator sport.

So we arrive at the central dilemma facing the 1986 campaign. It could not succeed by amplifying public opinion nor by fostering a national debate on this issue. Rather, the publics relevant to vulnerable members of Congress had to be isolated and manipulated. This is the strategy laid out in Dolan's proposal of January 1986, which planned to "frame the debate" rather than engage the issues. Rather than make the President or the Secretary of State the focus, Dolan advocated "hir[ing] a Hollywood personality or sports figure to head up this drive." "Congressmen and legislative staff should be voting right," Dolan strategized, "not purely based on the persuasiveness of our positions, but on the real fear that if they break their word, they will pay a political price for doing so."

Dolan's plan contained "a two-track effort," a term often used in U.S. foreign policy to tie a publicized diplomatic initiative to an unpublicized threat of military action or covert destabilization. In addition to "a strong Washington lobbying presence," "the first track consisted of a national effort focused primarily in opinion-making

---

all four regions to have "yes" responses within the 34 to 37 percent band. See Gallup, *The Gallup Poll,* 65.

61. "The Age of Indifference: A Study of Young Americans and How They View the News," paper prepared for and distributed by the Times Mirror Center for the People and the Press (Washington, D.C., June 1990), 2.

62. "The Bush Team Recruits From the Hard-Ball League," the *Washington Post National Weekly Edition,* February 17, 1992, 15.

Table 5.1   Public opinion on giving the Contras military aid, 1984–1986

Yes or For	No or Against	Don't Know

October 23–25, 1984.   Do you think the United States government should provide military assistance to the people trying to overthrow the government of Nicaragua, or not? CBS News and *New York Times.*

30%	44%	27%

May 29–June 2, 1985.   Should we send military supplies and weapons to the people trying to overthrow the government of Nicaragua? CBS News and *New York Times.*

24	66	11

March 6, 1986.   President Reagan is asking Congress for new military aid for the Nicaraguan rebels known as the "Contras." Do you agree or disagree with Reagan that Congress should approve the money? ABC News.

34	59	8

March 25, 1986.   Same question as above. ABC News.

42	53	5

April 6–10, 1986.   Do you think the U.S. should give $100 million in military and other aid to the Nicaraguan rebels known as the *contras*? CBS News and *New York Times.*

25	62	13

April 13–15, 1986.   The Reagan administration has proposed giving $100 million in military, medical and economic aid to the rebels fighting the Sandinista government in Nicaragua. Do you favor or oppose this proposal? NBC News and *Wall Street Journal.*

33	55	12

April 24–28, 1986.   Do you generally favor or oppose the U.S. granting $100 million in military and other aid to the Nicaraguan rebels known as the *contras*? ABC News and *Washington Post.*

28	65	7

June 19–24, 1986.   Same as above except for not mentioning $100 million this time. ABC News and *Washington Post.*

29	62	8

SOURCE: Brad Lockerbie and Stephen Borrelli, "Question Wording and Public Support for Contra Aid," *Public Opinion Quarterly* 54 (Summer 1990), app. 1.

centers, such as New York, Washington, and Los Angeles." The second track consists of "a strong grass-roots response in the form of in-district lobbying," targeted on the fewest representatives possible so as to maximize the pressure brought to bear on each. In referring to these members of Congress Dolan uses such words as target, intimidate, and threaten. Each targeted representative should receive fifty lobbying contacts a week, preferably "in the form of personal group meetings with the Congressman in his district office," supplemented by letters and phone calls to his Washington office. To Dolan "grass-roots pressure" meant visits from "high-dollar contributors" along with "business, labor, and media leaders" from the home district.

In what Dolan accurately foresaw as "a five-month campaign" coordination would tie what happened nationally to the pressure members of Congress felt locally. "Contra leaders and victims of Nicaraguan atrocities" are to be paraded through "opinion-making centers" and then into the home districts. Expensive television commercials will be designed on the "donut" format where a hole is left in a professionally designed ad for inserting material tailored to individual representatives. "It is important that each of these advertising programs be well coordinated with each other and with direct mail activities. This will maximize the amount of grassroots activities generated and will increase the perception of the Congressman that he will have political problems if he votes wrong." Finally, "as many functions as possible" should be farmed out to "consulting agencies," a.k.a. the cutouts.[63]

The 1986 Campaign Plan

Consistent with Dolan's recommendations, the Ninety-Day Plan that emerged from the S/LPD begins with public opinion polls and research into "buzz words." Delegated to White House pollsters is the task of identifying "current American attitudes toward Sandinistas, including key words, phrases, or images . . . that affect those attitudes." "Private sector groups" are to "sponsor" speaking tours of defectors and other Central American personalities. A "media blitz" starts with public officials calling editorial boards in key media centers, then providing

---

63. Dolan, "Central American Proposal."

newsrooms with "one-pagers on Nicaragua," "op-ed pieces" drafted by the S/LPD, and "key administration officials" for talk shows. Specifically aimed at members of Congress and their staffs was a day-long conference at the Department of State, visits to Washington by select Central American presidents, "resource packets" geared to the floor debate, and phone calls from the President right before the vote. Specific interest groups are targeted for special pressure, including labor and religious organizations.

A month after the drafting of the Ninety-Day Plan in mid-December 1985, minutes of Raymond's Public Diplomacy Group refer to a "60-Day Plan" being "thoroughly reviewed."[64] The major difference between the two plans is the higher visibility of the President and the Secretary of State found in the latter. "To kick-off support for aid legislation," the Secretary of State will testify before the appropriate committees of Congress and give a major address before the Veterans of Foreign Wars. Accompanied by his Secretaries of State and Defense, the President will brief "TV commentators and anchormen" and also hold a televised meeting with Contra leaders and a televised inspection of captured weapons and documents. A presidential address on prime-time national television, "to be presented at [a] time deemed most likely to favorably influence [the] vote," emerged as a key element.[65]

Obviously the purpose of the cutouts would be defeated if administration plans detailed the advertising, lobbying, and mobilizing of home districts found in Dolan's strategy and prominent in Channell's documents. These less seemly aspects leave their tracks on the official record, nonetheless. They are present in North's log and lists of things to do, as well as implied by meetings that Reagan and his aides held with the staff of NEPL, where the White House was informed not only of what NEPL had done but of what it planned to do.[66] One of four points in Channell-financed lobbyist Bruce Cameron's "Plan of Action" is: "We

64. "Minutes of the Public Diplomacy Meeting," January 14, 1986, National Security Archive 2148. North is noted as playing a vigorous role in this discussion, proposing "thematic changes" that the minutes do not describe.

65. "Update of Time-Line for Sixty-Day Public Diplomacy Plan," March 3, 1986, National Security Archive 2437; "Nicaragua Resistance Funding: Public Diplomacy Actions," February 27, 1986, National Security Archive 2410.

66. A memo from David Fischer to Chief of Staff Donald Regan indicates that transcripts of the televised "attack ads" were made available to the White House, and possibly videotapes of the ads themselves. See "Aid to Contras Meeting," January 5, 1986, National Security Archive 2091.

will maintain continuous liaison with the Administration." Through Poindexter, North instructs Vice President Bush to turn his Washington meeting with Contra leaders into an opportunity for them to address the media, "as a means of gaining visibility." Minutes of a campaign planning meeting held by representatives of NEPL, IBC, and Edelman Public Relations read: "State have purchased $250,000 worth of markets," an apparent reference to the S/LPD.[67] And so on.

The "Central American Freedom Program," which IBC's Richard Miller drafted for Channell, makes clear that "[w]e are using the methodology of national political campaigns."[68] Using these and other documents we learn that a two million dollar media purchase (much of it in the form of televised attack ads) is projected to reach 135 million people.[69] Combined with these ads was the still novel practice of offering television stations across the country, free via satellite, footage taped in Central America that had been edited to advance the campaign. Local stations uncritically use such footage inasmuch as it allows them to "upgrade" their news programming.[70]

This "Central American Freedom Program" paralleled Dolan's proposal: simultaneously working the nation at large and the swing districts; pairing presidential appeals to patriotism and bipartisanship—what Cameron called "the high moral ground"[71]—with less lofty attacks on individual members of Congress. A January list of 72 targeted members was pared down to 30, then to 21. By April lobbyists could pinpoint representatives to take on trips to Central America or to receive focused treatment from the White House. Maps with such

67. "Meeting with the National Endowment for the Preservation of Liberty," January 30, 1986, National Security Archive 2288; "Plan of Action to Lobby Congress," January 24, 1986, National Security Archive 2205; "Meeting with the UNO Leadership," March 5, 1986, National Security Archive 24448; "Meeting re Central American Freedom Program," February 24, 1986, National Security Archive 2381.

68. The plan that Miller wrote for Channell is "Central American Freedom Program," February 16, 1986, National Security Archive 2354. The skeletal version is "Components of the Central American Freedom Program," drafted by Channell, February 27, 1986, National Security Archive 2402.

69. "Meeting re Central American Freedom Program."

70. This practice grew to become a major feature of the Clinton and Bush campaigns, leading one reporter to call 1992 "the year of satellite dish politics," adding that "[s]ometimes local stations run what are essentially campaign advertisements on their news programs" since they are free. See "Satellite Technology Allows Campaigns to Deliver Their Messages Unfiltered," *New York Times,* October 23, 1992, A13.

71. Bruce Cameron's memo to Channell, "Why the President Won on Contra Aid," July 2, 1986, National Security Archive 3094.

"Components of the Central American Freedom Program" apparently was drafted by Carl (Spitz) Channell on February 27, 1986. This document was found in the files of Channell's organization, the National Endowment for the Preservation of Liberty," and is reproduced from National Security Archive Document 2402.

Channell's Brief Plan

1. *Objective:*
   - Target democrat swing votes in the house (63 total, 36 are in just eight states).
   - Maintain flexible strategy to respond to events as they occur.

2. *District Level Public Education Program:*
   - A spokesperson for the Freedom Fighters speaks at local organizations (shows film).
   - Visits religious and labor leaders.
   - Interviews with local newspaper and/or TV/radio stations for editorial board meetings.
   - Articles and/or news broadcasts are generated.
   - A spokesperson will be in *each* target district at least three times during the campaign.

3. *District Level Advertising Campaign:*
   - District-wide TV spots designed to generate response back to the congressman.
   - Letter writing campaign within the district coordinated through veteran, social, religious and business organizations (grass roots effort).

4. *National Media:*
   - To reach other 27 swing vote districts, especially D.C. and New York because of national press and networks.
   - Arrange for spokespeople to be interviewed or appear on TV (talk shows and political shows).
   - Op-Ed pieces written by UNO leaders and placed in leading press, i.e., Wall Street Journal, New York Times and Washington Post.

5. *Special Media for D.C.:*
   - To broadcast every 10 days, never before seen video news releases (we have two film crews, one in Managua and one with the Freedom Fighters who send us film weekly which we edit and distribute via satellite).
   - There are fifty top stations, thirty took our first distribution.

6. *Lobbying:*
   - We have hired two democrat lobbyists, PRODEMCA and Bruce Cameron, formally of Americans for Democratic Action who was fired due to his support for the Freedom Fighters.
   - Daily monitoring of how swing vote congressmen feel about aid to the Freedom Fighters.
   - Help the democrats find a face saving intellectual justification for a vote change.

titles as "Advertising Campaign" and "Media Markets" show media purchases and speaking tours targeted on key congressional districts.[72] For the more important of them Channell purchased "action plans" researched by public relations firms, such as the plan Daniel J. Edelman, Inc., developed for Texas's twelfth congressional district represented by House Majority Leader Jim Wright. This document directs NEPL to emphasize Fort Worth over Dallas in its media picks, to send a different message to elites with local power bases from that given conservatives already active on this issue, and to keep a low profile, a caution found in many Channell documents.[73]

Lobbying activity was identified by the skeletal document printed above as one of the six "components of the Central American Freedom Program." "We have hired two democrat lobbyists, PRODEMCA and Bruce Cameron, formally of Americans for Democratic Action."[74] According to the House Foreign Affairs Committee report, Channell and IBC's Miller had "close financial and personal ties" to PRODEMCA (Friends of the Democratic Center in Central America), whose president, Penn Kemble, "was involved in a broad array of activities related to Channell's Central American Freedom Program." PRODEMCA received $88,000 from Channell. "At the PRODEMCA offices, Kemble hosted legislative strategy sessions, in at least one of which State Department official Robert Kagan was a participant, prior to the 1986 Congressional votes on Contra aid."[75] Kagan worked with the S/LPD and was named its coordinator in April 1986—further evidence of a close working relationship between public officials and the cutouts.

Recommended to IBC and then to NEPL as an effective lobbyist, Bruce Cameron received a contract from Channell's NEPL in January 1986. Then taking Robert Owen's organization as his vehicle and renaming it Center for Democracy in the Americas, with Kemble as chairman and himself president, Cameron received an additional $66,000 from Channell's organizations to lobby Democrats and another

72. "The National Endowment for the Preservation of Liberty, Advertising Campaigns, Media Markets," February 27, 1986, National Security Archive 2397; "The National Endowment for the Preservation of Liberty, Media Speaking Tours, Media Markets," February 27, 1986, National Security Archive 2398.

73. "Action Plan for the Congressional District Program," December 15, National Security Archive 1932.

74. "Components of the Central American Freedom Program."

75. "Final Staff Report," 26–7. On Channell's funding of PRODEMCA see Gutman, *Banana Diplomacy*, 332.

ten thousand from IBC.[76] Because he had been an aide to Democratic Congressman David McCurdy, who remained influential with moderates on this issue, Cameron was particularly effective (in McCurdy's words) in "slic[ing] away the guys."[77]

With the money that Reagan and North helped raise for Channell, Cameron and another lobbyist (Robert Leiken) orchestrated a trip that fourteen representatives took to Central America, where they were exposed to Sandinista "tyranny" and met the presidents of neighboring countries.[78] As with Cameron, Leiken was effective in lobbying moderate Democrats due to past affiliations. Along with North they participated in the face-lift of the Contra leadership that created the illusion of an option in between the Sandinistas and the FDN's actual command. Once again Channell's discretionary funds proved useful, as Nicaraguan civilians who fronted as Contra leaders sometimes were paid from those accounts.

Lobbying sought to force targeted members of Congress off the fence and out of the complexities, to make them define themselves as either procommunist or anticommunist in an election year. While Cameron and Leiken worked to give the fence sitters a soft place to land by playing up a reformed Contra leadership, others (including White House Communications Director Pat Buchanan) kept rattling the fence. Eleven days before a major Reagan address presented this theme to the nation in suitably presidential language Buchanan woke up the audience with a widely printed op-ed that said: "With the vote on *contra* aid, the Democratic party will reveal whether it stands with Ronald Reagan and the resistance—or Daniel Ortega and the Communists."[79]

76. Kornbluh, "The Contra Lobby"; Gutman, *Banana Diplomacy,* 331, 334. In a letter to Channell Cameron describes two organizations of his, each with a different tax status. He also asks for money to continue his lobbying "over the next seven to nine months." See "Proposal to Carl Channell to Fund Pro-Contra Lobbying," June 12, 1986, National Security Archive 2998.

77. Gutman, *Banana Diplomacy,* 331, 334.

78. Ibid., 332, 334. Some of this money Leiken returned to Channell after it became known that Channell had abused the tax-exempt status of his organizations in raising money for the Contra cause. Cameron later publicly stated that "I was fundamentally in error in 1985 and 1986 in my assessment of the Contras, the Reagan Administration, liberals and the Soviet Union." He came "to reject the Contra policy as a response to the Sandinista challenge." See "Second Thoughts and Third Thoughts," in *Second Thoughts: Former Radicals Look Back at the Sixties,* ed. Peter Collier and David Horowitz (Lanham, Md.: Madison Books, 1989), 122–23.

79. "The Contras Need Our Help," the *Washington Post National Weekly Edition,* March 17, 1986, 29.

But Did It Work?

When it was over and the Congress had reversed itself, Channell's lobbying organization Sentinel claimed credit for six of the eleven representatives who switched positions between the March and June votes. "The efforts by Sentinel began more than one year ago to help President Reagan change the climate on Capitol Hill from weak support for humanitarian assistance to a strong message of military and humanitarian aid to the United Nicaraguan Opposition."[80] In a memo drafted for Chief of Staff Donald Regan, Channell claimed his organizations had "carried the support program for the president successfully into 32 of the 51 Democratic districts that ultimately stood with Ronald Reagan on this issue."[81] Lists generated by the Goodman Agency indicate that all but three of the eleven representatives who switched were subject to televised attack ads in their home districts.[82]

In his postmortem memo to Channell, Cameron was more nuanced. Influences on swing votes were multiple, he said, and parliamentary maneuverings complex. Thus individual "switches," Cameron recognized, were overdetermined. (A coordinated advertising campaign tries to give the customer many reasons to make the right choice.) Three who switched had been influenced by direct pleas from the President, Cameron believed, including one Democrat. Reagan had been effective both in speeches appealing for bipartisan support and in one-on-one conversations.[83] Three Democrats had responded favorably to the advertised changes in the Contras' leadership along with administration promises that more reforms would follow. Four of those who had been on the trip to Central America changed their votes as a result of that experience, concluded Cameron, while three switchers found the cover they needed in an amendment that increased economic support for the

---

80. "News Release," June 25, 1986, National Security Archive 3054.

81. Kornbluh, "The Contra Lobby," 28.

82. It is hard to be precise about this since the Goodman Agency laid out options, not all of which Channell may have purchased. The cheapest option included six of the eleven on Cameron's list of switchers, the most expensive option included eight. See "American Conservative Trust," January 1, 1986, National Security Archive 2186; "N.E.L.P. 'Freedom Fighters' TV National Spot Placement Television Analysis," June 1986, National Security Archive 2931.

83. One Democrat who switched said "it was a real thrill to meet him," referring to fifteen minutes with Reagan, while a Republican echoed, "One of the better things that's happened in my life [was] the opportunity to visit with him just for a brief time." See Arnson, *Crossroads*, 198.

"democracies" surrounding Nicaragua. Decisive for one representative but no doubt a factor with others was the desire to get the President's men off their backs before returning home to campaign for the November election.[84]

As a lobbyist reporting to his sponsor, Cameron naturally emphasized those activities in which he took part, so we hear nothing about the television and radio commercials, the planted op-eds, etc. Also, swing votes tell only part of the story. Holding previous supporters in line also qualifies as a success given the polls' indication that less than half the public backed the administration on this issue.

Visible in the plans laid for the 1986 campaign are the elements that Cameron singles out in his postmortem: Reagan's speeches and personal appeal; the repackaging of the Contra leadership for display stateside; threats of punishment for representatives who vote "wrong." Also visible is the explanation that William LeoGrande emphasizes, having frequented the House during these months: the campaign's ability to impose its frame on the debate, to shift the terms of the argument.[85]

While little has been said thus far about this issue, a theme of the next chapter, we have seen campaign organizers being attentive to "framing" issues. Several documents have described the importance of using polling data and lobbying reports to recast the question in such a way that targeted audiences faced a choice they could not refuse. We have run into such phrases as "see what turns Americans against the Sandinistas" and "frame the debate about Central America on our terms, not on the opposition's terms." Otto Reich, who led the S/LPD into the campaign, later claimed that that agency had "played a key role in setting out the parameters and defining the terms of the public discussion on Central American policy."[86]

Blumenthal reminds us that at the White House Ronald Reagan was surrounded by "the most sophisticated team of pollsters, media masters and tacticians ever to work there. They helped him to transcend entrenched institutions like the Congress and the Washington press corps to appeal directly to the people."[87] Tracing that appeal through the loop that Blumenthal implies—from administration strategists to

---

84. "Why the President Won on Contra Aid."

85. LeoGrande, "The Contras and Congress," 222.

86. Parry and Kornbluh, "Iran-Contra's Untold Story," 27.

87. Sidney Blumenthal, *The Permanent Campaign* (New York: Simon and Schuster, 1982), 284.

the public and then to the legislators who switched positions—is impossible. The plan that envisaged this, however, has been documented here.

By hitting a few representatives hard, the campaign sought to remind the others of Reagan's ability to mobilize a formidable array of forces against them. With an election looming such reminders were not lost on many in the House. Compounding that fear was the confusion created by the shift in the terms of debate (which the next chapter details). Some mixture of being caught off balance and of fearing retaliation lay behind reactions such as the following, from a Democratic member of Congress in March 1986: "[W]e're scared to death that he'll [Reagan] pull another rabbit out of his hat, turn another loser into a winner, and leave us totally vulnerable."[88] Reagan's popularity, combined with the advertising skills of his aides, added up to a "power" that even the Democratic Speaker of the House found "absolutely awesome."[89]

88. "Mudslinging over Contras," *New York Times,* March 12, 1986, A5.
89. Arnson, *Crossroads,* 214.

6

The Campaign as an
Ad Drawing on the Myth

*[W]e cannot conceive of a language without the possibility of
lying, as there is no speech which does not know metaphor. But
a society may favor or, quite the contrary, strongly discourage
any discourse that, rather than faithfully describing things, is
chiefly concerned with its effect and therefore neglects the dimen-
sions of truth.*

—Tzvetan Todorov[1]

This chapter confronts core questions of this book: To what extent did
the 1986 campaign function as an advertising campaign, and in what
ways did it reproduce the America/Américas myth? In advertising,
framing the choice for the customer is all important. Impose the
question and the answer takes care of itself. We shall begin, then, by
identifying four frames that appear in texts as varied as ten-second
television commercials and the most widely viewed televised address by
President Reagan on this topic. Next, using the latter as a representative
text, a more detailed analysis asks, To what extent can this text be read
as an advertisement, given the model spelled out in Chapter 3?

1. *The Conquest of America,* trans. Richard Howard (New York: Harper & Row
Colophon, 1985), 90.

Recurring Frames

In the first of four frames evident in the campaign Sandinistas are presented as communists controlled by Cuba and the Soviet Union. Members of Congress are then asked to define themselves as *procommunist or anticommunist*. The popularity of U.S. air attacks on Libya in March and April 1986 added the variant of being tough or soft on terrorists. Within the discourse the nearly universally loathed Ayatollah Khomeini of Iran and Muammar Qaddafi of Libya increasingly substituted for the more ambiguous Soviet leader, Mikhail Gorbachev, as the Sandinistas' mentors and associates. Fresh in the public's memory was the killing of a U.S. tourist on the cruise ship *Achille Lauro*. Terrorism introduced a vulnerability that, if properly played upon, could break through the U.S. citizen's sense of safety at home. One thirty-second commercial warned viewers that Libyan leader Muammar Qaddafi has threatened to strike "American citizens in their own streets" and "now sits on our doorstep." (The storyboard for this ad is reproduced below.)

Over the previous year a reporter had noted how, in discussing Central America, officials were trying to "replace the term 'leftist guerrilla' with the much more negative word 'terrorist' in the public mind."[2] In a planning document written for Channell, IBC's Richard Miller suggested adding narcotrafficking to this mix to create "a single issue which no one can publicly disagree with."[3] In January 1986 Reagan stated that "[t]he link between the governments of such Soviet allies as Cuba and Nicaragua and international narcotics trafficking and terrorism is becoming increasingly clear. These twin evils—narcotics trafficking and terrorism—represent the most insidious and dangerous threats to the hemisphere today."[4] This three-in-one framing of the

2. Joanne Omang, "Where's the Evidence . . . ," *Washington Post National Weekly Edition*, August 5, 1985, 17.

3. "Action Plan for 1986 Programs of the American Conservative Trust and the National Endowment for the Preservation of Liberty," National Security Archive 2353. For a full explanation of this source see note 8 of Chapter 4.

4. As cited in Peter Dale Scott and Jonathan Marshall, *Cocaine Politics: Drugs, Armies, and the CIA in Central America* (Berkeley and Los Angeles: University of California Press, 1991), 23. According to testimony at the Robert Gates confirmation hearings in 1991, CIA Director "Casey wanted a memo that would link drug dealers to international terrorists." Casey's deputy Gates kept reassigning the research until he found a CIA analyst who would deliver the desired conclusion (ibid., xi).

Sandinistas will be evident in the March speech analyzed later in this chapter.

Polarization was part of the plan, as was apparent in Patrick Buchanan's attack on Democrats in an op-ed widely published in early March. Impugning the loyalty of members of Congress backlashed, however, even from Republicans. So in the major televised speech of this campaign President Reagan used more diplomatic language to keep the choice binary. "My fellow Americans, you know where I stand," the avuncular President intoned. "Now the Congress must decide where it stands." Then quoting Clare Booth Luce, Reagan continued: "Only this is certain. Through all time to come, this, the 99th Congress of the United States, will be remembered as that body of men and women that either stopped the Communists before it was too late—or did not."[5]

Attack ads aimed at individual members of Congress and broadcast in their home districts took their cues from Buchanan. Typical was one that bore the headline: "Congressman Alexander, why are you letting the Communists take over Central America?"[6] In television and newspaper ads "communism" lost its national qualifiers to become simply "communism" and "the communists," as in "the Communists are now completing this huge submarine base in Nicaragua."[7] In analyzing the impact of wording on responses to questionaires, Lockerbie and Borrelli discovered "that identifying the Sandinistas as leftist, Marxist, or pro-Soviet increases support for the Contras."[8] After the April bombing of Libya proved popular, Reagan speeches leading up to the second vote emphasized the Sandinistas' "trying to build a Libya on our doorstep."[9]

Next, frame two *makes the vote a referendum on Sandinista performance,* not on Contra performance. For every charge laid at the

5. "Address to the Nation on the Situation in Nicaragua, March 16, 1986," *Public Papers of the Presidents of the United States: Ronald Reagan, 1986* (Washington, D.C.: U.S. Government Printing Office, 1988), 1:356. This address is reproduced in the Appendix.

6. "Inside Washington," *Human Events,* March 1, 1986, 3.

7. This example is from the ten-second "spots" purchased by Channell's Sentinel organization. See "Sentinel: 'Fact Checks,' " June 1986, National Security Archive 2933.

8. Brad Lockerbie and Stephen Borrelli, "Question Wording and Public Support for Contra Aid," *Public Opinion Quarterly* 54 (Summer 1990), 197, 199–200. Such "ideological labeling" increased support for the President's policy by an estimated 4.4 percentage points during 1983–86. The association is statistically significant at the .05 level.

9. "Reagan Says Sandinistas Seek to 'Build a Libya,' " *New York Times,* April 23, 1986, A7.

Contras' door the campaign found a countercharge to lay at the Sandinistas', and used those countercharges preemptively. The choice was framed as one of "liking" or "approving of" the Sandinistas, an unusual criterion for foreign relations. Attempts were made to engross the public in such personal details as a Sandinista leader buying designer eyeglasses while in New York or Marx appearing on Nicaraguan postage stamps (along with George Washington). "Gluing black hats" on the Sandinistas not only shifted attention from the Contras' claim to "white hats" but appealed to the public's personalized approach to foreign affairs, a trend evident in the attention given Manuel Noriega's "witchcraft" and sex life during the U.S. invasion of Panama three years later.

Reagan's televised March address described the Sandinistas as "an outlaw regime" dealing drugs, torturing clergy, maintaining "secret prisons," and serving as "a command post for international terror." Frame two depictions were linked to frame one through such expressions as "like Communist governments everywhere," giving Sandinista behavior the force of inevitability. In the speech with which a similar campaign had been launched the year before Reagan referred to the "institutionalized cruelty that is the natural expression of a Communist government, a cruelty that flows naturally from the heart of totalitarianism."[10] During one of his Saturday radio broadcasts of the 1986 campaign the President described the Sandinistas as "a cruel clique of deeply committed Communists at war with God and man."[11] One television spot made by the Goodman Agency spoke of "the inevitable betrayal of the Nicaraguan people" by the Sandinistas, while another referred to "what we now know is the pattern of every communist takeover in the world."[12] So frames one and two reinforce each other.

Whether viewed as a separate frame or as part of number two, there was a conscious effort to portray the Contras as underdogs, as one may hear in this strategy drafted at Channell's National Endowment for the Preservation of Liberty and reproduced here as it appears in the original:

10. Roy Gutman, *Banana Diplomacy: The Making of American Policy in Nicaragua, 1981–1987* (New York: Simon and Schuster, 1988), 284.

11. "Reagan Aides Oppose Compromise Talks," *New York Times*, March 9, 1986, A1.

12. Goodman Agency commercial entitled "No Wonder" (no. 86-130). See "American Conservative Trust," January 21, 1986, National Security Archive 2186; National Endowment for the Preservation of Liberty, Title: 'Refugees,' " February 27, 1986, National Security Archive 383.

> And they [the Contras] need to be seen under attack; they need
> to be seen as wounded they need to be seen as the victims rather
> than the victimizers. . . . we need to cast them as the underdog.
> . . . But those kinds things need to be created that mystique of
> the Alamo the out-numbered; out-gunned, out-flanked under-
> armed forces in desperate battle. We need pictures of the Hind
> helicopters coming over the hill and in some cases getting
> shot down. That's why the afgan, the mystique of the Afgan
> Mujahadeen. That's where it all comes from.[13]

The Alamo comparison had been discussed within the White House as
a theme for Reagan speeches on Contra aid.[14] Reagan's televised speech
presents the Contras as a brave, outnumbered French Resistance holding
world communism at bay.

A third frame presented full U.S. support for the Contras as *the only
solution standing between two unacceptable alternatives:* letting the
communists take over and having to send in U.S. troops. All competing
solutions were tied to Reagan's Contra aid proposal. Negotiations can
only succeed when the Sandinistas are under the pressure of a Contra
military victory, democracy can only come when the Sandinistas are
forced to share power with the armed opposition. Elliott Abrams
positioned the administration's policy in between what he termed
"two quick fixes": "direct U.S. military intervention" and accepting
Nicaraguan proposals for security arrangements, the latter being "a
prescription for disaster camouflaged as a diplomatic solution."[15]

Both the commercials and the President's speeches play down the risk
of U.S. troops being involved—if the Contras are fully supported. One
sees this in the storyboard of a thirty-second "spot" that aired between
the first and second House votes, an ad that ignored what two-thirds of
the aid was earmarked to buy (ellipses are in the original):

13. "NEPL Strategy Ideas for Political Advertisements and Lobbying," February 1, 1986,
National Security Archive 2305.

14. Peggy Noonan, *What I Saw at the Revolution: A Political Life in the Reagan Era* (New
York: Ivy Books, 1990), 245.

15. In January 1986 the *New York Times* quoted Abrams as saying, "You can use American
military force, which is the last thing we wish to do, or you can surrender, which is, I would
think, unacceptable." See "Now that Contadora is Dead," January 8, 1986, A22. In fairness
to Abrams, I have quoted a less silly version of his formula, even though it is from remarks
given a year later. See Abrams's remarks to the Senate Committee on Foreign Relations,
February 5, 1987, as printed in the State Department's *Current Policy* 915, 1.

President Reagan wants to help the people of Nicaragua . . . not with guns . . .

. . . but with food and medicine. Giving them the chance to find their own future . . .

. . . without American boys fighting or dying on foreign soil. If we support our . . .

. . . President today, our boys won't be sent to die tomorrow.[16]

Failing to help the Contras now, viewers were told, means U.S. troops will have to do the job later. One television "spot" showed a young U.S. soldier writing home:

Dear Mom, it might be awhile before you hear from me again. We're shipping out tomorrow and it's no secret to anybody where we're going. All I know about Nicaragua is what I read in the papers. But don't worry, Mom, I'll take good care of myself.

The voice-over added: "If Congress will act while there's still time, thousands of Americans will never be sent to fight and die in Nicaragua."[17] Opinion polls which implied that "somebody other than Americans will be doing the actual fighting" were likely to elicit nine more percentage points in favor of Reagan's policy than polls that omitted this information.[18]

As a part of the strategy to win over Democrats, Reagan appointed the respected diplomat Philip Habib as his Special Envoy to search for "a diplomatic solution." (White House instructions, however, prevented Habib from talking to the Sandinistas.) The campaign tied "diplomatic solutions" to military aid, as when Reagan said, "What we're asking Congress for is the tools so that Ambassador Habib can do the job."[19] After drawing an analogy between Sandinista documents and *Mein Kampf* while speaking to the Senate Foreign Relations Committee,

16. "American Conservative Trust, 'Freedom Can't Work,' " June 1986, National Security Archive 2929.

17. "Backers: Avoid Sending GIs," *Washington Post*, March 19, 1986, A29.

18. Lockerbie and Borrelli, "Question Wording and Public Support for Contra Aid," 197, 199–200.

19. "Habib: The Man with the Golden Suitcase," *New York Times*, March 12, 1986, A24; "Reagan Appoints Habib as Envoy to Central America," *New York Times*, March 8, 1986, A4.

Secretary of State Shultz said: "Pressure is the one way to bring them [the Sandinistas] to the bargaining table. . . . military pressure is . . . essential."[20]

A fourth and final frame suffuses the rest: the *direct threat to the United States* that opinion polls had indicated the public did not take seriously. Here is part of the storyboard for a thirty-second spot, preserving its pauses:

> Muammar Kaddafi has plans for America.
> He's already threatened to strike at "American citizens in their own streets." Kaddafi used to be far away . . .
> . . . but now he sits on our doorstep—supplying arms and terrorist experts
> to the communists in Nicaragua, only two hours away from our borders.[21]

According to one of the ten-second "spots":

> Communist planes can strike us in only two hours from this new base in Nicaragua. And still Congressman Ed Jones won't support the President. Call him.[22]

In his March speech Reagan asked, "What in the world are Soviets, East Germans, Bulgarians, North Koreans, Cubans, and terrorists from the PLO and the Red Brigades doing in our hemisphere, camped on our own doorstep?"

Proximity plays a role in frame four, as references to "our own doorstep" and "our hemisphere" suggest. Several of the texts generated by the campaign refer to Central America as part of North America.[23] Here is one thirty-second spot:

20. "Nicaragua: Will Democracy Prevail?" the State Department's *Current Policy* 797.

21. "National Endowment for the Preservation of Liberty, Title 'Terrorist Influence,' " February 27, 1986, National Security Archive 2405.

22. "Sentinel: 'Fact Checks.' "

23. Geographers include Mexico as part of North America but usually treat Central America as a separate region, as do most other social scientists, diplomats, and journalists. Indeed calling the region "Central America" was standard Reagan administration practice, as may be seen in the title of the blue ribbon commission Reagan convened to propose a bipartisan policy and in the report it issued. In extending North America as far south as Panama, Reagan wordsmiths were reverting to the practice of John Quincy Adams and James Polk described in Chapter 2.

Each day there are more of them. They are Cuban-supplied, Soviet-built Mi-24's. And they are here . . . in numbers . . . on our North American continent in Nicaragua.[24]

In his televised address of March 16 the President described Nicaragua as "a Soviet ally on the American mainland only two hours' flying time from our own borders," adding, "the United States must deny the Soviet Union a beachhead in North America." Pointedly, one of the televised spots claimed: "The communists in Nicaragua—they don't want our money. They want *us*!"[25]

Frames one and four reinforce each other. If the threat comes from international networks of "communists" and "terrorists" rather than from the government of a small underdeveloped country the threat to the United States is more credible. As a threat to its neighbors and a justification for increasing the Contras' arms, the Sandinista regime is portrayed as powerful. But as a threat to the United States, Nicaragua is only the space on which the truly powerful operate: "a beachhead" of the Soviet Union. By arguing that "Nicaragua is literally already a satellite of the Communist bloc, and its goal is the continued expansion of Communism worldwide," as Reagan told *The New York Times* in March 1986,[26] the administration raised the danger level to the point where the Contras no longer provided a rational solution. Thinking he was speaking off the record, Henry Kissinger—Republican yet logical—wondered how $100 million supporting twenty thousand Contras could stop the determined march of the Soviet Union.[27]

Taken together these frames reveal many of the characteristics of advertising outlined in Chapter 3. Strong, culturally shared emotions are evoked (e.g., anticommunism) with hooks that play on the public's fear of terrorism, drugs, and illegal migrants. The emotions and convictions aroused are then transferred to objects less familiar to the audience. As we saw in the last chapter most citizens had little real knowledge of the Contras and the Sandinistas. Presented as "freedom

24. Goodman commercial 86-230, as found in "American Conservative Trust—'Freedom Fighters Television'—National Spot Program," January 21, 1986, National Security Archive 2186.

25. "The National Endowment for the Preservation of Liberty: 'Throw Money,' " February 27, 1986, National Security Archive 2404.

26. "Transcript of Interview with President at the White House," *New York Times*, March 23, 1986, A23.

27. " 'Off the Record' Kissinger Talk Isn't," *New York Times*, April 20, 1986, A20.

fighters" and "communists," however, these forces became recognizable in ways that promoted the sale.

The product being sold was the policy of aiding the Contras militarily, which was positioned as low-cost and risk-free: the Contras will do the fighting, their military pressure delivering (here the citizen is invited to customize the ad) national security, a blow to communism, democracy in Nicaragua, an end to terrorism, peace in Central America, a halt to drug trafficking, and so on.

The skeptical reader may still wonder, however, whether I have not fabricated these frames and then selected bits of campaign texts to illustrate them. The only way to answer such legitimate skepticism is to choose one text that everyone would agree was central to the campaign, reproduce it so that the reader has unedited access to it (see the Appendix), and then proceed to demonstrate how it functions as an ad, using the criteria spelled out in Chapter 3. Since many campaign texts, we have seen, were the creations of advertising agencies, the ideal text for this test is one created inside the White House that would be least likely to be considered an advertisement, conventionally speaking. I have chosen President Reagan's televised speech of March 16, 1986.

Transmitted live from the Oval Office by major news networks, this primetime address presented itself as reasoned, nonpartisan, and presidential. It is a fair sample of the campaign in that it capped a two-week blitz in which Reagan delivered seven speeches on Contra aid that either were broadcast nationally or given to audiences large enough to attract major media coverage. Language found in this speech appears in those other presentations as well as in Reagan's other major speech, which he gave right before the June vote and which the networks refused to air precisely because by then the arguments had been repeated so often.

A Major Presidential Address

Shaped by Oliver North as well as by White House speech writers, the March 16 speech used graphics and text prepared by the Office of Public Diplomacy that turned up in other presentations, such as Shultz's before the Senate Foreign Relations Committee. Reagan's televised version attracted the largest audience of any single piece of the 1986 campaign.

Chapter 3 listed seven elements that characterize successful ads. Taking them in two clusters, we can look for their presence or absence in Reagan's March 16 address:

1. capture attention by any means consistent with 2, usually with one or more attention-grabbing "hooks";
2. arouse fears, fantasies, and loyalties already present in the audience, leaving enough ambiguity so that most can read their desires into the ad;
3. transfer those aroused emotions and memories to whatever is being sold, taking care to do so through juxtapositions and substitutions (metaphors and similes) rather than through methods that might spark critical reflection.

Reagan's speech contains vivid hooks intended to arouse the fear and indignation regarding communism and terrorism widespread at that time. As these emotions were aroused, they were transferred to the Sandinistas through describing them as close allies of the Soviet Union, of Libya, of the PLO, and of Khomeini, as well as by using the generic terms "communist" and "terrorist." Nowhere does the more ambiguous term "Marxist" appear in Reagan's speech, while variants on "communism" recur a dozen times in association with the Sandinistas. An opinion poll taken secretly for the White House had indicated strong public support for a U.S. military attack on Libya, then considered a major sponsor of terrorist incidents in Europe and the Middle East.[28] So it is not surprising to find the President saying in this speech: "Gathered in Nicaragua" are "all the elements of international terror," invoking the names of Qaddafi, Arafat, and the Ayatollah Khomeini. "Will we permit the Soviet Union to put a second Cuba, a second Libya, right on the doorstep of the United States?"[29]

Proximity to the United States kept the audience's emotions engaged. Nicaragua was described as "a Soviet ally on the American mainland only two hours' flying time from our own borders." Reagan portrayed

28. Jane Mayer and Doyle McManus, *Landslide: The Unmaking of the President, 1984–1988* (Boston: Houghton Mifflin, 1988), 221–23.

29. In his March 16 speech Reagan linked the Sandinistas to the killing of four U.S. servicemen in a San Salvador cafe and cited Qaddafi statements praising the Nicaraguan regime. No evidence has been produced of a Sandinista role in that killing, although it is clear that the Sandinistas aided Salvadoran guerrillas in various ways including armaments. A CIA official told Woodward that Libyan support for Nicaragua was "more solidarity than anything." See Bob Woodward, *Veil: The Secret Wars of the CIA, 1981–1987* (New York: Simon and Schuster Pocket Books, 11988), 371.

it "as a privileged sanctuary" from which global enemies of the U.S. launch "their struggle against the United States." After describing the "support" Nicaragua had given "radicals" throughout Latin America, the televised speech recalled "an old Communist slogan that the Sandinistas have made clear they honor: 'The road to victory goes through Mexico.'"

For more personal hooks the speech turned to religion, drugs, and illegal immigrants, using stories such as the following, concerning an evangelical pastor caught by a Sandinista patrol who was "tied to a tree, struck in the forehead with a rifle butt, stabbed in the neck with a bayonet—finally his ears were cut off, and he was left for dead. 'See if your God will save you,' they mocked. . . . He lived to tell the world his story—to tell it, among other places, right here in the White House." Evidence of Sandinista religious persecution included Catholics, Protestants, and Jews.

The recent death of basketball star Len Bias from a cocaine overdose had given drugs added salience. Wirthlin's polls "showed a surging public concern about drug abuse"—an ideal issue for advertising, being "long on emotion and short on specifics."[30] So in the televised address the President said, "I know every American parent concerned about the drug problem will be outraged to learn that top Nicaraguan Government officials are deeply involved in drug trafficking." As evidence Reagan pointed to a photograph that he claimed showed "a top aide to one of the nine comandantes who rule Nicaragua, loading an aircraft with illegal narcotics bound for the United States. No, there seems to be no crime to which the Sandinistas will not stoop—this is an outlaw regime" (Fig. 3).

Another hook was fear of illegal immigrants flooding the United States, which White House polls also indicated to be salient, especially in sunbelt states. Reagan's speech describes a chain of events in which

> [u]sing Nicaragua as a base, the Soviets and the Cubans can become the dominant power in the crucial corridor between North and South America. Established there, they will be in a position to threaten the Panama Canal, interdict our vital

30. Mayer and McManus, *Landslide*, 279–80. Political scientist Ann Crigler found "Miami Vice" to be an important source of voter information on drugs. See "Political Experts Offer 3 Views," *New York Times*, October 29, 1988, A10. In the popular culture drugs and criminality are frequently linked to Latins.

Fig. 3. This photograph apparently had been appropriated by Oliver North from a confidential U.S. Drug Enforcement Administration (DEA) briefing held at the NSC. North used it in his fund-raising and lobbying talks, thereby halting further DEA investigations. Testimony at the 1991 trial of deposed Panamanian leader Manuel Noriega indicates that the Medellín drug cartel indeed had a "Managua connection" in Federico Vaughn, the "top aide" mentioned in Reagan's speech and the man seen in the striped shirt handling boxes in this photograph. Vaughn was a minor official who had been named in an indictment by a Miami grand jury almost two years before Reagan's speech. The Sandinistas had denied the accusation. The news was old.

Besieged by the press the day after the President's speech, the DEA acknowledged its earlier investigation, pointing out that "no evidence was developed to implicate the minister of the interior or other Nicaraguan officials." Minister of the Interior Tomás Borge was the comandante referred to in Reagan's speech. Privately, DEA officials were livid: "All these guys give a shit about is the Contra thing, trying to get the funding passed through Congress by blaming [the Sandinistas] for being dope traffickers." Whatever cocaine flowed through Nicaragua to the United States was minuscule compared to that smuggled into the United States by Contra suppliers, a connection Oliver North is thought to have prevented the DEA from investigating. See "Former Smuggler Ties Top Official of Cuba and Nicaragua to Drug Ring," *New York Times*, November 21, 1991, A10; "Accused Nicaraguan No Longer at Ministry," *Washington Post*, August 9, 1984, A31; Elaine Shannon, *Desperados: Latin American Drug Lords, U.S. Lawmen, and the War America Can't Win* (New York: Viking, 1988), 153–60; Peter Dale Scott and Jonathan Marshall, *Cocaine Politics: Drugs, Armies, and the CIA in Central America* (Berkeley and Los Angeles: University of California Press, 1991), 100–103, 117, 172–73, 180.

Caribbean sealanes, and, ultimately, move against Mexico. Should that happen, desperate Latin peoples by the millions would begin fleeing north into the cities of the southern United States.

This elaborate chain of if/then assumptions probably was lost on most viewers, who may only have heard Nicaragua, Soviets, Cubans, desperate Latin peoples fleeing to the United States. "Latin peoples" disguises the tenuous logic tying this hook to reality. When the President spoke, there were nearly two million deportable aliens in the United States, 95 percent of them *Mexicans* who had left a country Reagan considered democratic, capitalist, and friendly.[31]

The purpose of interjecting such contextual information is to signal that these were advertising truths: not literally false yet highly misleading due to missing context. Without context, proportionality and probability are lost. Supplying the missing context for all claims made in this speech would divert us from our goal, which is to see how this speech functioned as an ad. Suffice it to say, Reagan's claims regarding the Sandinistas' religious persecution, military capability, and refusal to negotiate were all misleading. The White House staffer who checks presidential speeches for accuracy admitted that she was not sure "if any of the speech was true."[32] Some newspapers ran stories challenging the speech's claims, but only a small proportion of the audience would have seen those rebuttals.[33]

To work as an ad Reagan's address also had to transfer positive associations to the Contras, making them seem worthy of U.S. support and competent enough to deliver the promised solution. The President

31. Throughout the 1980s nine out of every ten deportable aliens caught in the United States was Mexican. If we ask which country in Central America was sending the largest proportion of its population to the United States illegally at the time the President spoke, the answer is El Salvador. If we focus on immigrants seeking asylum, where the connection to the political regime is most clear, then El Salvador and Guatemala top the list of hemispheric states. In the Reagan lexicon these were democratic regimes. See *Statistical Abstract of Latin America*, Committee on Latin American Studies, vol. 27 (University of California, 1989), table 1505. Testimony of Nancy Kingsbury of the General Accounting Office before the Subcommittee on Immigration of the House Judiciary Committee, March 9, 1989 (GAO/T-NSIAD-89-16).

32. Mayer and McManus, *Landslide*, 211.

33. For example, "Claims on Contras in Dispute," *Washington Post*, March 18, 1986, A6.

did this using the narrative form of a fairy tale, which not only invites the listener in but evokes a battle between good and evil.

> You see, when the Sandinistas betrayed the revolution, many who had fought the old Somoza dictatorship literally took to the hills and, like the French Resistance that fought the Nazis, began fighting the Soviet-bloc Communists and their Nicaraguan collaborators. These few have now been joined by thousands. With their blood and their courage, the freedom fighters of Nicaragua have pinned down the Sandinista army and bought the people of Central America time. . . . But now the freedom fighters' supplies are running short, and they are virtually defenseless against the helicopter gunships Moscow has sent to Managua.

The World War II analogy, evident in pitting the French Resistance against the Nazis and their collaborators, would elicit from viewers an association between the Contra war and a patriotic war in which U.S. motives were pure and its allies valiant. In "these few" who "bought time" there is even an echo of Winston Churchill's eulogy of the RAF pilots who held the Nazis at bay during the Battle of Britain.

Turning to the remaining characteristics of successful ads, we have:

4. position whatever is being sold as, if not the sole panacea, the most satisfying one, framing the choice so that competing alternatives are either excluded or co-opted;
5. motivate the sale by promising an appropriate catharsis through a sense of triumph or acceptance or some other positive feeling;
6. encourage the customer to feel that the decision to buy originates with him/her, that s/he automously wishes to do what the ad asks be done;
7. and do this by offering consumers multiple opportunities to participate in the ad, to own it by completing it with their own associations.

We already have seen the President drawing his audience in with a friendly, colloquial style. The "You see" above is part of a pattern of interjecting "Well," "You know," "Now let me show you," "So we're clear," "I could go on," "Let me give you," and "That's a good question." Reagan also appealed to audience by giving it rhetorical questions to solve, such as: "Why did Nicaragua's dictator go to the Communist Party Congress in Havana and endorse Castro's call for the worldwide triumph of communism?" He flattered his viewers, comparing the task before them with that Lincoln faced when "he freed the slaves and preserved the union" or with that of Churchill at the Battle of Britain. Care was taken to cite Democrats who had risen to similar challenges in the past, notably President Truman and Senator Henry Jackson.

While the critical step was Congress's to take, the President asked his public for its help, as a personal favor. Reagan functioned as a celebrity endorsing a product: "So, tonight I ask you to do what you've done so often in the past. Get in touch with your Representative and Senators and urge them to vote yes; tell them to help the freedom fighters. Help us prevent a Communist takeover of Central America." "Explicitly associating President Reagan with Contra aid," Lockerbie and Borrelli discovered, routinely added five points to public approval of the policy.[34]

By contacting his or her representative the viewer would "help us prevent a communist takeover of Central America" and would join those who have "the vision, the courage, and the good sense to come together and act." Later generations will thank you for leaving "America safe . . . secure . . . free." To this gratification is added the catharsis of striking back at America's nemeses abroad. "The Soviets have made their decision—to support the [Nicaraguan] communists. Fidel Castro has made his decision—to support the communists. Arafat, Qadhafi, and the Ayatollah Khomeini have made their decision—to support the communists. Now, we must make our decision."

An ad must guide the consumer past competing options to the seller's product. Usually obliquely but sometimes directly, the competition is dismissed as substandard, outdated, or beneath us. The President made a passing reference to a negotiated solution, blaming the Sandinistas for failure. "Ten times we have met and tried to reason with the Sandinistas; ten times we were rebuffed." Further decreasing the attractiveness of this option is language demonizing the Sandinistas as "the malignancy in Managua," an "outlaw regime," "mortal threat," and "command post for international terror." One does not negotiate with outlaws or coexist with malignant tumors; nor are enemy posts on one's soil long tolerated.

34. Lockerbie and Borrelli, "Question Wording and Public Support for Contra Aid," 196–97, 200. This association is statistically significant at the .05 level and, as with the other associations they discovered, based on public opinion surveys conducted between 1983 and 1986.

While excluding the competition, Reagan presented his solution as cheap, first stating "We're not asking for a single dime of new money. We are asking only to be permitted to switch a small part of our present defense budget" before adding "I'm not asking about American troops. They are not needed; they have not been requested." The alternative, however, will be expensive: not only "a Communist takeover of Central America" but an ignoble entry in the history books. "We still have time to do what must be done so history will say of us: We had the vision, the courage, and the good sense to come together and act—Republicans and Democrats—when the price was not high and the risks were not great."

What ads do, we have seen, is tap meanings already embedded in the culture and emotions already present in the consumer, redeploying both toward the sale of what otherwise would not be bought. The consumer is promised gratification on carrying out the ad's suggestion, even though objectively the purchase is only tangentially connected to that gratification. Objectively, how could anyone think that U.S. military assistance to Contras fighting to topple Nicaragua's government could stop terrorism in the world or drug abuse in the United States? Would a rival superpower intending "to bring Communist revolution home to the Western Hemisphere" be deterred by ten, even twenty thousand Contras?

Reagan's speech worked as an ad because it achieved this transfer from the well of emotions to a specific product (policy) through layered juxtapositions of familiar and novel images, bypassing a reasoned exploration of the alternatives. How do I know? ABC News polled the nation ten days before Reagan's speech and nine days after, using the exact same question. Support for "new military aid for the Nicaraguan rebels known as the 'contras'" rose from 34 to 42 percent, the sharpest gain of the entire Reagan period: eight points in one month against a secular trend (June 1983 through June 1986) of one point every four months.[35] By any criteria used in the corporate world that was a sale.

Completing the Sale on the Hill

Where a political sale differs from a commercial one is in market share. Politics focuses on achieving a plurality of the customers, not just

35. Ibid., 199, app. 1.

gaining more than we had yesterday. In this case enlarging the customer pool by eight percentage points would count for naught if a majority of those in Congress did not vote for the aid. So, while the texts described above were directed at representatives through their constituents, individual representatives also were singled out for what the corporate world calls "promotion" and "public relations": special trips, inside information, individually tailored deals. In launching a new painkiller a pharmaceutical firm will both advertise to the public at large and send special packets of information and samples to physicians. It may even invite physicians to seminars in attractive locales. So it was with this campaign.

Reading the debates within the House of Representatives that preceded the final vote in June, we are able to see whether language directed at the public found its way into the thinking of representatives—or, more precisely, into the rationales they used to explain their vote and to urge others to vote likewise. Let's begin with Republicans who supported the President, for if they were not using his language the influence of the ad on the final sale would seem weak.

From Republican members of the subcommittee that deals with the Western Hemisphere—representatives presumably more aware of the complexity of this issue than the average congressperson—we hear clear echoes of Reagan's words.[36]

> MICHAEL DEWINE (OHIO): Mr. Speaker, the real question that we are facing today . . . is: are we willing to see the Soviet Union become the dominant power between the Panama Canal and Mexico?
>
> DAN BURTON (INDIANA): There is a cancer down there that is spreading out of Nicaragua that will engulf all of Latin America if we do not take action right away.
>
> JOHN MCCAIN (ARIZONA): We will be faced today if we turn down the proposal with two options: one, accepting a Cuba in the Western Hemisphere . . . or two, eventually sending in American troops to eradicate that cancer.

36. Unless otherwise indicated, all of the remarks attributed to members of Congress come from the "House" portion of the *Congressional Record,* vol. 132, June 25, 1986, pages marked H 4159-4220 and H 15522-15581.

Having extended North America into Central America, Cuba was excluded from the hemisphere, so politicized was geography.

Turning to other Republicans, we hear more comments in the same vein. Here is a sampling from all regions of the country.

> Don Ritter (Pennsylvania): It is a vote for or against the Ortega-Qadhafi-Khomeini terrorist alliance.
>
> David Dreier (California): [T]hat revolution to which the President referred yesterday, the revolution without borders, being strengthened by Mu'ammar Qadhafi, Yasser Arafat, Fidel Castro, and the Soviet Union.[37]
>
> William Broomfield (Michigan): [T]he pressure from the Contras keeps reminding the comandante that there is a solution. There is a peaceful way. A negotiated settlement is the answer.
>
> Bob Livingston (Louisiana): [O]ur undefended border with Mexico, some 2,000 miles, could one day become the equivalent of the Korean DMZ or the Berlin Wall.
>
> Henry Hyde (Illinois): Do we really want to permit the Soviet Union to become the dominant force on the land bridge between South America and North America? . . . [I]f you need a rationale for our helping freedom fighters, read the Declaration of Independence. . . . Ought we not [to] help these freedom fighters? The struggle is the same whether it is Angola, Afghanistan, or Cambodia.

While holding and expanding the "yes" vote was important, disabling the critics was equally so, for this helped tip the fence sitters in Reagan's

---

37. Here Dreier is referring to a phrase Reagan used the day before: "Can we responsibly ignore the long-term danger to American interests posed by a Communist Nicaragua, backed by the Soviet Union and dedicated—in the words of its own leaders—to a 'revolution without borders'?" See "Excerpts from Reagan's Speech," New York Times, June 25, 1986, A12. The President misquoted a phrase lifted from a 1981 speech by Sandinista comandante Tomás Borge: "Our revolution goes beyond our borders." In butchered versions this phrase was much cited by administration sources as evidence of the Sandinistas's intention to export their revolution by force. Actually Borge had talked of the Sandinistas's moral example for and their sense of solidarity with revolutionaries elsewhere, explicitly ruling out export of revolution by force. Since Borge's speech had been translated and published by the Foreign Broadcast Information Service on July 21, 1981, continued misuse of it by Reagan, Shultz, and others constitutes advertising.

direction. Opponents offered less effective arguments than they might have, had they been willing to attack assumptions built into the frames of the ad, such as that Marxism is unacceptable in Central America, that this region is vital to U.S. security, that dislike of the Sandinistas is sufficient reason for promoting war in Central America, or that regional diplomacy was stalled from a lack of military pressure. By June most opponents were reduced to criticizing Reagan's proposal by questioning its cost, its effectiveness, or the precedent it might set. They had conceded what one House aide called "the big arguments."[38] As Arnson notes, by now the opposition had "abandoned a challenge to the Reagan administration's definitions of what was at stake in Nicaragua."[39]

Some opponents pointed to domestic priorities or to public opinion polls running against military aid to the Contras. Those arguments were not effective against the "put up or shut up" challenge of frame one. We hear such arguments in the following voices. First, Indiana Democrat Harold Ford: "No one wants to see the Central American region become a base for the projection of Soviet or Cuban military power. However, the means through which the administration has fought this threat have become counterproductive." Ford advocated either spending the money "to help the less fortunate here at home" or "to promote democracy through peaceful means." The former did not address the problem at hand and the latter lacked specificity. "To really cut off Marxists in Central America," argued David Obey, Democrat of Wisconsin, "we need to help those countries tackle their mountain of debt." By sweetening the bill with economic assistance to Central America's democracies, the administration marginalized critics such as Ford and Obey.

Berkeley Bedell, a Democrat from Iowa, cautioned that once the door of military aid to the Contras was reopened the flow of money would be hard to stop: "[I]s $100 million enough to let them get the job done or will [we] be asked again in the near future to infuse another $100 million, $200 million, or worse, to infuse American blood in a campaign doomed to failure?" To this the reply was "now is cheaper than later." To John Rowland of Connecticut, one of the Republicans who switched from "no" to "yes," it was time "to fish or cut bait," a sentiment shared

38. Quoted in Cynthia Arnson, *Crossroads: Congress, the President, and Central America, 1976–1993*, 2d ed. (University Park: Pennsylvania State University Press, 1993), 210.
39. Ibid.

by a Democrat from South Carolina, Robin Tallon, who argued against an amendment to postpone a determination on military assistance until October: "Why not agree to do it now, when it is needed and when it will make a difference?"

The campaign succeeded in creating a climax that, given the prevailing paradigm, meant that the United States must act, one way or the other. If the President was willing to take the rap, why not let him have his way. A Democrat who switched his vote, Mario Biaggi (New York), said that if "the contras are scoundrels and the Sandinistas are scoundrels," as long as "the national interest" is implicated, "a tie has to go with the President."[40] The third option of noninvolvement with all scoundrels was ignored, since it lay outside the activist impulse of deep sentence three of the Americas myth.

Paving the way for Biaggi-like choices were the many Democrats who joined the Republicans in Sandinista-bashing. Thomas Foley (Democrat, Washington) preceded his remarks opposing the aid package by saying "the Government of Nicaragua . . . has no supporters in this body" and by conceding that the President's description of the Sandinistas was correct. Adopting such a line reinforced the presumption that liking Latin leaders is central to a coherent hemispheric policy.

Where Is the Americas Myth in All This?

The House debate imparts a strong sense of how deep and bipartisan is the adherence to the America/Américas myth. Politicians on both sides of the aisle expressed little confidence in the capacity of Latin Americans to solve their own problems. They conflated a U.S. consensus that Marxism is alien with a hemispheric consensus that on this point simply did not exist. The vanguard itch may explain why a brief trip to Central America by a half dozen of what Robert Michel (Republican of Illinois) called the "younger members" led three to switch to Reagan's side. Seeing the situation at first hand, these members returned convinced that "something must be done," "something" meaning action by the

---

40. Biaggi as quoted by the *New York Times* in Bruce Cameron's account of who switched and why: "Why the President Won on Contra Aid," July 2, 1986, National Security Archive 3094.

U.S. government. "Our goal—no, our responsibility," argued Maine's Olympia Snowe, a Republican trip taker who switched, "is to help them [the Central American countries] prove that democracy will lead to peace, stability, and prosperity." She cited President Oscar Arias of Costa Rica in arguing that U.S. military aid for the Contras would promote this goal. As we shall see in the next chapter, that was not Arias's position at all.

To further evaluate this book's contention that it is through advertising campaigns such as this one that the America/Américas myth is reproduced, I list the four "deep sentences" introduced in Chapter 2 and for each offer representative language from the 1986 campaign. This provides evidence of the myth's presence in the 1986 campaign, commingled with mythic elements drawn from World War II and the early years of the Cold War. The commingling should not surprise us, as myths are incorporated into political discourse opportunistically to form the verbal collage considered most persuasive at the time.

Sentence 1: "The Western Hemisphere is the geographical *tabula rasa* on which God (Providence, History) demonstrates civilization's advance through agents understood to be the descendants of Europeans." In campaign texts we have seen the borders between the United States and Latin America dissolve, literally. A Marxism physically located in the Western Hemisphere is banished from it (Cuba) while Central America is described as North America or simply America. That "America" is more than geography is clear from the Reagan address immediately preceding the June 1986 vote: "Let us send this message to the world: that America is still a beacon of hope, still a light unto the nations. A light that casts its glow across the land and our continent and even back across the centuries—keeping faith with a dream of long ago."[41] That city-on-a-hill language also appears in the televised Reagan speech of March, which ends: "We still have time to do what must be done so history will say of us: . . . We left America safe, we left America secure, we left America free, still a light unto the nations."

Sentence 2: "The content of this advance is freedom and progress: forms of association favoring the self-determination of peoples and the liberty of individuals, which are linked to advances in material well-

---

41. "Address to the Nation on United States Assistance for the Nicaraguan Democratic Resistance, June 24, 1986," *Public Papers of the Presidents of the United States: Ronald Reagan, 1986,* 1:838.

being." In a press release issued in the President's name after the June vote, that victory was compared to "our own Independence Day": "The cause is freedom, the cause is just, the cause will triumph."[42] On March 21 Reagan compared the Contras to John Paul Jones, "another famous freedom fighter," while in the televised address he stated, "The Soviets and the Sandinistas must not be permitted to crush freedom in Central America," adding that "We have sought, and still seek . . . a democratic future in a free Nicaragua." What made the Sandinista regime an "outlaw" was that beneath its mask of pseudodemocracy lay "the face of totalitarianism."

Reagan speech writer Peggy Noonan had jotted down themes for speeches as they emerged in White House planning sessions during the 1986 campaign. One Noonan sketch reads: "This is more than a vote, more than an appropriation of money. This is a sign, a declaration, a commitment. We have drawn a line in the sand: this far and no farther. The Communists and communism must be expunged from the clean, free lands of the Americas."[43] While sentence three and four are evident in Noonan's sketch, they are linked to sentences one and two by the image of "the clean, free lands of the Americas," a continent unsullied by Old World tyranny, the *tabula rasa*. "This hemisphere is truly the cradle of democracy," President Reagan told reporters in January 1986, "Communism is an unwanted, foreign ideology."[44]

Sentence 3: "The United States of America is where this project first began and where it still excels. The United States is the vanguard of a hemisphere that, following its leadership, is the vanguard region of the world." During the March 16 address Reagan said: "The Soviets have made their decision—to support the Communists [meaning the Sandinistas]. . . . Now we must make our decision. . . . If we fail, there will be no evading responsibility—history will hold us accountable." Washington assumed the full burden of speaking for and protecting the hemisphere.

Throughout the campaign the U.S. public was told that the Contras "are willing to lay down their arms and negotiate to restore the original goals of the revolution" that "the Sandinistas betrayed." In another

42. "Statements: Victory of Contra Aid Legislation," June 25, 1986, National Security Archive 3056.
43. Noonan, *What I Saw at the Revolution,* 245–46.
44. "Responses to Questions Submitted by *Noticias de México,* January 2, 1986," *Papers of the Presidents of the United States: Ronald Reagan, 1986,* 1:6.

variant of the prodigal son theme peace depends on the Sandinistas "restor[ing] the original goals" of the 1979 revolution. Decoded: the authoritative interpreter of Nicaragua's choices is neither the Nicaraguan people nor their (by 1986) elected government; rather it is those whom the Sandinistas defeated in 1979 and *their* patrons in Washington.[45] That's the vanguard pretension behind Reagan's saying, extemporaneously at a 1985 press conference, "if they'd say 'uncle,'" meaning: if they'd admit their mistake and do it over my way, the right way.[46]

Sentence 4: "Such an advance in civilization provokes enmity from an old world that clings to ways that are the antithesis of the new ways described in (2). The new world may be endangered by the old." In a dozen different ways the campaign characterized outsiders in Nicaragua as a "menace to the peace and security of our Latin neighbors" as well as a threat to "the security of the United States." We have heard too many references to Soviet designs and Islamic supporters to warrant repeating them here. Using the Reagan Doctrine, the campaign suggested a world divided in two, if not "old world versus new" then "world communism versus the free world." In Nicaragua U.S. leaders were defending Western civilization under the gun of totalitarian forces.

What made the Contras Americans (in the hemispheric sense) is that

---

45. Briefly in this and more fully in other speeches Reagan claimed that the Sandinistas were permitted to come to power only after they promised the Organization of American States that they would hold elections and respect human rights. Reagan later explained his famous "if they'd say 'uncle'" remark as "what we want is that they finally give in to saying we will restore the original goals of the revolution," goals Reagan claimed the Sandinistas "put in writing to the Organization of American States . . . when they asked for [its] help . . . to persuade Somoza to step down and end the bloodshed." On July 12, 1979, as Washington was trying to head off an exclusively Sandinista victory and to preserve some role for the National Guard *sin Somoza,* the revolutionary front responded to an OAS resolution by promising to respect human rights and to hold free elections without specifying when. Probably because so little bloodletting followed the transfer of power a week later, both the OAS and the U.S. government forgot about this "pledge" until Reagan resurrected it several years later. By the time of the 1986 campaign the Sandinistas *had* held national elections, which Washington had compromised by encouraging the most visible opposition candidate to withdraw midway in the race. See "The President's News Conference, February 21, 1985" and "Interview with Morton Kondracke and Richard H. Smith of Newsweek Magazine, March 11, 1985," *Public Papers of the Presidents of the United States: Ronald Reagan, 1985* (Washington, D.C.: U.S. Government Printing Office, 1988), 1:200, 263. For the 1984 election see Gutman, *Banana Diplomacy;* for the 1979 diplomacy see Robert Pastor, *Condemned to Repetition: The United States and Nicaragua* (Princeton: Princeton University Press, 1987).

46. "The President's News Conference, February 21, 1985," *Public Papers of the Presidents of the United States: Ronald Reagan, 1985,* 1:200.

they were the equivalent of the U.S. founding fathers, the French Resistance, Texans fighting at the Alamo.[47] Reagan publicly identified himself as a Contra and called them his brothers.[48] Here we witness the identity theme explored in Chapter 2. Good Nicaraguans are Americans as we understand Americanness. As we saw in that chapter, the flip side is the criminalization of difference. The Ninety-Day Plan described Sandinista Nicaragua as "a renegade nation . . . clearly distinct from the other Central American countries."[49] In Reagan's speeches Sandinistas become "outlaws," "at war with God and man," revolutionaries who "betray" their revolution.[50] "Renegade" comes from the Spanish word for Christians who converted to Islam when the Moors conquered Spain. The renegade betrays his cause by abandoning its values. The only solution is for the renegade to return to the fold *a la* the prodigal son or be eliminated. Father can wait only so long. "Ten times we have met and tried to reason with the Sandinistas; ten times we were rebuffed."

47. Reagan used various versions of this idea, which Peggy Noonan claims to have originated: "moral equivalents," "moral equals," "moral descendants" of the U.S. Founding Fathers. The phrase became so well known that two years later it was used ironically in a headline to a story about Washington's abandoning the Contras: "The Moral Equivalent of Deserted," *Washington Post National Weekly Edition*, October 24, 1988. For an example of Reagan's use, see "Remarks to Jewish Leaders during a White House Briefing . . . , March 5, 1986," *Public Papers of the Presidents of the United States: Ronald Reagan, 1986*, 1:297.

48. "President Declares He's 'a Contra, Too,'" *Washington Post*, March 15, 1986, A20.

49. "Public Diplomacy Plan Central America," December 17, 1985, National Security Archive 2006.

50. I do not deny that the Sandinistas violated human rights and placed limits on political dissent, nor do I deny that Nicaragua's neighbors, including the United States, had reason to be concerned about the military aid the Sandinistas received from the Soviet bloc. Holding the Sandinistas to some collective standards of behavior, however, required two things that the Reagan administration not only ignored but frustrated. One is that the standard be spelled out in agreements that member states of the relevant group adopt; the other is that standards be enforced impartially. The Reagan administration's claim to be enforcing a hemispheric standard was undercut by the majority of Latin American governments interpreting that standard differently (witness the positions taken by the Central American states at Esquipulas II and by the Contadora Support Group). Washington's unwillingness to work through the Organization of American States revealed a lack of interest in using existing treaty law and collective organizations. Lack of comparability in the administration's treatment of Guatemala (among others) and Nicaragua undercut the impartiality rule. That the Reaganites ended up being chastised by the World Court and cut out of Central American diplomacy is testimony to their unilateral and discriminatory approach to these issues. Of the OAS, Walter LaFeber notes: "The United States did not bring in the Organization of American States at all. . . . Any public OAS consideration of U.S. policy would have brought overwhelming condemnation." See *Inevitable Revolutions* (New York: W. W. Norton, 1993), 283.

This bipolarity leaves most Latin Americans little room. In January 1986 eight Latin governments, including all regional powers, agreed on the "Message of Carabelleda," which the five Central American governments endorsed before it was delivered to the U.S. Secretary of State. Among other things Carabelleda called for "the termination of all foreign assistance to irregular forces" (e.g., U.S. aid to the Contras), which for the foreign ministers would constitute "an indispensable contribution to the achievement of peace."[51] To their U.S. audience, however, Reagan officials explained this away by claiming that privately the Latin American officials thought otherwise. Some were too intimidated by the Sandinistas to speak their mind, claimed the Reaganites, while others were trapped in a cultural reflex against outside intervention.[52] In fact, many Latin American officials were more angry at Reagan policy than their diplomatic messages conveyed.[53]

During his March speech the President pointed to a map of Latin America that turned progressively red as he linked Sandinista subversion to a dozen Latin American countries, including distant Brazil, Argentina, Uruguay, and Chile. The Brazilian government shot off a complaint, pointing out that the military regime there had wiped out subversives long before the Sandinistas came to power. Prior to the speech Reagan claimed that "almost 90 percent" of Central Americans supported his policy, based on opinion polls commissioned by the United States Information Agency. In fact, those polls had turned up only modest majorities in support of "U.S. aid to the Nicaraguan resistance" at a time when all such aid was "humanitarian" (June to November 1985).[54] A Costa Rican researcher discovered that the USIA poll automatically eliminated respondents with less than seven years of education, a major class barrier in Central America. Compared to

51. "A Plea for Contadora," in *The Continuing Crisis: U.S. Policy in Central America and the Caribbean*, ed. Mark Falcoff and Robert Royal (Lanham, Md.: Ethics and Public Policy Center in Association with University Press of America, 1987).

52. For example see Abrams's press briefing of March 3, 1998, 2 P.M., and Senator Richard Lugar's comments at a briefing organized by Larry Speakes on March 20 at 4 P.M., both in *American Foreign Policy: Foreign Affairs Press Briefings 1986 Supplement* (Washington, D.C.: Department of State, Office of the Historian, 1989), pt. 2.

53. Congressional leaders who met with Latin officials in Latin America reported that, in private, those officials were *more* critical of Reagan's policy, not less. Journalists corroborate this version rather than the administration's. See "Latin Mood Shifts against Washington," *Washington Post*, March 17, 1986, A18; "Doubts Still Hang over Contadora Peace Accord," *Latinamerica Press*, May 1, 1986, 7.

54. "Majority Is Held to Back Aid Plan," *New York Times*, March 18, 1986, A6.

Reagan's figure of 69 percent support in Costa Rica, a poll that sampled the entire population and asked about military aid drew only 10 percent approval.[55] The White House was (mis)using polling data to discredit Latin American presidents while refusing to be bound by public opinion in its own venue.

These *contretemps* illustrate the central question that the America/ Américas myth sidesteps: Who speaks for the hemisphere? The most significant aspect of the myth reproduced by the 1986 campaign was the answer, Washington does. We saw this assumption reproduced through the many references to Central America as "the American mainland" and "North America." It was present in the pledge that Reagan's March address asked the audience to make: "We left America safe, we left America secure, we left America free." Who knows to which America the President was referring, nation or hemisphere, as he closed his most effective speech? Finally, speaking for the hemisphere appears in the "explaining away" of those Latin officials who raised their voices to offer an alternative policy. "They don't mean what they seem to say; we know what they really intend" is a form of silencing the other through assuming a common identity.

55. "All Things Considered," National Public Radio, March 24, 1986.

7

A Different Discourse

The key to President Reagan's Central American policy has been
a realistic commitment to democracy. It sounds so obvious: who
can be against democracy?

—Constantine Menges
National Security Council staff member for Latin America[1]

At the core of this book's analysis is the constructed nature of the
Reagan administration's Nicaragua. This and any other book about a
U.S. president's construction of Latin America also is a construction.
Unconstructed reality eludes us. By comparing Reagan's construction
with that of another president who shared his values and who operated
in his time frame, however, it is possible to move this discussion out of
the study and into the "real world" of international politics. We can
discuss how different constructions of apparently similar situations play
themselves out in the actions of governments. Discourse shapes policy
shapes activity. Are the ensuing results those that the discourse points
to and the policy seeks?

For this comparison I have chosen Oscar Arias Sánchez, whose tenure
as president of Costa Rica overlapped Ronald Reagan's second term

---

1. Constantine Menges, *Inside the National Security Council* (New York: Simon and
Schuster, 1988), 96. From October 1983 until May 1986 Menges worked at the National
Security Council. In July 1985, however, he was removed from responsibility for Nicaraguan
affairs.

and whose stated goals mirrored Reagan's. The Sandinista threat pre-occupied Arias at least as much as it did Reagan and his aides; Arias was as dismissive of Marxism as were they, and public opinion within Costa Rica was even more hostile than U.S. opinion toward the Sandinistas.[2] After spending several hours together at the White House on December 4, 1986, President Reagan sent President Arias on his way with these words: "As you've said: Democratization is the key to peace in Central America. Well, the United States agrees."[3]

Moreover, Reagan policymakers frequently extolled Costa Rica as the model of what Central America should be, as in this statement of Secretary of State Shultz: "What we seek is a Central America more like Costa Rica than Cuba."[4] Costa Rica was perceived as having long been "a democratic island in a sea of dictatorship," its people having "labored for decades to cultivate the habits of civil society—habits of freedom and responsibility."[5] Rarely does one encounter a case in which the stated goals of two governments seem so similar and their political regimes so much alike (stable liberal democracies).[6]

From early 1987 on, however, these two governments competed for the leadership of regional diplomacy, pulling third parties in different directions, including the U.S. House of Representatives. While Reagan pressured Congress to continue underwriting the Contras' military capability, Arias lobbied in the United States and Europe as well as in

2. An opinion poll taken in November 1986 revealed that 70 percent of the Costa Rican public viewed the Sandinistas as a major threat, not just the mild threat selected by another 15 percent. As we saw in Chapter 7, within the United States most citizens perceived the Nicaraguan regime as a mild threat but not a serious one. See "Ticos dudan de elecciones en Nicaragua," *La nación,* December 13, 1989, A8. *La nación* is the leading conservative newspaper in Costa Rica published in San José.

3. "Remarks Following Discussions with President Oscar Arias of Costa Rica, December 4, 1986," *Public Papers of the Presidents of the United States: Ronald Reagan, 1986* (Washington, D.C.: U.S. Government Printing Office, 1989), 2:1603.

4. Shultz's statement is found in a sidebar in the Department of State's publication *Current Policy* 687 (1985), 1.

5. Schultz's "Letter of Transmittal," *The U.S. and Central America: Implementing the National Bipartisan Commission Report,* U.S. Department of State special report 148 (August 1986). See also "U.S.-Costa Rican Friendship," *U.S. Department of State Dispatch,* October 14, 1991.

6. In 1989 Costa Rica celebrated one hundred years of democracy. Interruptions in that pattern occurred prior to 1949, as happened also in the United States (e.g., the Civil War). Along with Canada, the United States and Costa Rica are the oldest and stablest democracies in the hemisphere. Canada joined Costa Rica in opposing Reagan's continuation of the Nicaraguan war.

Latin America for an end to military aid to both sides in the Nicaraguan civil war. A year after December 1986's amicable exchange at the White House, as Arias dominated the news on receiving the Nobel Peace Prize, Reagan's Assistant Secretary of State for Inter-American Affairs told associates that Arias made him sick to his stomach.[7]

Discourse links values to policies. That the same values can be used to construct different policies supports this book's contention that discourse matters. In this chapter we shall see that the presumption of identity perpetuated by the America/Américas myth is dangerous for U.S. policymakers who assume that those who share "our values" must support "our policies." This is the control-through-sameness discussed in Chapter 2. What seems "so obvious" in Washington, D.C.—as in "who can be against democracy?"—turns out to be highly contested.

Arias's Costa Rica

Oscar Arias comes from a well-heeled family, is fluent in English, was educated in England as well as Costa Rica, and has been a university professor. He is predisposed to identify with the United States, which has come to Costa Rica's defense in the past. In 1948 Costa Rica placed its defense in the hands of inter-American organizations and disbanded its army. Given Washington's dominant role in those organizations, not to mention its role as the primary source of economic and military assistance to the region, any Costa Rican president must think twice before alienating his U.S. counterpart.

So it was not surprising that Arias would say in a televised speech of August 1986 that "peace in Central America was menaced by the Nicaraguan dictatorship" that had replaced the Somoza tyranny only to "swear loyalty to the Marxist empire." Arias publicly chastised the Sandinistas for betraying their revolution, turning dictatorial, and becoming militarized; he blamed them for introducing the east-west conflict into the region.[8] As we have seen, Ronald Reagan was saying

7. Guido Fernández, *El desafío de la paz en Centroamérica* (San José: Editorial Costa Rica, 1989), 167. Formerly a journalist, Fernández served the Arias administration in various capacities, including Ambassador to the United States during this period.

8. Oscar Arias Sánchez, *El camino de la paz,* ed. Manuel Araya Incera (San José: Editorial Costa Rica, 1989), 108, 118–22. All translations are mine.

virtually the same things at the same time. On assuming the Costa Rican presidency in May 1986 Arias described his policy toward Latin America as "maintaining the liberty achieved [in the wake of military regimes] and consolidating democracy and peace in all the region," language similar to Reagan's many second-term references to democracy sweeping the world. Arias called on other governments to join Costa Rica in "an alliance for liberty and democracy."[9] The peace plan that Arias shaped differed from the Contadora draft treaties that preceded it precisely in its insistence that Central American governments democratize themselves.

Yet within months of the five Central American presidents signing Arias's plan—evolved by August 1987 into the mutually authored Esquipulas II peace accords—Oscar Arias was persona non grata with those in charge of U.S. Central American policy.[10] The rift was apparent by May of that year, when Arias's plan "was threatening a diplomatic disaster to the Reagan policy."[11] During a trip to Washington that June, Arias was invited to the Oval Office only to encounter the President flanked by the Vice President, Secretary of State, Chief of Staff, Assistant Secretary of State for the hemisphere, and four other policymakers. Arias advisor John Biehl found it "very scary stuff. . . . Oscar appeared like Spartacus going before the Roman generals." The position Arias was asked to adopt was one that the Reagan team had clung to for three years: that the Sandinistas "had to move toward verifiable and genuine democratization before any pressure could be taken off them by reducing or ending aid to the Contras." Arias knew that this was a nonstarter and refused to endorse it.[12]

Three interwoven events shed light on Arias's willingness to confront Washington on Nicaraguan policy. We shall review each briefly in order to understand the Costa Rican context before preceeding to the construction of the Nicaraguan situation in Arias's discourse. First,

9. Ibid., 97, 117, 177.

10. Frank McNeil, *War and Peace in Central America* (New York: Charles Scribner's Sons, 1988), 204, 253–54, 276–77; Fernández, *El desafío de la paz en Centroamérica* 78, 118–26, 152.

11. William Goodfellow and James Morrell, "From Contadora to Esquipulas to Sapoa and Beyond," in *Revolution and Counterrevolution in Nicaragua*, ed. Thomas W. Walker (Boulder: Westview Press, 1991), 377.

12. Jack Child, *The Central American Peace Process, 1983–1991* (Boulder: Lynne Rienner, 1992), 46. Child cites Holly Sklar, *Washington's War on Nicaragua* (Boston: South End Press, 1988), for Biehl's comment.

there was Arias's decision, during the 1985–86 presidential campaign, to recommit his party to its historic position of neutrality in foreign wars. The race was close and it was not clear whether Arias would benefit more from stressing his party's commitment to neutrality or from playing to the anti-Sandinista, pro-U.S. sentiment evident in the Costa Rican press.[13] In choosing the former Arias actually borrowed elements from both. He combined the emphasis on democracy found in the right's attacks on the Sandinistas with the left's rejection of military intervention. He offered the Costa Rican public an ideologically engaged and diplomatically energetic neutrality. With regard to U.S. policy toward Nicaragua he embraced its goals while rejecting its methods. It was a winning combination that reflected Arias's own views of the matter, as may be seen in his perfecting this formula and imposing it on Costa Rica's foreign policy professionals during the year that followed.[14]

Closely associated with neutrality was Arias's commitment to protect Costa Rican territory from the foreign intrigues that swirled around the Contra war and the drug trafficking linked to it on the southern front. On becoming president, Arias discovered the threat to Costa Rican sovereignty emanating from the U.S. government, specifically from Oliver North's Project Democracy. While this threat expressed itself in a series of events, the following is emblematic and will provide the second part of the background we are reviewing.

During the winter of 1985–86, while Arias was campaigning, Project Democracy worked to reopen a southern front for the Contras, which meant supplying them along Costa Rica's northern border with Nicaragua. Supply flights flew from San Salvador on a loop around Nicaraguan air space. Air drops in this region were problematic, due to weather conditions, jungle terrain, and the less than state-of-the-art aircraft Project Democracy owned. Thus Project Democracy sought use of a landing strip in Costa Rica for refueling its planes, offloading supplies to be flown to John Hull's inland airstrip by smaller craft, and for permitting aircraft to make emergency landings. John Hull was an American with dual citizenship whose ranch served as a staging base

---

13. Guido Fernández, *El primer domingo de febrero* (San José: Editorial Costa Rica, 1986), 304. Subsequent citations of Fernández are to his later book, *El desafío de la paz en Centroamérica*, not to this one.

14. Carlos Sojo, *Costa Rica: Política exterior y sandinismo* (San José: Facultad Latinoamericana de Ciencias Sociales, 1991), 183–200.

for Contras operating along the southern front. He has acknowledged his ties to the CIA and was apparently considered by Bill Casey "a 'John Wayne' type, a true patriot."[15]

A U.S. firm based in Panama, Udall Research Corporation, was used to acquire *hacienda* "Santa Elena" from a U.S. owner, through the work of North's associate Robert Olmstead. Located on Costa Rica's Pacific coast just south of the Nicaraguan border, this cattle ranch had a long, dirt landing strip in an isolated location, known as Potrero Grande. Project Democracy improved the strip, added barracks, then stocked it with aviation fuel. North's notebook entries document his hands-on role supervising this project.[16] Help on the Costa Rican end came from longtime North aide Robert Owen and from CIA station chief Joseph Fernández (a.k.a. Tomás Castillo) with the full cooperation of U.S. Ambassador Lewis Tambs. Since the Potrero Grande project was discussed in the Central American restricted interagency group (RIG), it was an official, if secret, part of U.S. policy.[17] Tambs told associates then, and testified later, that his major function as U.S. Ambassador to Costa Rica was to help reopen the southern front.

The cooperation of Costa Rican authorities necessary for the Santa Elena project was provided by Benjamín Piza, Minister of Public Safety under Arias's predecessor, Luís Alberto Monge. Piza was the founder of a rightist movement in Costa Rica affiliated with John Singlaub's World Anti-Communist League. With Arias's inauguration as president, Project Democracy lost this asset.[18]

15. Interview with Joseph Fernández, the CIA's station chief in Costa Rica, conducted by the CIA's Office of Inspector General, reproduced as document 40 in Peter Kornbluh and Malcolm Byrne, eds., *The Iran-Contra Scandal: The Declassified History* (New York: The New Press, 1993), 154.

16. A good example is "North Notebook Entries for January 20, 1986," National Security Archive 2185. This project allowed North to take his family on vacation to Costa Rica, to a beach near Santa Elena. See Oliver North with William Novak, *Under Fire: An American Story* (New York: Harper Paperbacks, 1992), 199.

17. On occasion and when empty, Project Democracy airplanes landed at the international airport just outside the Costa Rican capital. The smaller air strip on John Hull's property has been noted. A fishing operation also served as cover for CIA projects on Project Democracy's behalf, financed by laundered drug money. In addition to Joseph Fernandez's testimony a fairly complete picture of these operations on Costa Rican soil can be found in Peter Dale Scott and Jonathan Marshall, *Cocaine Politics: Drugs, Armies, and the CIA in Central America* (Berkeley and Los Angeles: University of California Press, 1991), chap. 6.

18. When Piza visited Washington in the spring of 1986 to iron out issues connected with Santa Elena, he was rewarded with a photo opportunity with the President. Reagan conveyed to Piza his "sincere gratitude for your efforts on behalf of those who struggle for freedom in

Monge later told a previous U.S. ambassador, Francis (Frank) McNeil, that in approving the project he had been manipulated by disinformation supplied by the U.S. government. Monge claims he was told the Sandinistas were preparing to invade Costa Rica from the north. Would Monge permit the Pentagon's Southern Command to prepare the Santa Elena strip for that contingency? Following further pressure from U.S. officials, including a visit from National Security Advisor Poindexter, who kept President Reagan informed about the project, Monge agreed. A quid pro quo for Monge may have been the removal of Contras from Costa Rican territory into Nicaragua and increased U.S. economic assistance.[19]

The first Project Democracy airplane to actually use Santa Elena did so two weeks after Arias's inauguration in May 1986. By then Arias had communicated to Fernández, Tambs, or both that the airstrip could not be used for supplying the Contras. Arias's insistence was conveyed to North and the RIG, but with no effect. Project Democracy continued to use the air strip to supply the Contras. Early in September poachers stumbling on the strip exposed its existence, leading Costa Rican authorities to call a press conference at which, North and others feared, their role in reestablishing the southern front would be exposed.

North mobilized U.S. officials in an effort to intimidate Arias into silence. The Costa Rican president was threatened with "poor relations" with Washington by both Elliott Abrams and North, including cancellation of an upcoming meeting with President Reagan. When Arias had tried to shut the Potrero Grande strip down in June Abrams apparently told Tambs "We'll have to squeeze his balls."[20] In September, reporting to National Security Advisor Poindexter, North advocated similar pressure. "[W]e agreed to the following sequence:—North to call Pres. Arias

---

Nicaragua" and expressed his hope that "this support will continue after May 8," when Arias was inaugurated. In essence Reagan is asking a Costa Rican official soon to return to private life to continue clandestine activities on behalf of the Contras. See "Meeting with Costa Rican Security Minister Benjamin Piza," March 17, 1986, National Security Archive 2496. For a full explanation of this source see note 8 of Chapter 4.

19. McNeil, *War and Peace in Central America,* 235–37; U.S. Congress, joint committees of the Senate and House, *Report of the Congressional Committees Investigating the Iran-Contra Affair,* 100th Cong., 1st sess., H. Rept. 100-433, S. Rep. 100-216 (Washington, D.C.: U.S. Government Printing Office, 1987), 64–65.

20. Joseph Fernández interview, 161; see also document 41: "Sequence of Events" (see note 15).

and tell him that if the press conference were held, Arias [excised] would never see a nickel of the $80M that McPherson had promised him earlier on Friday."[21] M. Peter McPhearson directed the U.S. Agency for International Development. Along with other Latin American countries, Costa Rica had been caught in the backwash of the Reagan recession of the early 1980s and was particularly hurt by the Central American conflicts' impact on regional trade. The $80 million in balance of payments assistance for Costa Rica was held up for almost a year, an action McNeil believes was linked to Arias's lack of cooperation.[22]

In response to a call by Tambs—apparently not by North—the press conference was canceled. Within weeks, however, Costa Rican security forces raided the Potrero Grande airstrip, impounded its fuel supply, and blocked the runway. This action made the local papers and, while no U.S. officials were named, the dummy corporation was cited and had to be shut down. A Project Democracy operative who quickly left Costa Rica notified North, adding: "Pres. Arias will attend Reagan's dinner in New York September 22. Boy needs to be straightened out by heavy weights."[23]

This event provides a glimpse into the HP mentality (see Chapter 4) of key U.S. players while revealing the ends-means confusion that has plagued Washington's promotion of democracy in Latin America. To install democracy in one country by force—always a dubious prospect— Washington was jeopardizing the sovereignty of the country it considered the region's democratic model. Sovereignty is integral to democracy since democracy assumes, among other things, that important national decisions are made by elected national leaders or their staffs. What

21. "Iran [Report on President Oscar Arias's Planned Press Conference]," September 6, 1986, National Security Archive 3380. North's notebook entry for September 6 adds: "[T]ell Arias . . . never set foot in Wton [Washington]," a reference to the upcoming meeting between the two presidents. See "North Notebook Entries for September 6, 1986," September 9, 1986, National Security Archive 3381. In his testimony to the Iran-Contra investigators Abrams admitted sending this threat to Arias. Abrams got Tambs to phone Arias to "dissuade him from this press conference," although Tambs appears not to have passed along the threats that North listed. Whether North himself actually called Arias is doubtful. See *Report*, 143; McNeil, *War and Peace in Central America*, 238–39.

22. McNeil, *War and Peace in Central America*, 239, 241.

23. "Costa Rica Seizure of Santa Elena Airstrip," September 10, 1986, National Security Archive 3393. The operative was Rafael Quintero, who worked for Secord. He is one of several Cuban exiles who were involved in Project Democracy and the 1986 campaign, including S/LPD's Otto Reich and Félix Rodriguez (who managed the Contra supply flights).

would Arias conclude from these events? If he interpreted Abrams's, Tambs's, and North's behavior as rogue, that Reagan's policy was in disarray. If, on the other hand, Abrams, Tambs, and others accurately reflected administration policy, Arias would know that there was no common understanding between his government and Reagan's on how to promote democracy and peace in Central America.

The second interpretation was confirmed when Arias visited Washington in December 1986, our third event. The Costa Rican entourage spent several hours with Reagan, Secretary of State Shultz, Assistant Secretary Abrams, and other top U.S. officials. Separately Arias talked with CIA Director Casey and Vice President Bush.[24] Now that Congress was backing full military aid to the Contras Arias found U.S. officials intent on prosecuting the war. Since he already had decided that such a policy reinforced Sandinista intransigence, dooming negotiations and delaying democratization, Arias had little choice but to launch his own counterinitiative. Inaction was ruled out since Costa Rica, in Arias's view, was staring at a flood of refugees, falling foreign investment, and declining exports, all due to the Nicaraguan war.

Within two months of his return from Washington, Arias launched his diplomatic initiative.[25] At first his call for a meeting of four Central American *democratic* presidents seemed to follow Washington's strategy of deepening Nicaragua's isolation. When Arias's plan was shown to the other presidents on February 15, however, it linked the democratization of Nicaragua to a prohibition on aiding the armed opponents of any government. "Simply by asserting the fundamental premise of diplomacy—concessions by both sides—[Arias] had wandered far off the reservation."[26] He was followed first by Guatemala, then by El Salvador, with Nicaragua showing strong interest. Washington no longer had a majority of the "democratic" governments supporting its policy.

Arias's Construction of the Issue

As was suggested above, the differences between Arias's and Reagan's construction of the Nicaraguan issue largely dealt with means, not ends.

24. Fernández, *El desafío de la paz en Centroamérica*, chaps. 3 and 4.
25. Ibid., chaps. 2–5.
26. Goodfellow and Morrell, "From Contadora to Esquipulas to Sapoa and Beyond," 377.

The classic Arias position was stated in his address to the Organization of American States in September 1987: "If we democracies of the world show ourselves afraid of liberty, afraid of using our own tools, such as dialogue and persuasion, we will be following the methods of the tyrants, the path of the oppressors."[27] In the same breath that he said "liberty" is "on mankind's agenda," Arias stated that "nonintervention" also is "a sacred right." If, as Arias believed, self-determination is a component of liberty, then imposing liberty on another country by force is a contradiction. Similarly, if democracy is a process of give-and-take within a framework of norms, imposing democracy through force is likely to fail.

Eschewing liberty or democracy imposed by violence did not render Arias passive. There are choices other than laissez faire and intervention, he insisted, including the "dialogue and persuasion" mentioned in the OAS speech. "One must put an end to the absurd divorce between liberty and reconciliation," a divorce he saw in the Reagan position on negotiations.[28] A persistent theme in Arias's discourse, then, is one noticeably absent from Reagan's: ends-means congruence. Democracies should encourage democracy using democratic means (advocacy, persuasion, negotiation). Twenty years before Reagan's inauguration as president, Martin Luther King Jr. had pointed out that "ends are preexistent in the means."[29]

Arias rejected communism but chose to combat it much as the young Reagan had when, as president of the Screen Actors Guild in 1947, Reagan told the House Un-American Activities Committee that rather than outlawing the U.S. Communist party the better course "is to make democracy work."[30] While in the thick of politics, wheeling-and-dealing with people he knew, the young Reagan came close to embodying Jefferson's notion of democracy. Arias never abandoned that stance.

As a practical matter Arias did not believe that lasting democracy in Central America could be built on force, a contention that the history of U.S. interventions in Latin America sustains. Of *el derecho* (law or right) Arias said, "When we put our trust in it, we know that through its equal application to all it will neither generate hatred nor sow rancor." In contrast, war "brings with it death, suffering, ruin, misery

27. Arias, *El camino de la paz*, 319–20.
28. Ibid., 198, 250.
29. James Cone, *Malcolm & Martin & America* (Maryknoll, N.Y.: Orbis Books, 1993), 78.
30. Lou Cannon, *Reagan* (New York: G. P. Putnam's Sons, 1982), 83.

and moral degradation."[31] This was not abstract reasoning; suffering was Central America's daily reality, as Arias frequently commented. The wars in Central America, being largely civil wars, will not stop until opponents of existing regimes see an option to toppling governments by force, Arias reasoned: that option being fair elections. "Only democracy can end wars between brothers."[32] But meaningful elections, he also understood, rarely occur in the midst of civil war. To escape this conundrum progress is needed on both fronts: opening up the political process to dissidents while persuading rebels to stop fighting. Practically, this requires a *series* of negotiations through which all sides slowly gain trust in each other. In the meantime outside governments should stop throwing fuel on the fire, as Arias perceived Washington to be doing following Reagan's victory over Congress in June 1986. For the same reason Arias was critical of the Soviet Union. Thus, while for the Reaganites, democratizing Nicaragua had become a *precondition* of peace, for Arias the two remained *reciprocal*. Peace and democracy are "inseparably linked" in Arias's discourse. "Peace is a force for democracy" no less than democracy is the opening required for peace.[33]

While Arias called spades spades, he avoided labels that demonize the adversary or lock anyone into their past. A collection of his speeches does not yield a single reference to another leader, party, or movement as aliens, beasts, diseases, or occupied territory, stock Washington metaphors for Latin American Marxists. Instead, Arias categorizes people and stances he dislikes as retrogressive or mistaken. His faith in the possibility of change can be seen in Arias's frequent use of *camino* or *ruta* (road, way, path), as found in the title chosen for the collected speeches, "El camino de la paz" (The Road to Peace).

In this connection two aphorisms familiar to Costa Ricans are relevant: *Se hace camino al andar* and *Arrieros somos y por el camino vamos:* the path is made by walking it, and (loosely translated) we are all in the same boat.[34] Cubans and Nicaraguans, Arias felt, were

---

31. Arias, *El camino de la paz,* 262, 290.
32. Ibid., 107.
33. Ibid., 259.
34. The first aphorism is universal and quite old. It appears, for example, in the ancient Chinese sage Chuang Tsu's observations in *Inner Chapters,* trans. Gia-fu Feng and Jane English (New York: Vintage Books, 1974), 30. A Spanish incarnation caught the eye of a Bush speech writer: "There's a poem called Machado's *Caminante.* There's one line that stands out; here it is: 'Traveler, there is no road; you make the road in traveling.' " See Bush's remarks on greeting Chilean President Aylwin, May 13, 1992, *U.S. Department of State Dispatch,* May 18, 1992, 387.

traveling *los dolorosos caminos* (painful roads), but travel implies movement. The peace plan "has opened a new road for Central Americans," Sandinistas included.[35] To be on the wrong road is still to be in the terrain, not an alien. History is open-ended. While Reaganites talked of "white hats" and "black hats," Arias rejected the "demand that we see the whole world as black or white."[36] How the opponent is characterized obviously influences the success of negotiations. In the September 1987 speech to the U.N. General Assembly in which he acknowledged that the peace process had little to show as yet, Arias voiced a characteristic appeal to move forward. "No one has a right to judge exclusively on the basis of past conduct. None of the actors, including the big powers, has the moral authority to throw the first stone."[37]

Demonizing images and the associated theme of betrayal are less likely to arise from a discourse that does not homogenize the Americas as Reagan's did. Reagan's use of "America" harbored the conflation of nation and continent that allowed U.S. leaders to assume that they knew what Latin Americans need. While Arias occasionally referred to America in the singular, this is the *nuestra América* of José Martí, a Latin historical-cultural entity rather than a current ideological bloc. Most often Arias used the plural *las Américas* or *las tres Américas y el Caribe.* Thus the United States and Canada comprise one of four regions within the Western Hemisphere, one of three "Americas."

Negotiations, Arias believed, require commitments and deadlines. He criticized the Contadora diplomacy for its lack of a timetable. But it is equally counterproductive, Arias insisted, to make too much of missed deadlines. He chided those who pronounced the Esquipulas process dead whenever a target was not met on schedule. If a deadline was missed, his response was to have the presidents set another in a time frame that did not reward delay. As a negotiator, Arias also left the most difficult items out of initial agreements. Start with the solvable, build trust; then problems once deemed intractable will appear in a different light. While this is how the Reagan administration dealt with the Soviet Union from 1985 on, in Central America after 1984 the White House refused to even meet with Nicaraguan authorities, insisting

35. Arias, *El camino de la paz,* 356, 383.
36. Ibid., 292.
37. Ibid., 329.

that the Sandinistas first negotiate with the Contras. Arias, in contrast, asked the Sandinistas first to negotiate with the unarmed opposition inside Nicaragua. Having taken that step, the Sandinistas eventually took the more difficult one of negotiating with Contra leaders despite years of rejecting that option.

Other leaders made significant contributions at critical moments, especially El Salvador's José Napoleon Duarte and Nicaragua's Daniel Ortega.[38] The Canadian government's role in organizing a joint U.N.-OAS peacekeeping operation was important.[39] Soviet leader Mikhail Gorbachev leaned on the Sandinistas to negotiate and then cut off all Soviet military aid to Nicaragua at the close of 1988.[40] Our purpose here is to understand Arias's construction of the Central American situation, not to do justice to the complex negotiations that eventually brought peace to the region.[41] There is surely a connection, however, between the way Arias framed the situation and his ability to involve others in finding a solution.

The White House Loses Control

After meeting around the clock in Guatemala, on August 7, 1987, the five Central American presidents signed the agreement that they converted into reality through a one-step-backward, two-steps-forward process requiring half a dozen meetings over the next two and a half years. The Nobel Peace Prize awarded Arias later that year brought international support for this process. Inside the Reagan administration, however, Arias's initiative was perceived as "destructive," "a trap," "another phony peace plan." Writing in early 1988, former NSC staffer Constantine Menges claimed that "the Arias plan had failed."[42]

While the Reagan policy continued to tie U.S. strategy to the Contras, the Esquipulas II accords attracted sufficient congressional support that

38. Jim Morrell, *The Nine Lives of the Central American Peace Process*, International Policy Report (Washington, D.C.: Center for International Policy, 1989).
39. Child, *The Central American Peace Process*, 65.
40. Jan S. Adams, *A Foreign Policy in Transition: Moscow's Retreat from Central America and the Caribbean, 1985–1992* (Durham: Duke University Press, 1992), chap. 5.
41. For the latter see Child, *The Central American Peace Process*.
42. Menges, *Inside the National Security Council*, 320–25, 330, 374, 389.

the White House could no longer publicly fund the Contras' military needs. Having exposed the extralegal means used from 1984 to 1986, the Iran-Contra investigations closed down that alternative from early 1987 on. Outmaneuvered by Oscar Arias and House Speaker James C. (Jim) Wright Jr. working in tandem, the Reagan administration first tried to co-opt Esquipulas by identifying it with a plan the White House hastily worked out with Wright and then issuing "clarifying" language to bring the Reagan-Wright plan back in line with administration policy. That failing, President Reagan pronounced the Central American presidents' plan "fatally flawed" and retreated into ritual requests to Congress for continued military aid to the Contras. Recalling that the impression of U.S. "impotence" was what the 1984 Kissinger Report most sought to avert in Central America, it is ironic that the Reagan administration ended on this note.[43]

Violence fed by centuries of inequality and repression is never quickly ended, nor are tyranny and corruption. A war that left at least 30,000 Nicaraguans dead *did* wind down, however, albeit in fits and starts, allowing diplomatic efforts to refocus on El Salvador, where a similar pacification was achieved in 1992 and where ex-guerrillas participated in the 1994 election. Noting the return of civilian governments in Haiti, Guatemala, El Salvador, and the southern cone of South America, President Reagan frequently reminded domestic audiences of the "one tragic, glaring exception to that democratic tide—the Communist Sandinista government in Nicaragua."[44] However, according to Frank McNeil, who spent 1984–87 as second in command of the State Department's Bureau of Intelligence and Research, on this score "more was accomplished inside Nicaragua in the first eight months of the Guatemala Accords [Esquipulas II] than in seven years of Contra insurgency."[45] Having covered Central America for eight years, *Washington Post* reporter Julia Preston similarly concluded that "concessions the Sandinistas made under the two-year-old peace plan authored by

---

43. The Kissinger Commission urged Washington to prevent "the erosion of our power to influence events worldwide that would flow from the perception that we were unable to influence vital events close to home." The fear of being perceived "impotent" is on the same page. See *The Report of the President's National Bipartisan Commission on Central America* (New York: Macmillan, 1984), 111.

44. "Address to the Nation on United States Assistance to the Nicaraguan Democratic Resistance, June 24, 1986," *Public Papers of the Presidents of the United States: Ronald Reagan, 1986* (Washington, D.C.: U.S. Government Printing Office, 1988), 1:833.

45. McNeil, *War and Peace in Central America*, 265.

Costa Rican President Oscar Arias have expanded political freedom."[46] Human rights expert Aryeh Neier agreed, in early 1988 finding more of an opening in Nicaragua than in Guatemala or El Salvador and attributing this to the Arias peace plan.[47]

It was within the context of the Esquipulas II plan that the Sandinistas made the most significant moves toward pluralizing their regime, paving the way for the domestic opposition's victory in the 1990 elections behind Violeta Chamorro, an outcome that few beside Arias predicted.[48] Reporting that election, the *New York Times* stated that the outcome "is seen by diplomats as a vindication of President Oscar Arias Sánchez of Costa Rica and his Central American peace plan. The plan appears to have achieved by peaceful democratic means what years of United States military and economic pressure could not."[49]

Left here the story has its moral: Central American negotiation triumphs over U.S. intimidation, a *process*-oriented discourse succeeds where a discourse heavy on imposed solutions fails. Real world outcomes, of course, are rarely so tidy. Apologists for the Reagan administration claim credit for the political opening in Nicaragua. Had the White House not played "bad cop" to Arias's "good cop," they argue, the Sandinistas would not have made concessions. In October 1987 Ronald Reagan claimed: "Without the freedom fighters, the Sandinistas never would have signed the Guatemala accord."[50] In January 1994 Oliver North told an audience that he "deserved credit . . . that there was a democratically elected government in Nicaragua."[51]

While the collapse of communist regimes in Eastern Europe induced the Sandinistas to veer toward social democracy, it is debatable how

---

46. Julia Preston, "Nicaragua's Ten-Year Transformation," *Washington Post National Weekly Edition,* July 17, 1989, 6–7.

47. Aryeh Neier, "Has Arias Made a Difference?" *New York Review,* March 17, 1988.

48. Chamorro's coalition, it should be noted, was heavily funded by the U.S. government, which also helped foot the costs of the electoral process. There is no need here to sort out the factors responsible for the Sandinista defeat. The reader should not assume, however, that it can be reduced to a simple preference among Nicaraguan voters for Chamorro's policies over Sandinista policies.

49. "Sandinistas' Loss to be Felt by Other Leftist Movements," *New York Times,* February 27, 1990, A14.

50. "Address to the Permanent Council of the Organization of American States, October 7, 1987," *Public Papers of the Presidents of the United States: Ronald Reagan, 1987* (Washington, D.C.: U.S. Government Printing Office, 1989), 2:1145.

51. "Oliver North Looking to Join the Senate He Once Defied," *New York Times,* January 28, 1994, A1.

much credit the Reagan administration deserves for those European events. Focusing on Central America, Arias's intervention was necessary (if insufficient); it is not clear that the Reagan administration's was either. Even when the Contras were finished as a fighting force, the Sandinistas proceeded toward the elections that cost them power. Why?

> Nicaragua was hearing from Democrats in Congress what it had just heard in Caracas: an end to the U.S. trade embargo and the credit embargo that had prevented Nicaragua from getting any funds from the Inter-American Development Bank, the World Bank, and the International Monetary Fund would only come after Nicaragua held the election. Given the high priority of rebuilding its war-shattered economy, Nicaragua went to the [1989 El Tesoro] summit with plans to announce that not only the municipal elections, but elections for president, vice president, the legislature, and the Central American Parliament would be moved up to February 25, 1990.[52]

In short, economic pressure was the only stick needed. At the El Tesoro meeting of the Central American presidents Nicaragua accepted conditions for a free and monitored election.

The Power of Words

The good cop/bad cop approach had been tried by the Reagan administration during Thomas Enders's and Langhorne Motley's stints as Assistant Secretary of State for the region, and had failed. Known as "two tracks," this first-term Reagan policy sought a diplomatic settlement based on concessions the Sandinistas would make when confronted with escalating hostilities. One reason this policy failed is that Reagan's directives were used by second-level officials to undermine the efforts of Secretary of State Shultz to reach an accommodation with the Sandinistas in 1984.

52. Goodfellow and Morrell, "From Contadora to Esquipulas to Sapoa and Beyond," 385–86.

Constantine Menges recounts how "false" peace agreements with the Sandinistas were averted when "loyal" Reaganites like himself, located further down the foreign policy hierarchy, mobilized trusted associates of the President to bring to his attention the discrepancies between proposed diplomatic solutions and his own less compromising rhetoric. One of Menges's (by his count) seven eleventh-hour interventions came in October 1984, when his faction was able to "kill the Shultz election-eve 'peace in our time' treaty."[53] (Note the invocation of Munich.) That particular intervention put an end to Shultz's active engagement in finding a diplomatic solution. Journalist Roy Gutman's reconstruction of what happened in 1984 corroborates Menges's insider account while giving Jeane Kirkpatrick star billing as spoiler.[54] After 1984, Reagan administration strictures on who could negotiate what with whom effectively ruled out any solution that failed to produce a change of regime within Nicaragua, that being the operational meaning of "democratization" among those Menges called Reagan loyalists.

Menges claimed that he was able to stop the foreign policy profession-als in their tracks by waving the talisman of Ronald Reagan's words. Of one Assistant Secretary of State for the hemisphere Menges wrote: "Motley felt defensive about getting into a debate with me because I had the annoying habit of bringing along copies of the president's National Security Decision Directives or excerpts from his major public statements. I'd show them to Motley and the other subcabinet members in order to document and clarify the president's foreign policy, which we were *all* supposed to be implementing."[55] Menges eventually got himself "promoted" out of the NSC core for quoting Reagan's language at those trying to effect a workable policy. As he and Kirkpatrick left the circle of policymakers, however, Casey, North, and Abrams contin-ued the tactic, obstructing negotiated solutions while feeding President Reagan optimistic accounts of the Contras' capabilities.[56] At the end of his meticulous study Jack Child voiced a judgment that others shared: ["T]he United States under the Reagan administration attempted to block the Contadora/Esquipulas process" down to the day it left office.[57] Discourse kept the Reaganites locked into a failing policy that the

53. Menges, *Inside the National Security Council*, 166.
54. Gutman, *Banana Diplomacy*, 216–19.
55. Menges, *Inside the National Security Council*, 154.
56. Gutman, *Banana Diplomacy*, 297, 313–4.
57. Child, *The Central American Peace Process*, 151–52.

scarcely less conservative George Bush changed on assuming the presidency.

Another product of the Reagan discourse was the imperial style that policy-makers brought to their dealings with Central American leaders, a style evident in the Potrero Grande airstrip episode. Steeped in the "HP" syndrome described in Chapter 4, this style remained unchecked due to the influence of myth on Central American policymakers, particularly myths with strong vanguard presumptions. Along with Abrams, Casey and North ignored protocol in badgering Central American officials to cooperate with "Project Democracy." In a typical incident, on flying uninvited to Costa Rica Casey demanded to see Arias secretly and then turned down Arias's offer of a less sequestered meeting at his house. Recalls Arias adviser Biehl of a progression of U.S. officials intent on pressuring Arias, "They all walked in and out, always nervous and hurried, always wanting immediate results."[58] "Subtly imperial" is how the Costa Rican Ambassador to Washington remembers Elliott Abrams.[59] Traveling to five Latin American countries in April 1987, Frank McNeil found "frustration" with the inflexibility of the United States and "what many saw as an arrogant refusal to listen to its neighbors' views."[60]

Far from being a matter of manners, Central American leaders understood the role assigned to their countries by the Reagan Doctrine and rejected it. Who wants to serve as a battleground on which superpowers fight it out using locals as proxies? In a Costa Rican television interview in February 1986 Arias foresaw "more war and more deaths, where some are providing the arms and we, the Central Americans, are providing the dead."[61] Speaking to a U.S. audience in 1987, Arias invited "those who preach war, who think that it is the only solution . . . to send their own children into that war rather than pay to have other mothers' sons killed."[62] Arias repeated this sentiment

58. Morrell, "The Nine Lives of the Central American Peace Process," 3.

59. Fernández, *El desafío de la paz en Centroamérica*, 78, chaps. 3 and 8; McNeil, *War and Peace in Central America*, 241.

60. Frank McNeil, "The Road to Esquipulas," paper delivered at the Sixteenth Congress of the Latin American Studies Association, Washington, D.C., April 1991, 23.

61. Televised interview of February 20, 1986, San José, Costa Rica, translated and reprinted by Mark Falcoff and Robert Royal, eds., *The Continuing Crisis: U.S. Policy in Central America and the Caribbean* (Lanham, Md.: Ethics and Public Policy Center in association with University Press of America, 1987), 177.

62. Arias, *El camino de la paz*, 346.

to the other Central American presidents—then to the world at large through his Nobel Prize address that castigated world powers for congratulating themselves on nuclear arms control while fueling *conventional* wars in the Third World.[63] It was a sentiment Latin American leaders had uttered before and would do so again, as when Colombia's president commented that "[t]he United States has decided to declare war on drugs until not one Colombian is left standing."[64] The perception that the vanguard nation was being careless with other peoples' lives and sovereignty, even those of its allies, strengthened the Central American leaders' conviction that, as the Costa Rican Foreign Minister put it, "it is time for Central Americans to solve their own problems."[65]

To some impossible-to-measure extent, then, the way Reagan officials conceived of their role in the hemisphere (vanguard) and conceptualized democracy (as the right people in power rather than the right processes in place) prevented them from executing not just the "two-track" policy of the first term but its one-track sequel. Reagan discourse served to marginalize those within the executive who were not hard-liners while enhancing the authority of those who were. The marginalization of Philip Habib, the President's Special Envoy to Latin American leaders, is a prime example.[66] Seeing this, Central American allies turned away from the White House's direction, leaving the U.S. executive with a reduced role in shaping the outcome of a conflict on which it had expended great resources.

A myth-driven policy influenced the selection of personnel and options so as to deliver control of the policy to HP officials who thought they already knew all that they needed to know about Central America. In the end they did not know enough.

---

63. Ibid., 384–85. "En nuestras manos está la esperanza," speech given to the Central American presidents meeting at Alajuela, Costa Rica, January 15, 1988 (San José: Imprenta Nacional, 1988), 8.

64. "Colombia: U.S. Arming Traffickers," *Washington Post,* June 12, 1990, A16.

65. Jeffrey Toobin, *Opening Arguments* (New York: Viking, 1991), 108.

66. Habib resigned when, in the wake of the Esquipulas II breakthrough, the White House refused the Secretary of State's suggestion that Habib return to Central America, which he had visited several times since assuming his position in March 1986.

8

Beyond the
America/Américas Myth

*To respect differences, to hear discrete voices, to recognize the
right of fellow human beings to act, live and let live . . . may turn
into a strategic characteristic of our time.*
    —Orlando Fals-Borda and Muhammad Anisur Rahman[1]

Throughout these chapters we have seen the Americas myth, in conjunc-
tion with lessons drawn from Europe in the 1940s, used to mobilize
Congress and the public behind the contention that the national security
of the United States was endangered by the Sandinistas' ideology and
their choice of foreign partners for trade, aid, and advice. "Having this
regime in Central America imperils our vital security interests," President Reagan said in the 1986 speech analyzed in Chapter 6, adding:
"Central America is strategic to our Western alliance."[2]

Interviewing Washington officials in the mid-1980s, Lars Schoultz
found widespread agreement with that proposition. On investigating
the factual assumptions underlying it, however, Schoultz found the

---

1. Orlando Fals-Borda and Muhammad Anisur Rahman, eds., "A Self-Review of PAR,"
in *Action and Knowledge: Breaking the Monopoly with Participatory Action Research* (New
York: Apex Press, 1991), 33.
2. "Address to the Nation on the Situation in Nicaragua, March 16, 1986," *Public Papers
of the Presidents of the United States: Ronald Reagan, 1986* (Washington, D.C.: U.S.
Government Printing Office, 1988), 1:354.

evidence shaky. One had to assume an illogical Soviet plan to invest scarce resources in this corner of the globe, or outmoded technologies, or worst-case scenarios of extremely low probability.[3] Changes evident in the Soviet leadership since 1982, reinforced by Gorbachev's ascendancy in early 1985, weakened the credibility of this line of reasoning.[4]

Perhaps it was convenient for U.S. interests to remove the Sandinistas from power. Perhaps it sent a message to other governments that (as President Reagan put it) the United States was "back" and "standing tall." Whatever it was, removing the Sandinistas was not "necessary" or "vital," and failing that test it is hard to view Reagan's policy as proportional. Proportionality means that the good sought ought not to be outweighed by the harm done obtaining it.[5] This is not only an ethical judgment: when proportionality is absent, alliances weaken and publics grow fractious. In short, the costs mount. Our case provided ample evidence of this.

The Nicaraguan civil war *did* threaten the territorial integrity, trade, and prosperity of several Central American states, but only indirectly can the Sandinistas be held responsible for prolonging that conflict. How long would the Contras have fought without continued U.S. backing? The Reagan administration claimed that U.S. military support for them was indispensable. And so it proved when, early in 1988, Congress made it clear that it would not supply further military aid and the Contras went "on strike." To use Central America's warfare as justification for U.S. acts prolonging that war is circular reasoning.[6]

This case study illustrates, then, the transformation of a problem into

3. Lars Schoultz, *National Security and United States Policy toward Latin America* (Princeton: Princeton University Press, 1987).

4. Jan S. Adams, *A Foreign Policy in Transition: Moscow's Retreat from Central America and the Caribbean, 1985–1992* (Durham: Duke University Press, 1992), 23–27, 110.

5. Proportionality long has been one aspect of theories of just war. Another that the Reagan administration violated in sponsoring the Contras is "last resort" (exhausting all peaceful alternatives before fighting).

6. Subtracting the war, it is difficult to argue that Sandinista Nicaragua presented a security threat to its neighbors. Claims that the Contra war was needed to induce the Sandinistas to stop supplying guerrillas in El Salvador are not persuasive, while Sandinista incursions into Honduras qualify as the "hot pursuit" that Washington accepts when its allies engage in it. United States Ambassador to Nicaragua Lawrence Pezzullo succeeded in using diplomatic pressure to get the Sandinistas to stop supplying the Salvadoran guerrillas in 1981 but was removed by the Reagan administration. Following Washington's invasion of Grenada, the Sandinistas once more cut this supply link. Their support for the Salvadorans remained a "card" Sandinista leaders were prepared to play in negotiations, and ultimately did.

a crisis. A discourse that taps into the America/Américas myth is likely to do this. As both opportunities and threats take on world-historic proportions and moral obligation, the perceived stakes overwhelm prudence and proportionality. One of the S/LPD's several "white papers" on Central America made the front page of the *New York Times* on February 10, 1985: "U.S. Says Russians Try to Make Satellite of Central America." In the *Rochester Democrat and Chronicle* on that day—typical of newspapers across the land—that story produced a banner headline on the front page: "A Soviet-Cuban Plot."

Also evident in this case is the homogenizing impact of this myth. Democracy and freedom were assumed to be unitary, universal, and well understood by U.S. policymakers. Unpacking these terms is difficult when they carry the teleological momentum given them two centuries ago. If God ordains that freedom prevail, it is easy to slip into thinking that freedom is as independent of human culture and choice as the tides and the winds. But that surely is not the case. In the ways that *governments* engage freedom, democracy, and development, there is nothing anonymous, timeless, and given about them. There are only trade-offs and options.[7]

As organizing devices political myths may continue to be useful, just as dreams are for the individual who does not confer authority upon them or confuse them with ordinary reality. It is when we invest political myths with transhistorical authority—forgetting authorship, losing sight of alternatives, letting fantasy fly unchecked—that we invite trouble.

All social reality is constructed through discourse and none of it is free from the bias of interest and perception. That does not mean, however, that one discourse is just as good as another. Discourses may be judged by their functions and contexts: Who shares this language for what purpose? What is it we want our language to do when we practice democracy? Is it what we want when we are engaged in commerce or entertainment? What kind of relations do we want with Latin America today? Are they the same as when the America/Américas myth took form?

---

7. The trade-offs confronting many Latin American nations today are described by John Sheahan, *Conflict and Change in Mexican Economic Strategy* (San Diego: Center for U.S.-Mexican Studies, University of California, 1991), especially the chapter entitled "Some Implications and Questions for Latin America."

Democratic theorists argue that democracy needs participants who are aware of their interests and agency, and who accept the legitimacy of others having different interests expressed through different readings of reality. As for regional relationships, students of successful ones, such as Western Europe's, point to the importance of common rules from which no nation is exempt, rules flexibly applied out of an understanding that "equal" is not "same." So while the America/Américas myth remains an option, by virtue of all the baggage it carries it would seem a poor choice for building an interactive, freedom-supporting hemispheric order in the twenty-first century.

A myth reproduced through the techniques of advertising has the resilience of a weed. Nonetheless, while advertising deadens our capacity to reflect, it also can provoke a critical response. Like the shape-shifter of preliterate myths, language tricks even those who think they have it mastered. Chief of Staff Donald Regan recalls President Reagan telling a group of senators, "If you're not for the contras, you're for communism."[8] "No more Cubas, no more Vietnams" is how influential Senator Richard Lugar brought history to bear on U.S. choices in Central America.[9] As the deposed leaders of Eastern Europe's communist regimes learned, such hard sells can backfire. When political ads stress *the one* answer or frame *the one* choice, those very claims stir the skepticism they were intended to silence. The problem is that while ads self-destruct or audiences tire of them, what replaces one ad tends to be a more cunning one. Developing a discourse appropriate for U.S.-Latin American relations involves more than waiting for the old language to exhaust its permutations.

Beyond the America/Américas Myth

Before rushing to the drawing boards, we should revisit the original concern with order. Today not just postmodern aesthetics but neoliberal economics challenge the myth's assumption that the only alternative to a unity-based order is chaos. Both argue that a relaxation of controls,

8. Donald Regan, *For the Record: From Wall Street to Washington* (New York: St. Martin's Press, 1988), 59.

9. George Black, *The Good Neighbor* (New York: Pantheon Books, 1988), 143.

including "standards," creates the possibility of alternative orders more flexible, more engaging, more inspiring, perhaps, than those inherited from the past. Both ask, in effect, how many different voices can be included before things get out of hand. Both assume that order can be *implicit*—generated from within the process.

From the natural sciences and the arts we know that one century's dissonances give rise to the next century's harmonies—or must we speak of decades now? The space that lies between static order and entropy is the very space where creativity and productivity thrive. We ask that political systems protect and enlarge that space, not confine it. Where is creativity currently found in inter-American relations? Hardly in warmed-over homilies about a common mission. The "new world" of that discourse no longer seems new or singular. New ideas and identities are being generated in music, dance, film, theater, and fiction—and in trade, investment, and environmental conservation. "Fusion" and "crossover" abound. Let Pablo Neruda be our guide: poet and politician, Marxist and romantic, Chilean and, yes, American.

Challenging the rules as given, as the Latin imagination has done in many realms, has proven destructive as well as creative. The universe packages things that way. But why should U.S. elites clutch at the thought of destructive outcomes in Latin America when it is the Latins who primarily pay for these and who many times learn from them? It is not as if Washington's record in promoting development and democracy in Latin America is a string of successes.[10] Here we approach what Gabriel García Márquez had in mind when, in his 1982 Nobel Prize acceptance speech, he asked why the powerful nations of the world applaud Latin America's innovations in the arts while checking, even sabotaging, its experiments in politics and economics. "You do *that* so

10. Even today, as U.S. leaders congratulate themselves for fostering democracy in Latin America, the "real, existing democracy" evident in Brazil, Argentina, Venezuela, and elsewhere in the early 1990s showed the limits of U.S.-style campaigns. The slick and photogenic Fernando Collor modeled his rise to the Brazilian presidency on Joe McGinniss's account of Nixon's campaign, *The Selling of the President 1968*. In Costa Rica the winner of the 1990 presidential election hired Roger Ailes, the consultant who scripted Bush's 1988 campaign commercials, taking attack ads to a new low. In Costa Rica this importation of a U.S. model threatens a vibrant tradition of community involvement in national politics. There an election rally still provides an occasion for half a town to turn out, listen to speeches, and mingle in the plaza talking about it. Eight out of ten Costa Ricans vote in their national elections compared to five in ten in the United States.

well" is the praise that suggests its completion—"well for a Latin American." Washington keeps affirming Latin America's performance in limited realms but not its identity, its intrinsic worth, or its creativity.

"Differences are vital," states William Irwin Thompson. The reason for emphasizing "diversity, individuation, integrity," Thompson suggests, is not to be nice to others but to learn from them.[11] This book is hardly the place to work through all the opportunity costs of clinging to a nineteenth-century concept of order through (presumed) identity, but the costs are real. The United States has much to gain by substituting Thompson's "participation in the universal through the unique" for its historic pattern of "identifying the other purely and simply with one's own 'ego ideal' " (Todorov).[12] The America/Américas myth rose in response to insecurities early U.S. leaders felt about their society as well as in response to preindustrial concepts of generating wealth. Historicizing the myth is one way to escape it. It was then, we are now.

Attempted Solutions

The present moment in hemispheric relations, in which democracy and capitalism are ascendant, resembles the years immediately following World War II. Spurred by the formation of the United Nations and the niche it offered regional organizations, treaties laying the foundation for the present inter-American system were signed and regional organizations created. While signing treaties and funding organizations, Washington refused to tie its hands by granting real power to hemispheric entities governed by any form of majority rule, even one that recognized the United States' greater power. Washington was wary of limiting its autonomy.[13]

That postwar moment was a missed opportunity, leaving the old discourse to bear too much of the burden of managing an alliance of three dozen countries. While second-guessing the past is pointless, seizing the opportunity when it appears a second time is not. Greater institutionalization of the Americas would permit the toning down of

11. *Pacific Shift* (San Francisco: Sierra Club Books, 1985), 129.
12. *The Conquest of America*, trans. Richard Howard (New York: Harper & Row Colophon, 1985), 165.
13. David Green, *The Containment of Latin America* (Chicago: Quadrangle Books, 1971).

the vanguard pretensions in the myth, resulting in an alliance better suited to the realities of a multipolar world. The formation of the European Community (now Union) provides a useful model. That community included Portugal and Germany, Greece and Britain, when those nations were at different levels of development; it has managed economic and cultural diversity more through rules and institutions than through the managed consensus that characterizes the Western Hemisphere.

We forget that the United States Constitution joined states with divergent cultures and religions, different economic systems and ecologies, and disparate sizes. "The production of different parts of the union are very variant, and their interests, of consequence, diverse," observed the anti-federalist "Brutus."[14] The "procedural republic" was grounded in the federalists' faith in institutions and rules. Similarly, in the Western Hemisphere the corrective lies in managing *pluribus* through procedure rather than stressing *unum* through discourse. In a 1969 speech President Richard Nixon told an audience of U.S. and Latin American officials, "we are a community of widely diverse peoples. Our cultures are different."[15] Nixon did not reveal his motive for such uncharacteristic humility—a desire to complete the switch from a policy of supporting democracy to one of supporting military regimes—and he did not take his own advice in dealing with Chile. Nonetheless, there is a useful distinction to be recovered from Nixon's formulation. Difference is not deficiency. Differences can lead to toleration, even curiosity, rather than to judgment and corrective action. To take this benign turn, however, the deep sentences of the myth must be set aside along with the family metaphor.

Back to the Future

Real differences will continue to distinguish the interests and values of peoples on the multiple sides of the cultural, economic, and national

14. "Essay 1," in *The Anti-Federalist Papers and the Constitutional Convention Debates,* ed. Ralph Ketcham (New York: Mentor, 1986), 271.

15. "Remarks at the Annual Meeting of the Inter-American Press Association, October 31, 1969," *Public Papers of the Presidents of the United States: Richard Nixon, 1969* (Washington, D.C.: U.S. Government Printing Office, 1971), 894, 900.

frontiers that cross this hemisphere. When it comes to the choices governments make, "freedom" and "progress" will continue to be far from self-evident. What sounded like inclusion in the past often was control—unaccountable control by a vanguard government with a penchant for conflating its interests with everyone else's. The time for that has passed.

Rather than confront history, U.S. leaders have chosen to see the end of the Cold War as miraculously changing everything. So, a discourse based on the America/Américas myth continues to plug holes in the bridge of consent across which (U.S. leaders hope) hemispheric cooperation will continue to travel. But if differences are real and conflicts of interest genuine, ignoring these realities cannot work for long.

> *Language is a perfect reflection of what's happening, and when they say "This is America," this is America.*
> —Alfredo Jaar, Chilean who now lives in the United States.[16]

---

16. Alfredo Jaar, "Transcript of Remarks," in *Being América: Essays on Art, Literature, and Identity from Latin America,* ed. Rachel Weiss and Alan West (Fredonia, N.Y.: White Pine Press, 1991), 125. In 1987 Jaar projected, on an electronic billboard in Times Square, a 45-second animation juxtaposing a map of the United States with the words "This is not America."

Appendix: The Reagan Speech

President Reagan's address to the nation of March 16, 1986, is reproduced below so that readers can compare their reading to mine. Many
additional texts from the 1968 campaign likewise can be accessed
through the *Public Papers of the Presidents of the United States: Ronald
Reagan, 1986,* available in most college and university libraries. While
reading Reagan's speeches, keep in mind his flawless delivery born of
an actor's training. Reagan was the first president to read from a hidden
teleprompter while looking directly at the camera.

"Address to the Nation on the Situation in Nicaragua," broadcast from
the Oval Office of the White House by radio and television, March 16,
1986. Reproduced from pages 352–57 of volume one of the *Public
Papers of the Presidents of the United States: Ronald Reagan, 1986*
(Washington, D.C.: U.S. Government Printing Office, 1988).

My fellow Americans:
    I must speak to you tonight about a mounting danger in Central
America that threatens the security of the United States. This danger
will not go away; it will grow worse, much worse, if we fail to take
action now. I'm speaking of Nicaragua, a Soviet ally on the American
mainland only 2 hours' flying time from our own borders. With over a
billion dollars in Soviet-bloc aid, the Communist government of Nicaragua has launched a campaign to subvert and topple its democratic
neighbors. Using Nicaragua as a base, the Soviets and Cubans can
become the dominant power in the crucial corridor between North and
South America. Established there, they will be in a position to threaten
the Panama Canal, interdict our vital Caribbean sealanes, and, ultimately, move against Mexico. Should that happen, desperate Latin

peoples by the millions would begin fleeing north into the cities of the southern United States or to wherever some hope of freedom remained.

The United States Congress has before it a proposal to help stop this threat. The legislation is an aid package of $100 million for the more than 20,000 freedom fighters struggling to bring democracy to their country and eliminate this Communist menace at its source. But this $100 million is not an additional 100 million. We're not asking for a single dime in new money. We are asking only to be permitted to switch a small part of our present defense budget to the defense of our own southern frontier.

Gathered in Nicaragua already are thousands of Cuban military advisers, contingents of Soviets and East Germans, and all the elements of international terror—from the PLO to Italy's Red Brigades. Why are they there? Because as Colonel Qadhafi has publicly exulted: "Nicaragua means a great thing: it means fighting America near its borders, fighting America at its doorstep."

For our own security, the United States must deny the Soviet Union a beachhead in North America. But let me make one thing plain: I'm not talking about American troops. They are not needed; they have not been requested. The democratic resistance fighting in Nicaragua is only asking America for the supplies and support to save their own country from communism. The question the Congress of the United States will now answer is a simple one: Will we give the Nicaraguan democratic resistance the means to recapture their betrayed revolution, or will we turn our backs and ignore the malignancy in Managua until it spreads and becomes a mortal threat to the entire New World? Will we permit the Soviet Union to put a second Cuba, a second Libya, right on the doorstep of the United States?

How can such a small country pose such a great threat? Well, it is not Nicaragua alone that threatens us, but those using Nicaragua as a privileged sanctuary for their struggle against the United States. Their first target is Nicaragua's neighbors. With an army and militia of 120,000 men, backed by more than 3,000 Cuban military advisers, Nicaragua's Armed Forces are the largest Central America has ever seen. The Nicaraguan military machine is more powerful than all its neighbors combined.

This map—[indicating]—represents much of the Western Hemisphere. Now, let me show you the countries in Central America where weapons supplied by Nicaraguan Communists have been found: Hon-

duras, Costa Rica, El Salvador, Guatemala. Radicals from Panama to
the south have been trained in Nicaragua, but the Sandinista revolutionary reach extends well beyond their immediate neighbors. In South
America and the Caribbean, the Nicaraguan Communists have provided
support in the form of military training, safe haven, communications,
false documents, safe transit, and, sometimes, weapons to radicals from
the following countries: Colombia, Ecuador, Brazil, Chile, Argentina,
Uruguay, and the Dominican Republic. Even that is not all, for there
was an old Communist slogan that the Sandinistas have made clear they
honor: The road to victory goes through Mexico.

If maps, statistics, and facts aren't persuasive enough, we have the
words of the Sandinistas and Soviet themselves. One of the highest level
Sandinista leaders was asked by an American magazine whether their
Communist revolution will, and I quote, "be exported to El Salvador,
then Guatemala, then Honduras, and then Mexico." He responded,
"That is one historical prophecy of Ronald Reagan that is absolutely
true."

Well, the Soviets have been no less candid. A few years ago, then-
Soviet Foreign Minister Gromyko noted that Central America was,
quote, "boiling like a cauldron" and ripe for revolution. In a Moscow
meeting in 1983, Soviet Chief of Staff Marshal Ogarkov declared:
"Over two decades, there are Nicaragua"—I should say, "there was
only Cuba—in Latin America. Today there are Nicaragua, Grenada,
and a serious battle is going on in El Salvador." But we don't need their
quotes; the American forces who liberated Grenada captured thousands
of documents that demonstrated Soviet intent to bring Communist
revolution home to the Western Hemisphere.

So, we're clear on the intention of the Sandinistas and those who
back them. Let us be equally clear about the nature of their regime. To
begin with, the Sandinistas have revoked the civil liberties of the
Nicaraguan people, depriving them of any legal right to speak, to
publish, to assemble, or to worship freely. Independent newspapers have
been shut down. There is no longer any independent labor movement
in Nicaragua nor any right to strike. As AFL-CIO leader Lane Kirkland
has said, "Nicaragua's head-long rush into the totalitarian camp cannot
be denied by anyone who has eyes to see."

Well, like Communist governments everywhere, the Sandinistas have
launched assaults against ethnic and religious groups. The capital's
only synagogue was desecrated and firebombed—the entire Jewish

community forced to flee Nicaragua. Protestant Bible meetings have been broken up by raids, by mob violence, by machineguns. The Catholic Church has been singled out; priests have been expelled from the country, Catholics beaten in the streets after attending mass. The Catholic primate of Nicaragua, Cardinal Obando y Bravo, has put the matter forthrightly. "We want to state clearly," he says, "that this government is totalitarian. We are dealing with an enemy of the Church."

Evangelical pastor Prudencio Baltodano found out he was on a Sandinista hit list when an army patrol asked his name. "You don't know what we do to the evangelical pastors. We don't believe in God," they told him. Pastor Baltodano was tied to a tree, struck in the forehead with a rifle butt, stabbed in the neck with a bayonet; finally, his ears were cut off, and he was left for dead. "See if your God will save you," they mocked. Well, God did have other plans for Pastor Baltodano. He lived to tell the world his story—to tell it, among other places, right here in the White House.

I could go on about this nightmare—the black lists, the secret prisons, the Sandinista-directed mob violence. But as if all this brutality at home were not enough, the Sandinistas are transforming their nation into a safe house, a command post for international terror. The Sandinistas not only sponsor terror in El Salvador, Costa Rica, Guatemala, and Honduras—terror that led last summer to the murder of four U.S. marines in a cafe in San Salvador—they provide a sanctuary for terror. Italy has charged Nicaragua with harboring their worst terrorists, the Red Brigades.

The Sandinistas have been involved themselves in the international drug trade. I know every American parent concerned about the drug problem will be outraged to learn that top Nicaraguan Government officials are deeply involved in drug trafficking. This picture—*[indicating]*—secretly taken at a military airfield outside Managua, shows Federico Vaughn, a top aide to one of the nine commandantes who rule Nicaragua, loading an aircraft with illegal narcotics, bound for the United States. No, there seems to be no crime to which the Sandinistas will not stoop; this is an outlaw regime.

If we return for a moment to our map, it becomes clear why having this regime in Central America imperils our vital security interests. Through this crucial part of the Western Hemisphere passes almost half our foreign trade, more than half our imports of crude oil, and a significant portion of the military supplies we would have to send to the NATO alliance in the event of a crisis. These are the chokepoints where the sealanes could be closed. Central America is strategic to our Western alliance, a fact always understood by foreign enemies. In World War II only a few German U-boats, operating from bases 4,000 miles away in Germany and occupied Europe, inflicted crippling losses on U.S. shipping right off our southern coast. Today Warsaw Pact engineers are building a deep water port on Nicaragua's Caribbean coast, similar to the naval base in Cuba for Soviet-built submarines. They are also constructing, outside Managua, the largest military airfield in Central America—similar to those in Cuba, from which Russian Bear Bombers patrol the U.S. east coast from Maine to Florida.

How did this menace to the peace and security of our Latin neighbors, and ultimately ourselves, suddenly emerge? Let me give you a brief history. In 1979 the people of Nicaragua rose up and overthrew a corrupt dictatorship. At first the revolutionary leaders promised free elections and respect for human rights. But among them was an organization called the Sandinistas. Theirs was a Communist organization, and their support of the revolutionary goals was sheer deceit. Quickly and ruthlessly, they took complete control.

Two months after the revolution, the Sandinista leadership met in secret and, in what came to be known as the "72-hour Document," described themselves as the vanguard of a revolution that would sweep Central America, Latin America, and finally, the world. Their true enemy, they declared: the United States. Rather than make this document public, they followed the advice of Fidel Castro, who told them to put on a facade of democracy. While Castro viewed the democratic elements in Nicaragua with contempt, he urged his Nicaraguan friends to keep some of them in their coalition, in minor posts, as window dressing to deceive the West. "And that way," Castro said, "you can have your revolution and the Americans will pay for it." And we did pay for it. More aid flowed to Nicaragua from the United States in the first 18 months under the Sandinistas than from any other country. Only when the mask fell, and the face of totalitarianism became visible to the world, did the aid stop.

Confronted with this emerging threat, early in our administration I went to Congress and with bipartisan support managed to get help for the nations surrounding Nicaragua. Some of you may remember the inspiring scene when the people of El Salvador braved the threats and gunfire of Communist guerrillas, directed and supplied from Nicaragua, and went to the polls to vote decisively for democracy. For the Communists in El Salvador, it was a humiliating defeat. But there was another factor the Communists never counted on, a factor that now promises to give freedom a second chance—the freedom fighters of Nicaragua.

You see, when the Sandinistas betrayed the revolution, many who had fought the old Somoza dictatorship literally took to the hills and, like the French Resistance that fought the Nazis, began fighting the Soviet-bloc Communists and their Nicaraguan collaborators. These few have now been joined by thousands. With their blood and courage, the freedom fighters of Nicaragua have pinned down the Sandinista army and bought the people of Central America precious time. We Americans owe them a debt of gratitude. In helping to thwart the Sandinistas and their Soviet mentors, the resistance has contributed directly to the security of the United States.

Since its inception in 1982 the democratic resistance has grown dramatically in strength. Today it numbers more than 20,000 volunteers, and more come every day. But now the freedom fighters' supplies are running short, and they are virtually defenseless against the helicopter gunships Moscow has sent to Mangua. Now comes the crucial test for the Congress of the United States. Will they provide the assistance the freedom fighters need to deal with Russian tanks and gunships, or will they abandon the democratic resistance to its Communist enemy?

In answering that question, I hope Congress will reflect deeply upon what it is the resistance is fighting against in Nicaragua. Ask yourselves: What in the world are Soviets, East Germans, Bulgarians, North Koreans, Cubans, and terrorists from the PLO and the Red Brigades doing in our hemisphere, camped on our own doorstep? Is that for peace? Why have the Soviets invested $600 million to build Nicaragua into an armed force almost the size of Mexico's, a country 15 times as large and 25 times as populous. Is that for peace? Why did Nicaragua's dictator, Daniel Ortega, go to the Communist Party Congress in Havana and endorse Castro's call for the worldwide triumph of communism? Was that for peace?

Some Members of Congress ask me, why not negotiate? That's a good question, and let me answer it directly. We have sought, and still seek, a negotiated peace and a democratic future in a free Nicaragua. Ten times we have met and tried to reason with the Sandinistas; 10 times we were rebuffed. Last year we endorsed church-mediated negotiations between the regime and the resistance. The Soviets and the Sandinistas responded with a rapid arms buildup of mortars, tanks, artillery, and helicopter gunships.

Clearly, the Soviet Union and the Warsaw Pact have grasped the great stakes involved, the strategic importance of Nicaragua. The Soviets have made their decision—to support the Communists. Fidel Castro has made his decision—to support the Communists. Arafat, Qadhafi, and the Ayatollah Khomeini have made their decision—to support the Communists. Now we must make our decision. With Congress' help, we can prevent an outcome deeply injurious to the national security of the United States. If we fail, there will be no evading responsibility— history will hold us accountable. This is not some narrow partisan issue; it is a national security issue, an issue on which we must act not as Republicans, not as Democrats, but as Americans.

Forty years ago Republicans and Democrats joined together behind the Truman doctrine. It must be our policy, Harry Truman declared, to support peoples struggling to preserve their freedom. Under that doctrine, Congress sent aid to Greece just in time to save that country from the closing grip of a Communist tyranny. We saved freedom in Greece then. And with that same bipartisan spirit, we can save freedom in Nicaragua today. Over the coming days I will continue the dialog with Members of Congress—talking to them, listening to them, hearing out their concerns. Senator Scoop Jackson, who led the fight on Capitol Hill for an awareness of the danger in Central America, said it best: "On matters of national security, the best politics is no politics."

You know, recently one of our most distinguished Americans, Clare Boothe Luce, had this to say about the coming vote: "In considering this crisis," Mrs. Luce said, "my mind goes back to a similar moment in our history—back to the first years after Cuba had fallen to Fidel. One day during those years, I had lunch at the White House with a man I had known since he was a boy, John F. Kennedy. 'Mr. President,' I said, 'no matter how exalted or great a man may be, history will have time to give him no more than one sentence. George Washington, he founded our country. Abraham Lincoln, he freed the slaves and pre-served the Union. Winston Churchill, he saved Europe.' 'And what, Clare,' John Kennedy said, 'do you believe my sentence will be?' 'Mr. President,' she answered, 'your sentence will be that you stopped the Communists—or that you did not.' "

Well, tragically, John Kennedy never had the chance to decide which that would be. Now leaders of our own time must do so. My fellow Americans, you know where I stand. The Soviets and the Sandinistas must not be permitted to crush freedom in Central America and threaten our own security on our own doorstep. Now the Congress must decide where it stands. Mrs. Luce ended by saying: "Only this is certain. Through all time to come, this, the 99th Congress of the United States, will be remembered as that body of men and women that either stopped the Communists before it was too late—or did not."

So, tonight I ask you to do what you've done so often in the past. Get in touch with your Representative and Senators and urge them to vote yes; tell them to help the freedom fighters. Help us prevent a Communist takeover of Central America.

I have only 3 years left to serve my country; 3 years to carry out the responsibilities you entrusted to me; 3 years to work for peace. Could there be any greater tragedy than for us to sit back and permit this cancer to spread, leaving my successor to face far more agonizing decisions in the years ahead? The freedom fighters seek a political solution. They are willing to lay down their arms and negotiate to restore the original goals of the revolution, a democracy in which the people of Nicaragua choose their own government. That is our goal also, but it can only come about if the democratic resistance is able to bring pressure to bear on those who have seized power.

We still have time to do what must be done so history will say of us: We had the vision, the courage, and good sense to come together and act—Republicans and Democrats—when the price was not high and the risks were not great. We left America safe, we left America secure, we left America free—still a beacon of hope to mankind, still a light unto the nations.

Thank you, and God bless you.

Select Bibliography

When it comes to documentation for a specific claim, surely the appropriate place is the footnote. Similarly, a borrowed phrase that serves a specific rhetorical purpose belongs as close to the body of the text as possible; once more a footnote is indicated. The functions of a bibliography are different: to point readers to sources that shape the interpretation of a work and to acknowledge the labor of those who contributed more than a turn of phrase or an isolated datum. So, having taken care to provide in footnotes all the information needed to verify sources, I use this opportunity to guide readers to more general sources of data and ideas.

Books and Articles

Adams, Jan S. *A Foreign Policy in Transition: Moscow's Retreat from Central America and the Caribbean, 1985–1992.* Durham: Duke University Press, 1992.

Arias Sánchez, Oscar. *El camino de la paz.* Edited by Manuel Araya Incera. San José: Editorial Costa Rica, 1989.

Arnson, Cynthia. *Crossroads: Congress, the President, and Central America, 1976– 1993* 2d ed. University Park: Pennsylvania State University Press, 1993.

Baritz, Loren. *Backfire: A History of How American Culture Led Us into Vietnam and Made Us Fight the Way We Did.* New York: William Morrow and Co., 1985.

Barthes, Roland. *Mythologies.* Translated by Annette Lavers. New York: Noonday Press, 1990.

Black, George. *The Good Neighbor.* New York: Pantheon Books, 1988.

Blumenthal, Sidney. "Marketing the President." *New York Times Magazine,* September 12, 1981.

———. *The Permanent Campaign.* New York: Simon and Schuster, 1982.

Bowen, Gordon. "Presidential Action and Public Opinion about U.S. Nicaraguan Policy." *PS: Political Science and Politics* 22 (December 1989), 793–800.

Bradlee, Ben, Jr. *Guts and Glory: The Rise and Fall of Oliver North.* New York: Donald Fine, 1988.

Bushnell, David. "The Independence of Spanish South America." In *The Cambridge History of Latin America,* vol. 3. Cambridge: Cambridge University Press, 1985.

Byrne, Malcolm, and Peter Kornbluh, eds. *The Iran-Contra Affair: The Making of a Scandal, 1983–1988.* Alexandria, Va.: Chadwyck-Healey, 1990.

Cannon, Lou. *Reagan.* New York: G. P. Putnam's Sons, 1982.

Chamorro, Edgar. *Packaging the Contras: A Case of CIA Disinformation.* Monograph Series 2. New York: Institute for Media Analysis, 1987.

Child, Jack. *The Central American Peace Process, 1983–1991.* Boulder: Lynne Rienner, 1992.

Coleman, Kenneth M. "The Political Mythology of the Monroe Doctrine: Reflections on the Social Psychology of Hegemony." In *Latin America, the United States, and the Inter-American System.* Boulder: Westview Press, 1980.

Committee of Santa Fe. *A New Inter-American Policy for the Eighties.* Washington, D.C.: Council for Inter-American Security, 1981.

Cone, James. *Malcolm & Martin & America.* Maryknoll, N.Y.: Orbis Books, 1993.

Connolly, William. *Identity/Difference.* Ithaca: Cornell University Press, 1991.

Cortés, Carlos. "To View a Neighbor." In *Images of Mexico in the United States,* edited by John Coatsworth and Carlos Rico. San Diego: University of California Center for U.S.-Mexican Studies, 1989.

Der Derian, James, and Michael Shapiro, eds. *International/Intertextual Relations.* Lexington, Mass.: Lexington Books, 1989.

Draper, Theodore. *A Very Thin Line: The Iran-Contra Affairs.* New York: Hill & Wang, 1991.

Edelman, Marc, and Joanne Kenen. *The Costa Rica Reader.* New York: Grove Weidenfeld, 1989.

Edelman, Murray. *Constructing the Political Spectacle.* Chicago: University of Chicago Press, 1988.

Etheredge, Lloyd. *Can Governments Learn?* New York: Pergamon Press, 1985.

Falcoff, Mark, and Robert Royal, eds. *The Continuing Crisis: U.S. Policy in Central America and the Caribbean.* Lanham, Md.: Ethics and Public Policy Center in association with University Press of America, 1987.

Fernández, Guido. *El primer domingo de febrero.* San José: Editorial Costa Rica, 1986.

———. *El desafío de la paz en Centroamérica.* San José: Editorial Costa Rica, 1989.

Fukuyama, Francis. *The End of History and the Last Man.* New York: The Free Press, 1992.

Gallup, George, Jr. *The Gallup Poll: Public Opinion 1986.* Wilmington, Del.: Scholarly Resources, 1987.

Gleijeses, Piero. "The Limits of Sympathy: The United States and the Independence of Spanish America." *Journal of Latin American Studies* 24 (October 1992), 481–505.

Goodfellow, William, and James Morrell. "From Contadora to Esquipulas to Sapoa and Beyond." In *Revolution and Counterrevolution in Nicaragua,* edited by Thomas W. Walker. Boulder: Westview Press, 1991.

Green, David. *The Containment of Latin America.* Chicago: Quadrangle Books, 1971.

Gutman, Roy. *Banana Diplomacy: The Making of American Diplomacy in Nicaragua, 1981–1987.* New York: Simon and Schuster, 1988.

Haggard, Stephan. *Pathways from the Periphery.* Ithaca: Cornell University Press, 1990.

Hakim, Peter. "The United States and Latin America: Good Neighbors Again?" *Current History* 91 (February 1992), 49–53.

———. "NAFTA . . . and After." *Current History* 93 (March 1994), 97–102.

Hamilton, Alexander, John Jay, and James Madison. *The Federalist Papers.* Edited by Isaac Kramnick. Harmondsworth, Eng.: Penguin Books, 1987.

Harrison, Lawrence E. *Underdevelopment Is a State of Mind: The Latin American Case.* Lanham, Md.: Madison books in association with University Press of America, 1985.

Hartlyn, Jonathan, Lars Schoultz, and Augusto Varas, eds. *The United States and Latin America in the 1990s: Beyond the Cold War.* Chapel Hill: University of North Carolina Press, 1992.

Hersh, Seymour M. *The Price of Power: Kissinger in the Nixon White House.* New York: Summit Books, 1983.

Hill, Patricia. "Picturing Progress in the Era of Westward Expansion." In *The West as America,* edited by William Truettner. Washington, D.C.: The Smithsonian Institution Press, 1991.

Huntington, Samuel P. *Political Order in Changing Societies.* New Haven: Yale University Press, 1968.

The Inter-American Dialogue. *Convergence and Community: The Americas in 1993.* Washington, D.C.: The Aspen Institute, 1992.

Johnson, John J. *Latin America in Caricature.* Austin: University of Texas Press, 1993.

Kornbluh, Peter. "The Contra Lobby." *Village Voice,* October 13, 1987.

———, and Malcolm Byrne, eds. *The Iran-Contra Scandal: The Declassified History.* A National Security Archive Documents Reader. New York: The New Press, 1993.

LaFeber, Walter. *Inevitable Revolutions.* 1st and 2d eds. New York: W. W. Norton, 1984, 1993.

LeoGrande, William. "The Contras and Congress." In *Reagan Versus the Sandinistas,* edited by Thomas Walker. Boulder: Westview Press, 1987.

Lincoln, Bruce. *Discourse and the Construction of Society.* New York: Oxford University Press, 1989.

Lockerbie, Brad, and Stephen Borrelli. "Question Wording and Public Support for Contra Aid." *Public Opinion Quarterly* 54 (Summer 1990), 195–208.

Lowenthal, Abraham. "The United States and Latin American Democracy: Learning from History." In *Exporting Democracy: The United States and Latin America: Case Studies,* edited by Abraham Lowenthal. Baltimore: The Johns Hopkins University Press, 1991.

McNeil, Frank. *War and Peace in Central America.* New York: Charles Scribner's Sons, 1988.

———. "The Road to Esquipulas." Paper presented at the Sixteenth Congress of the Latin American Studies Association. Washington, D.C., April 1991.

Mayer, Jane, and Doyle McManus. *Landslide: The Unmaking of the President, 1984–1988.* Boston: Houghton Mifflin, 1988.

Menges, Constantine. *Inside the National Security Council.* New York: Simon and Schuster, 1988.

Morrell, Jim. *The Nine Lives of the Central American Peace Process.* International Policy Report. Washington, D.C.: Center for International Policy, 1989.

Nash, Roderick, and Gregory Graves. *From These Beginnings.* Vol. 1. 4th ed. New York: Harper, 1990.

Noonan, Peggy. *What I Saw at the Revolution: A Political Life in the Reagan Era.* New York: Ivy Books, 1990; Ballantine Books, 1991.

North, Oliver, with William Novak. *Under Fire: An American Story.* New York: Harper Paperbacks, 1992.

Ornstein, Norman, et al. *The People, the Press, and Politics.* Reading, Mass.: Addison-Wesley, 1983.

Pardo-Maurer, Rogelio. *The Contras, 1980–1989: A Special Kind of Politics.* The Washington Papers. New York: Praeger Publishers in association with the Center for Strategic and International Studies, 1990.

Parry, Robert, and Peter Kornbluh. "Iran-Contra's Untold Story." *Foreign Policy* 72 (Fall 1988), 3–30.

Pastor, Robert. *Condemned to Repetition: The United States and Nicaragua.* Princeton: Princeton University Press, 1987.

Perkins, Dexter. *The Monroe Doctrine, 1823–1826.* Cambridge: Harvard University Press, 1932.

Peterson, Merrill. *Adams and Jefferson: A Revolutionary Dialogue.* Athens: University of Georgia Press, 1976.

Pevar, Stephen. *The Rights of Indians and Tribes.* New York: Bantam Books, 1983.

Pike, Fredrick. *The United States and Latin America: Myths and Stereotypes of Civilization and Nature.* Austin: University of Texas Press, 1992.

Postman, Neil. *Amusing Ourselves to Death.* New York: Viking Penguin, 1986.

Przeworski, Adam. *Democracy and the Market.* Cambridge: Cambridge University Press, 1991.

———. "The Neo-Liberal Fallacy." In *Capitalism, Socialism, and Democracy Revisited,* edited by Larry Diamond and Marc F. Plattner. Baltimore: The Johns Hopkins University Press, 1993.

Rappaport, Armin, ed. *The Monroe Doctrine.* New York: Holt, Rinehart and Winston, 1964.

Regan, Donald. *For the Record: From Wall Street to Washington.* New York: St. Martin's Press, 1988.

Roberts, Kenneth. "Bullying and Bargaining: The United States, Nicaragua, and Conflict Resolution in Central America." *International Security* 15 (Fall 1990), 67–102.

Ropp, Steve. "Things Fall Apart: Panama after Noriega." *Current History* 92 (March 1993), 102–5.

Said, Edward W. *Orientalism.* New York: Pantheon Books, 1978.

Schoultz, Lars. *National Security and United States Policy toward Latin America.* Princeton: Princeton University Press, 1987.

Scott, Peter Dale, and Jonathan Marshall. *Cocaine Politics: Drugs, Armies, and the CIA in Central America.* Berkeley and Los Angeles: University of California Press, 1991.

Sheahan, John. *Conflict and Change in Mexican Economic Strategy.* San Diego: Center for U.S.-Mexican Studies, University of California, 1991.

Sojo, Carlos. *Costa Rica: Política exterior y sandinismo.* San José: Facultad Latinoamericana de Ciencias Sociales, 1991.

Thompson, William Irwin. *Pacific Shift.* San Francisco: Sierra Club Books, 1985.

Times Mirror Center for the People and the Press. "The Age of Indifference: A Study of Young Americans and How They View the News." Washington, D.C., 1990. Photocopy.

Todorov, Tzvetan. *The Conquest of America*. Translated by Richard Howard. New York: Harper & Row Colophon, 1985.

Walker, Thomas W., ed. *Reagan Versus the Sandinistas*. Boulder: Westview Press, 1987.

———. *Revolution and Counterrevolution in Nicaragua*. Boulder: Westview Press, 1991.

Wekesser, Carol, ed. *Opposing Viewpoints: Central America*. San Diego: Greenhaven Press, 1990.

Williams, William Appleman. *Empire as a Way of Life*. New York: Oxford University Press, 1980.

Williamson, Judith. *Decoding Advertisements*. New York: Marion Boyars, 1983.

Wittkopf, Eugene R. *Faces of Internationalism: Public Opinion and American Foreign Policy*. Durham: Duke University Press, 1990.

Wolin, Sheldon. *The Presence of the Past*. Baltimore: The Johns Hopkins University Press, 1989.

Woodward, Bob. *Veil: The Secret Wars of the CIA, 1981–1987*. New York: Simon and Schuster Pocket Books, 1988.

Official Documents

Speeches of U.S. officials on foreign policy are most readily accessed through a publication now known as *U.S. Department of State Dispatch*. Its forerunner was *Current Policy*. The source of both is the Bureau of Public Affairs of the U.S. Department of State. Presidential statements ranging from news conferences to major addresses are found in the *Public Papers of the Presidents of the United States*, edited by the National Archives and published by the Government Printing Office.

Press statements that do not make it into these compilations may be accessed by other means, including *Foreign Affairs Press Briefings* issued by the Department of State, Office of the Historian. Important official speeches also may be found in such publications as *Vital Speeches of the Day* and the *New York Times*. For earlier periods sources include the "American Republics" volumes of *Foreign Relations of the United States*, again edited by the Office of the Historian, Bureau of Public Affairs, Department of State.

Crucial in writing this book have been the many publications of the Select Committees of the House of Representatives and of the Senate, which jointly investigated the Iran-Contra affair. A key document is:

U.S. Congress, *Report of the Congressional Committees Investigating the Iran-Contra Affair,* 100th Cong., 1st sess., H. Rept. 100-433, S. Rept. 100-216 (Washington, D.C.: U.S. Government Printing Office, 1987).

"Annexes" to the *Report* include "depositions" (testimony) and "exhibits" that total some two dozen volumes and thirty thousand pages published over two years. The National Security Archive, a private research organization in Washington, D.C., selected from this mountain those documents that most illuminate the Iran-Contra affair and arranged them in ways that make research easier (indices, chronologies, etc.). An extensive selection is available on microfiche at the archive's office and through Chadwyck-Healey, which published them as *The Iran-Contra Affair: The Making of a Scandal, 1983–1988*, edited by Malcolm Byrne and Peter Kornbluh (Alexandria, Va., 1990). A more select group of documents has been published in book form as *The Iran-Contra Scandal: The Declassified History*, edited by Peter Kornbluh and Malcolm Byrne (New York: The New Press, 1993). With a few exceptions I identify documents by the title, date, and fiche number of the National Security Archive. Using title and date, most of these documents can be found in the "Annexes" described above. Some government documents remain sealed for twenty (Senate) or thirty (House) years, while many of those available now have been censored.

During the period covered by this study the U.S. government issued a number of so-called "white papers" on Central America. These bore the imprimatur of the Departments of State and Defense but were the work of the Office of Public Diplomacy for Latin America and the Caribbean (S/LPD), an agency described in Chapter 5. For an evaluation of these reports see my contribution to *Reagan Versus the Sandinistas*, edited by Thomas W. Walker (Boulder: Westview Press, 1987). Another important official document of this era is the report of the Kissinger Commission: *The Report of the President's National Bipartisan Commission on Central America*, first published by the Government Printing Office and then by the Macmillan Company of New York, 1984.

Finally, this study benefited from access to government documents that had not yet made their way into the archives. They were obtained through personal request from congressional staff members. A key example is:

> U.S. Congress, House, Staff of the Committee on Foreign Affairs, "Final Staff Report," *State Department and Intelligence Community Involvement in Domestic Activities Related to the Iran/Contra Affair*, September 7, 1988.

The Iran-Contra committees' staff began work on a separate chapter in the final *Report* dealing with the Reagan administration's manipulation of Congress and the public. After Republican members objected and Democrats threatened to include the information in a minority report a weak compromise was found in a brief summary of this material within the "Executive Summary" found at the beginning of the *Report*.

Index

Abrams, Elliott, 87, 118
  and Costa Rica, 148, 156, 157
  lack of knowledge of Latin America, 76
  and Potrero Grande project, 145, 146
ACT (American Conservative Trust), 92
Adams, John Quincy, 24, 25, 26–27
advertising
  agencies in the executive branch, 86–89
  ideal type, 48
  as news, 95
  and 1986 campaign, xv, 52, 81–113,
    114–39
  in politics, xiv, 38–53
  relationship to myth, 40–41
Ailes, Roger
  Costa Rican election, 163
  "no new taxes," 50
Alfonsín, Raúl, 74
Alvarez, Gustavo, 61, 67
ambiguity
  in advertising, 48, 123
  at the core of U.S. strategy, 66
America/Américas myth, xiv, xv, 1, 13
  and advertising campaign, 114–39
  beyond the myth, 159–66
  "deep sentences" of, 18–20
  and hardball politics, 80
American Conservative Trust (ACT), 92
American identity, 19–21, 25–26, 30
American Indians, 26
Americas project, 20, 21–22, 24, 25
anticommunism
  framing the choice, 115, 121
  in public opinion, 100–101

Argentina election, 74
Arias Sánchez, Oscar, 140–58
  construction of the Central American
    crisis, 142–43, 148–51, 157
  diplomacy, 148, 151–54
  Project Democracy, 144–48, 157
Arnson, Cynthia, 84, 132
association, and advertising, 45–46, 47
Atwater, Lee, 51

Baker, James A., III, 4–5, 82
Barthes, Roland, 13–14, 37
Beal, Richard, 49
Bedell, Berkeley, 132
Bermúdez, Enrique, 61, 62
Biaggi, Mario, 133
Biehl, John, 143, 157
Blacken, John, 89
Blaine, James, 28
Blumenthal, Sidney, 113
  permanent campaign, 48–49
Boland amendments, 54–55, 58, 85
Bolívar, Simón, 2
Borrelli, Stephen. See Lockerbie, Brad, and
    Stephen Borrelli
boundaries of myth, 19–20
Bradlee, Ben, Jr., 84
Broomfield, William, 131
Buchanan, Patrick
  attack on Democrats, 116
  contact with pollsters, 94
  lobbying of Congress, 83, 111
Burghardt, Ray, 89
Burnham, James, 71

Burton, Dan, 130
Bush, George
  Americas project, 21
  Central American policy, 157
  family metaphor, 31
  "new world" order, 5–6, 22
  "no new taxes" image, 50
  post–Cold War role, 4

Calero, Adolfo, 61, 62, 63
Cameron, Bruce
  Center for Democracy in the Americas,
    92
  as lobbyist, 108, 109, 110
  1986 campaign success, 111–12
  Plan of Action, 107
campaign, 1986, 89, 92, 99
  advertising, xv, 52, 81–113, 114–39
campaign, permanent
  election, 44
  1986 campaign, 89
  by White House, 48–49, 51
Carabelleda, Message of, 138
Casey, William, 69–72
  Costa Rica, 148, 156, 157
  covert policies during Reagan's first
    term, 54
  getting rid of Sandinistas, 60
  as hardball practitioner, 78
  lack of knowledge of Latin America, 76
  1986 campaign, 83
  Reagan and human interest, 68
  Special National Intelligence Estimates
    (SNIEs), 67
  World War II–style heroism, 75
Castillo, Tomás (Joseph Fernández), 145,
    146
Castro, Fidel, 34, 171, 173
catharsis, and advertising, 48, 127
Center for Democracy in the Americas,
    92, 110
Central American governments
  opposition to U.S. Contra aid, 138–39,
    152, 157–58
  summits, 152, 155

Central American Defense Council
    (CONDECA), 61, 67
Central American Freedom Program, 93,
    98, 107–11
Central American Public Diplomacy Task
    Force, 86–87, 88, 106
Central Intelligence Agency (CIA)
  and Congress, 54–55, 91
  control of Contra leaders, 62
  and hardball politics, 78
  and military aid, 57, 84
CFA (Citizens for America), 96–97
Chamorro, Edgar, 91
Chamorro, Violeta, 154
Channell, Carl (Spitz)
  Central American Freedom Program,
    107–10
  framing the choice, 117–18
  1985 plan, 96, 98
  1986 campaign, 92–93, 99, 111
Child, Jack, 156
choice, and advertising, 47–48, 127
CIA. See Central Intelligence Agency
Citizens for America (CFA), 96–97
Clarridge, Duane "Dewey," 76
Cleveland, Grover, 14
Clinton, Bill, 7, 9
coauthoring of advertisements, 47
Cold War, post–, 4, 82
Committee of Santa Fe, 15, 34, 71
communism
  and "deep sentences," 135
  framing the choice, 115–16, 121
  as hook in advertising, 123
  as perceived threat, 172, 173, 174
  and Reagan Doctrine, 70–74
CONDECA (Central American Defense
    Council), 61, 67
conflation, control through, 37
Congress
  comments on military aid, 130–33
  1986 advertising campaign by White
    House, xv, 52, 81–113, 114–39
  opposition to Contra aid, 54–56
  vote on military spending, 83–86, 168
Connolly, William, 37

construction of the Nicaragua issue, 140
  Oscar Arias Sánchez, 142–43, 148–51,
    157
  Ronald Reagan, 72, 148–52, 154
continuity in U.S. foreign policy, 7–8
Contra aid, 54–80
  Congressional approval, 83–86
  Congressional opposition, 54, 153
  framing the choice, 116–20
  "humanitarian" aid, 55, 58
  illegal funding methods, 57–58
contractors. *See* cutouts
Contras
  as Americans, 136–37
  intentions and capabilities, 60, 160
  number of soldiers, 67
control-through-sameness, xiv, 37, 142
Costa Rica, 140–58
Cruz, Arturo, Jr., 97
Cuba
  as threat, 168, 171, 173
  outside the hemisphere, 130–31
  U.S. economic blockade, 7, 12
cutouts, and advertising campaign, 89–93,
    105, 106

decision to buy, and advertising, 48, 127
"deep sentences," 29
  of America/Américas myth, 18–20
  and hardball politics, 80
  in 1986 campaign, 134–36
democracy
  and America/Américas myth, 161, 162
  and force, 149
  modern conceptions of, 25
  and "new world" order, 5, 6, 7, 8, 11
Democratic Leadership Council, 51
destiny, and the Americas project, 24, 36
DeWine, Michael, 130
difference
  importance of, 164, 165, 166
  vs. sameness, 37
discourse, 140–58
  and international relations, 8–13
  of Oscar Arias Sánchez, 140, 148–51
  power of, 155–58

process-oriented, 154
purpose of, 161, 162
unity through language, 36
vs. rules and institutions, 39
disease, as metaphor for communism, 34
disinformation, 98–99
Dolan, John Terry
  National Conservative Political Action
    Committee (NCPAC), 92
  "Ninety-Day Plan," 99–105
Dominican Republic, invasion of, 11
Dreier, David, 131
Drug Enforcement Administration (DEA),
  125
drug trafficking, 6, 35, 58
  Nicaraguan Government officials in,
    124, 125, 170
Duarte, José Napoleon, 152
Dulles, John Foster, 34

Eagleburger, Lawrence
  "new world" order, 23
  Panama, 4–5
economic policies, neoliberal, 7, 10
Edelman, Daniel J., Inc., 107, 109
Edwards, Jonathan, 23
Einaudi, Luigi, 4
election campaigns, and advertising, 44
Emerson, Ralph Waldo, 24
emotions, and advertising, 45, 46, 48, 49,
  123
Enterprise for the Americas Initiative, 20
equality, prejudice of, 35–37
Esquipulas II peace accords, 143, 151,
  152–54
Etheridge, Lloyd, and hardball politics,
  69, 77–80

family, as unifying symbol, 30–32, 35, 36,
  165
FDN (Nicaraguan Democratic Force),
  58–59, 60–63, 66
Fernández, Joseph (Tomás Castillo), 145,
  146
Fiers, Alan, 76
findings, presidential, 59

Flaco, Colonel (Jack Terrell), 60
Foley, Thomas, 133
Ford, Harold, 132
founding myths, 16–18, 36
framing the choice, in advertising, 48,
    114, 115–22
Franklin, Benjamin, 23
free trade, 6, 28
freedom, and America/Américas myth, 18,
    25, 36, 134–35, 161
"freedom fighters," 72
    Contras as, 73, 172
    myths about, 60
Freedom Research Foundation, 72
Friends of the Democratic Center in
    Central America (PRODEMCA),
    108, 109
Fukuyama, Francis, 21

Gates, Robert, 15
George, Clair, 75
Goodman Agency, 92–93, 117
Gorbachev, Mikhail, 74, 152
Gorman, Paul, 60
grandiosity, in policy making, 69, 78, 79,
    80
grassroots campaigning, 105
Grenada invasion, 11
    Casey's comments on, 73–74
    Nicaragua comparison, 66–67
Guatemala
    peace accords, 143, 151, 152–54
    U.S. intervention in, 34
Gutman, Roy, 66, 83, 156

Habib, Philip, 119, 158
Hakim, Peter, 2
Hamilton, Alexander, 25
    and course of nature, 24
    and new world, 27
hardball politics (HP), 69, 77–80
    in Costa Rica, 147, 157
hemispheric project, 7, 12. See also
    Americas project
America/Américas myth, 20
heroism, and Iran-Contra affair, 68–77

"hidden positives" of Monroe Doctrine, 3
Holocaust, as founding myth, 16
Honduras. See also Alvarez, Gustavo
    hosting of FDN camps, 59, 67
    Sandinista attacks on Contra bases, 61
    U.S. military construction in, 62
hooks in advertising, 45, 48, 123, 124
Hull, John, 144–45
"humanitarian" aid to Nicaragua, 55, 58
Huntington, Samuel, 25
Hyde, Henry, 131

IBC. See International Business
    Communications
identity, and advertising, 46–47, 137
images
    in advertisements, 45, 50
    and the America/Américas myth, 29–35
immigrants, illegal, 124, 126
infomercials, 44
Inter-American Dialogue, 2
International Business Communications
    (IBC), 90–91, 97
    Central American Freedom Program,
    93, 107
Iran-Contra investigations, xv, 153. See
    also Contra aid
isolationism, assumption in planning,
    100–101

Jacobowitz, Daniel "Jake," 89, 96
Jefferson, Thomas, 23, 25
    and American system, 3
    and new world, 27
Johnson, John, 30–31
Johnson, Lyndon, 31

Kagan, Robert, 109–10
Kemble, Penn, 109, 110
Kennedy, John F., 70
Kirkpatrick, Jeane, 156

language and power, 8–10
language in policy making. See discourse
Latin America, xv
    immigration to U.S., 124, 126

as part of hemispherewide community, 6
U.S. constructions of Latin Americans,
    25–35
Ledeen, Michael, 74–75
Lehder, Carlos, 57–58
Leiken, Robert, 110–11
LeoGrande, William, 83, 112
liberalism, Bush's vision of, 6
liberation, 25
liberty
    Oscar Arias Sánchez speech, 149
    recurring idea of America/Américas
        myth, 18, 134–35
Lincoln, Abraham, 27
Lincoln, Bruce, 16, 17
Livingston, Bob, 131
lobbying
    and campaign plan, 109–11
    in-district, 105
Lockerbie, Brad, and Stephen Borrelli,
    100, 103, 116, 119
Luce, Clare Boothe, 173–74
Lugar, Richard, 162

manipulation in advertising, 43
Marxism. See also communism
    ambiguity in Reagan's speech, 123
    public view of threat in Central
        America, 100–101
Mathes, Don, 89
Mayer, Jane, 77, 95
McCain, John, 130
McFarlane, Robert, 55, 96
    alteration of memos approving North's
        activities, 64
    Contra funding, 57
    influences and background, 74–75
    lack of knowledge of Latin America, 76
McManus, Doyle, 77, 95
McNeil, Frank, 76, 153, 157
McPhearson, M. Peter, 147
Medellín drug cartel, 58, 125
memories, and advertising, 46, 48, 123
Menges, Constantine, 152, 156
Michel, Robert, 133
military aid. See also Contra aid

Congressional approval, 83–86
Congressional opposition, 54, 152–53
Miller, Richard
    Central American Freedom Program,
        107
    International Business Communications
        (IBC), 93
"Miller Doctrine," 15
Moley, Raymond, 15
Monge, Luís Alberto, 145–46
Monroe, James, 2, 14, 17
Monroe Doctrine, 2–3, 4, 14–16
myth. See also America/Américas myth
    definition, 13–14
    founding myths, 16–18
    relationship to advertising, 40–41
    usefulness of, 161

narcotrafficking, 115. See also drug
    trafficking
National Conservative Political Action
    Committee (NCPAC), 92
National Endowment for the Preservation
    of Liberty (NEPL), 52, 106–7
    campaign plan, 109
    1986 campaign, 92–93
national security, perceived threat to,
    159–61, 167, 168, 170–71, 173
National Security Archive (NSA), xvi, 57
National Security Council (NSC)
    coordination to 1986 campaign, 86
    management of the Contras, 62, 88
    memos about Poindexter, 60
Nature, metaphor of Americas project,
    24, 37
NCPAC (National Conservative Political
    Action Committee), 92
negative campaigning, 51
"negative" elements
    of America/Américas myth, 13
    of Monroe Doctrine, 3
Neier, Aryeh, 154
neoliberal economic policies, 7, 10–11
NEPL. See National Endowment for the
    Preservation of Liberty
neutrality of Costa Rica, 144

"New Right," 99–100
"new world," 9, 22–23, 27
  and America/Américas myth, 18, 136
"new world" order, 4–8
  North American Free Trade Agreement,
    23
Nicaragua, 3, 12. See also Contra aid;
    Contras; Sandinistas
  civil war, 54–68, 152–55, 160
  elections, 66, 136, 154–55
  government officials in drug trafficking,
    124, 125, 170
Nicaraguan Democratic Force (FDN),
    58–59, 60–63, 66
  1985 plan, 96–99
  1986 advertising campaign, xv, 52,
    81–113, 114–39
  Ninety-Day Plan, 99–105, 105–6
Nixon, Richard, 6
  diversity of peoples, 165
  permanent campaign, 48
Nobel Peace Prize of Oscar Arias Sánchez,
    152
Noonan, Peggy, 135
North, Oliver, 75–76, 76–77
  on CIA role, 62
  Contra funding, 58–59, 63–64
  Costa Rica, 156, 157
  drug trafficking, 125
  and FDN, 63
  as hardball practitioner, 77–79
  1986 campaign, 89, 92, 96
  Project Democracy and threat to Costa
    Rica, 144, 146–47
  publicity, 64–65, 86
  Reagan Doctrine, 74
  sale of U.S. missiles to Iran, 59
  Special National Intelligence Estimates
    (SNIEs), 67
North American Free Trade Agreement, 29
NSA. See National Security Archive
NSC. See National Security Council

OAS. See Organization of American States
Obey, David, 132
Office of Public Diplomacy for Latin

America and the Caribbean (S/LPD),
    97
  contracts to IBC, 90
  and IBC, 90–91
  1985 plan, 96, 97
  1986 campaign success, 112–13
  Ninety-Day Plan, 99, 105
  "white papers" on Soviets in Central
    America, 161
old world vs. new world, 9–10, 18, 27,
    136
opinion, public. See public opinion
opinion-making centers, 105
Organization of American States (OAS)
  Dominican Republic invasion, 11
  Oscar Arias Sánchez speech, 149
  Panama, role in, 4
Organization of Eastern Caribbean States,
    11
Ortega, Daniel, 152. See also Sandinistas
otherness vs. sameness, 36–37
Owen, Robert, 58, 110
  assessment of Adolfo Calero, 61
  on FDN leaders, 62, 63
  lack of knowledge of Latin America, 76
  Potrero Grande project, 145

Panama, U.S. invasion, 2, 3, 4–6, 8, 11
Pan-American movement, 28
participation, and advertising, 47, 48, 127
patriotism, 78
peace plan, 150–52
Pearl Harbor, as founding myth, 16–17
permanent campaign, 48–49, 51
  election, 44
  1986 campaign, 89
Piza, Benjamín, 145
plans for 1986 advertising campaign
  1985 plan, 96–99
  1986 campaign, 105–11, 107
  Ninety-Day Plan, 99–105
  60-Day Plan, 106
Poindexter, John, 55
  influences and background, 74–75
  lack of knowledge of Latin America, 76
  replacing McFarlane, 96

targeting of Congress, 83
trip to Central America, 59–60
policy, U.S. toward Nicaragua. *See also*
    Reagan Doctrine
confusing and decentralized, 66
"two-track," 55, 59, 155, 158
political advertising industry, 44
polling of public opinion, 129, 138–39
    and policy packaging, 51, 52
    by White House, 94–95
"positive" elements
    of America/Américas myth, 13, 20
    of Monroe Doctrine, 3–4, 8
    post–Cold War, 4, 82
Potrero Grande project, 145–47
U.S. style in dealings with, 157
power
    and hardball politics, 79
    and language, 8–10
Prescott, William, 26
Preston, Julia, 153
private contributions
    and Contra aid, 57–58
    in 1986 campaign, 89
privatization of public goods and roles,
    51, 89
PRODEMCA (Friends of the Democratic
    Center in Central America), 108, 109
prodigal son, parable of, 32, 35, 136, 137
progress, and America/Américas myth,
    18, 134–35
Project Democracy, 63, 86, 87
    and Costa Rica, 144–47, 157
promotion, and advertising, 43
propaganda, 88, 91. *See also* advertising:
    in politics
protection of U.S. citizens abroad, 6
Providence, and assignment of leadership,
    23, 24
proximity to Nicaragua, and framing the
    choice, 120–21, 123–24
Przeworski, Adam, 10, 25
public diplomacy, 88. *See also* Central
    American Public Diplomacy Task
    Force; Office of Public Diplomacy for
    Latin America and the Caribbean

public ignorance, assumption in plan,
    100–101
public opinion
    generational differences, 104
    manipulation outside the U.S., 87–88
    opinion-making centers, 105
    opposition to Contra aid, 85, 102–3
    polling, 94–95, 129, 138–39
    polling and packaging of policy, 51, 52
    during Reagan years, 81, 82

Qaddafi, Muammar, 78, 168
    portrayed as threat in ad campaign, 120
Quayle, Dan, 20, 21, 58

Raymond, Walter, Jr., 86–88, 89
    Central American Public Diplomacy
        Task Force, 106
Reagan, Ronald, 69–70
    administrative style, 68, 73
    America/Américas myth, 20, 21, 34
    as consummate actor, 50
    and Costa Rica entourage, 148
    family metaphor, 32
    human interest stories, 68
    1986 campaign, 81–83
    permanent campaign, 48–49
    and private advertising agencies, 93
    Sandinista characterization, 37
    Sandinista threat, 159–60
    speech of March 16, 1986, 122–29,
        167–74
    World War II–style heroism, 75
    "yard" metaphor, 41
Reagan Doctrine, 70–74, 136
reality, and policy making in Central
    America, 68–69
Regan, Donald
    as Chief of Staff, 82–83
    contact with pollsters, 94
    influences, 69–70
    as professional salesman, 49
Reich, Otto, 88, 89
    coordinator, Office of Public Diplomacy
        for Latin America and the Caribbean
        (S/LPD), 87
    1986 campaign success, 112–13

renegades, Sandinistas as, 137
Rio Treaty, 61
Ritter, Don, 131
Roberts, Kenneth, 66
Rollins, Ed, 94
Rowland, John, 132
"rule of law," *vs.* democracy, 5

Said, Edward, xiv, 36
sameness
    control-through-, xiv, 142
    vs. otherness/difference, xv, 36–37
Sandinistas. *See also* Contra aid; Contras;
    Nicaragua
    activities, 169–70
    criticism by Oscar Arias Sánchez, 142
    framed as communists and
        terrorists,115–16
    negotiations, 65–66, 128, 172–73
    1979 revolution, 136
    number of soldiers, 67
    as renegades, 137
    signing of peace accord, 154, 155
    U.S. "two-track" policy, 55, 59, 155,
        158
Santa Elena project, 145–46
Saudi Arabia, and contra funding, 57
Schoultz, Lars, 29, 159–60
Secord, Richard, 63
    weapon supply, 64, 89
security, national. *See* national security,
    perceived threat to
self-determination
    Oscar Arias Sánchez speech, 18, 134–35
    recurring idea of America/Américas
        myth, 18, 134–35
semiotic system, advertising as, 39, 45–46
Sentinel, 92, 111
Shapiro, Michael, 40
Shultz, George, 85
    meeting with Costa Rica entourage, 148
    and military pressure, 119–20
    negotiations with Sandinistas, 155–56
Singlaub, John, 71, 72, 145
60-Day Plan, 106

S/LPD. *See* Office of Public Diplomacy for
    Latin America and the Caribbean
Snowe, Olympia, 134
Soviet Union
    aid to Nicaragua, 94, 167, 169, 172,
        173
    aid to Nicaragua, cutting off of, 152
    priorities and capabilities, 74, 101
    in Reagan Doctrine, 70, 71, 72
Special National Intelligence Estimates
    (SNIEs), 67
State Department
    humanitarian aid to Nicaragua, 58
    Office of Public Diplomacy for Latin
        America and the Caribbean (S/LPD),
        87
"strategic denial"
    America/Américas myth, 18
    of Monroe Doctrine, 2, 3
switching votes, reasons for, 111–12

tabula rasa, Western Hemisphere as, 18,
    134, 135
Tallon, Robin, 133
Tambs, Lewis, 145, 146, 147
terrorism, in 1986 campaign, 115, 123
El Tesoro summit, 155
Third World, and Reagan Doctrine, 71–74
Thompson, William Irwin, 164
Todorov, Tzvetan, 37, 114
transfer and emotion-evocation, in
    advertising, 49
Truman, Harry, 31
"two-track" policy, 55, 59, 155, 158

Udall Research Corporation, 145
United Nicaraguan Opposition (UNO), 63
unity through language, 36
UNO (United Nicaraguan Opposition), 63
U.S. Drug Enforcement Administration
    (DEA), 125

vanguard of the hemisphere, U.S. as,
    18–19, 133, 135, 136
Varas, Augusto, 2

Vaughn, Federico, 125, 170
Vietnam, compared to Central America, 75
Vietnam Syndrome, 82, 100, 104

Washington, George, 29
weapon supply, 57, 64, 89
Weinberger, Casper, 69–70
Western Hemisphere, as *tabula rasa,* 18, 134, 135
Wheeler, Jack, 72
Williamson, Judith, 45
Wilson, Woodrow, 3, 14
Winthrop, John, 22, 23
Wirthlin, Richard, 94–95, 124
Wolin, Sheldon, 14, 22

Woodward, Bob
  and CIA under Casey's direction, 67–68
  on Libya, 78
  on William Casey, 71, 75
World Anti-Communist League, 71, 72, 145
world order, 11, 12. *See also* "new world" order
World War II analogy, 127, 172
World War III projection, and Reagan Doctrine, 71
Wright, James C. (Jim), Jr., 153

"yard" as metaphor, 26, 40–42, 100

Zoellick, Robert, 29